Highland Style

FASHIONING HIGHLAND DRESS

Highland Style

c.1745–1845

Rosie Waine

First published in 2022
by NMS Enterprises Limited – Publishing
a division of NMS Enterprises Limited
National Museums Scotland
Chambers Street
Edinburgh EH1 1JF

www.nms.ac.uk

Text © National Museums Scotland 2022
Images © National Museums Scotland 2022, unless otherwise credited (see Acknowledgements page 210)

Every effort has been made to contact copyright holders for all images and text used in this book. No reproduction of images or text is permitted without first obtaining written permission from the publisher.

ISBN 978-1-910682-45-6

No part of this publication may be reproduced, stored in a retrieval system or transmitted, in any form or by any means, electronic, mechanical, photocopying, recording or otherwise, without the prior permission of the publisher.

The right of Rosie Waine to be identified as the author of this work has been asserted by her in accordance with the Copyright, Design and Patent Act 1988.

British Library Cataloguing in Publication Data.
A catalogue record for this volume is available on request from the British Library.

This product is made of material from well-managed forests and other controlled sources.

Printed and bound in Great Britain by Bell & Bain Ltd, Glasgow.
Cover design by Mark Blackadder.
Photography by Neil MacLean, Amy Campbell and Olga Tjukova for NMS Photography.
Cover illustrations:
    Front: Kilt suit, *c*.1815.
    Back: Jewelled plaid brooch, mid-19th century.
Text pages i, ii–iii: Silver ring brooch, *c*.1838.
    (Images © National Museums Scotland)

For a full listing of NMS Enterprises Limited – Publishing titles and related merchandise, see:

www.nms.ac.uk/books

Contents

Foreword by Professor Christopher Breward
    Director, National Museums Scotland VII
Foreword by David Grant
    William Grant Foundation IX
Introduction by Dr Rosie Waine
    National Museums Scotland XI

Chapters
1. Highland dress culture and the national collections 1
2. The rise and influence of the Highland societies 51
3. Designing and trading tartan in Georgian Britain 101
4. Highland style in Georgian society 135
    Afterword 191

List of sources 194
Index 200
Acknowledgements 210

Foreword

by Professor Christopher Breward

Director

NATIONAL MUSEUMS SCOTLAND

NATIONAL Museums Scotland holds an unrivalled collection of Highland dress and tartan costume. With origins as old as the museum itself, this extraordinary assembly of dress, textiles, weaponry, associated visual culture and documents, reveals much about the complex material history of a national icon. Supported by the William Grant Foundation, the museum has undertaken an ambitious project to reassess fundamentally the formation, scope and content of these unique holdings. Since our partnership began in 2018, we have conducted a programme of research, conservation and photography, which has enabled us to understand better the Highland dress collections in our care and to make them more accessible for future generations.

Highland Style is a landmark publication that situates Highland dress within the broader landscape of fashionable consumption in Britain during the eighteenth and nineteenth centuries. This richly illustrated volume brings the museum's earliest examples of Highland dress costume together in print for the first time and re-examines the cultural context in which they were made and displayed. Focusing on the experiences of manufacturers, wearers and collectors of the garb, the following pages offer a new perspective on the material and symbolic reinvention of Highland dress in Georgian Scotland.

I would like to thank the William Grant Foundation for its enthusiastic and generous support.

Edinburgh, 2022

Opposite: Targe, early 18th century

A targe is a type of shield. In the early modern period, they were considered an integral aspect of martial Highland dress. Targes were traditionally made of overlapping wooden planks covered by leather, studded with brass nail heads. They sometimes bore heraldic emblems of familial significance to the carrier. This was the first example of a Highland targe collected by the Society of Antiquaries of Scotland. It was donated by Edinburgh bookseller William Creech in 1781.

Foreword

by David Grant

WILLIAM GRANT FOUNDATION

As you will discover, Highland dress is both a complex and controversial topic. From a form of regional dress, the subject of curiosity and derision, it has slowly come to be regarded as a national costume for all Scots. There are those who quote rules about how it should – or *must* – be worn, while others prefer to take the individual creative approach and make the style their own. In this fascinating new book, Dr Rosie Waine shows us that it was forever thus.

Speaking on behalf of the William Grant Foundation, I have thoroughly enjoyed accompanying Rosie on her journey through the collections of National Museums Scotland, as she sheds light on its hitherto little-known riches of splendid tartan costumes, arms and accoutrements.

Rosie's work illuminates the unexpected degree to which a formalised culture of Highland dress had developed in Britain prior to the visit of King George IV to Edinburgh in 1822, an event of high tartan pageantry that has since been remembered as a doubtful expression of authentic Scottish identity. Her research challenges the accepted narratives of Highland dress history, from the commercial origins of clan tartans to the role of Highland clubs and societies in setting the sartorial standard.

Based on four years of scrupulous material culture research, this is a book for everybody who feels a sense of pride as they don their Highland wear.

Edinburgh, 2022

Opposite: Doeskin sporran, late 17th century (detail)

An evolution of the medieval purse, Highland sporrans were originally a form of practical accessory worn at the waist. As the centuries progressed, they became largely decorative in nature. This early example was purchased at auction in 1952 by the National Museum of Antiquities of Scotland and is part of the Major J. Milne-Davidson collection.

*The William Grant Foundation
is funded by family owned distiller
William Grant & Sons Ltd*

A Lady in the Highlands of Scotland.

Ja: Basire sculp.

The Plaid which is part of this Dress, is a Piece of chequered Silk or Woollen Stuff of about three Yards long and two Breadths wide; the Ladys generally dispose of it in such a manner as to reach the Waist behind, to let one Corner fall as low as the Ancle on one Side, and the other hang in Folds over the opposite Arm.

Introduction

by Dr Rosie Waine

NATIONAL MUSEUMS SCOTLAND

HIGHLAND dress history is composed of familiar footholds – the same characters and events are revisited time and again: Bonnie Prince Charlie and the Jacobites, Sir Walter Scott and the Royal Visit of 1822, the Balmoral heydays of Victoria and Albert. The story of tartan's rise is by now so ubiquitous, one might question the need to return to it. By delving into the surviving material culture of the period, this book aims to revisit and offer new perspectives on old tales.

What follows is not intended to be a chronological re-telling of the history of Highland dress, illustrated by a collection of surviving objects pulled from the stores of a national museum. Rather this book is an exploration of how Highland dress culture was reformed by the philosophies and material practices of the later eighteenth and early nineteenth centuries. It does not seek to claim, as others have, that the traditions of Highland dress were entirely 'invented' during this period. Instead, it argues that Highland dress culture was – and remains – a living tradition, which has been continuously remade and adapted to suit the social, cultural and political landscapes through which it moves.

Throughout the centuries, Highland dress culture has undeniably been appropriated, reclaimed and romanticised. However, it can also be said to have its roots in a historical, material reality. This study will explore how the late Georgian pursuits of amateur antiquarianism and conspicuous consumption converged with a popular taste for patriotic spectacle to create the archetypal Highland dress silhouette still recognised and referenced in contemporary Scotland. Through a series of object studies, we will examine how the Highland past was made material in the Georgian era, and how the acts of manufacturing, wearing and collecting Highland dress during this period should be considered fundamental to our understanding of the costume in the present day.

Opposite and page XIII: Costume prints, mid-18th century

In 1759 and 1760, John Barrow published *A New Geographical Dictionary*. The work was presented in two volumes and printed by J. Coote of London. Barrow's *Dictionary* contained more than 140 engravings, including maps, perspective views of places, structures and ancient ruins, and several plates depicting the traditional costumes of various regions around the world. Although Barrow's *Dictionary* contained detailed maps of Scotland, Ireland, England and Wales, only the regional dress of the Scottish Highlands was described and illustrated. Banned since the last Jacobite Rising of 1745–46, Highland dress was a subject of popular fascination in Georgian Britain.

This publication is based on the findings of a four-year research project funded by the William Grant Foundation, begun in 2018. The aim of the project was to map the contents of the tartan and Highland dress holdings of National Museums Scotland, with a view towards how the collection might be researched, exhibited and expanded in the future. In addition to a diverse array of men's, women's and children's wear, the collection also encompasses a significant body of domestic and commercial textiles, weaponry, paintings and prints, and papers relating to notable manufacturers and collectors of tartan. Together, these holdings can be used to trace the altering form and function of the garb.

As a living tradition, the material culture of Highland dress has been shaped not only by its wearers, but also by those who have chosen to study, collect and preserve its history. The study and collection of Highland dress artefacts has had a demonstrable impact on its aesthetic development, moulding its cultural legacy from the late eighteenth century onwards. Chapter 1 of this book provides a collecting history of the tartan and Highland dress objects acquired by the museum, from the foundation of the Society of Antiquaries of Scotland in 1780 through to the most recent curatorial practices of the twenty-first century. This chapter acknowledges the role of collectors, researchers and curators in determining the survival and interpretation of Highland dress within the museum world and asks, how have popular perceptions of the costume been influenced by the custodians of its material heritage?

The eighteenth and nineteenth centuries saw the rebranding of Highland dress in the public imagination, both within and outwith Scotland – from regional to national, rebellion to respectability, coarse stuff to finest worsted. Chapters 2, 3 and 4 present an object-driven discussion of Highland dress culture and its emerging place within British society, covering the period *c.*1745–1845. This was a formative era in the history of the costume. Over the course of a century, Highland dress was transformed from a marginalised traditional garb, associated with the warrior culture of the Gael, into an urbane fashion statement, a popular subject of antiquarian interest, and a patriotic icon of Scotland.

The surviving material culture of Highland dress has often been studied in isolation. It sits on the fringes of dress and fashion scholarship, regarded as a niche area of academic interest within an already specialised field. In antiquarian circles, approaches to the costume have tended towards the mythic and overly descriptive. Due consideration has seldom been given to the wider sartorial context within which these objects were made, used, inherited and displayed. An essential element of this study has been to reconceptualise the tartan and Highland dress collection in these terms – acknowledging the national distinctiveness of the costume, yet appreciating its stylistic relationship with the everyday, ceremonial and fancy dress cultures of Georgian Britain.

Habit of a Gentleman in the Highlands of Scotland.

This Gentlemans Garment is called a Trowse, consisting of Breeches & Stockings all of one Piece, something like those worn by Rope Dancers. They have also a short Coat & Waistcoat something longer, over which is thrown a kind of Cloak of chequer'd Tartan, called a Plaid. Instead of the Trowse they sometimes wear a short Stocking, which comes little higher than the middle of their Calf.

CHAPTER 1

Highland dress culture and the national collections

'Highland dress is still very much a living thing. Nothing that lives stands still, and growth or change is a sign of life.'

H. F. McClintock to John Telfer Dunbar (17 May 1948)

Pages xiv–1: Tartan cloak (detail)

The tartan used to construct this cloak does not have an official name. The pattern pre-dates the rise of clan tartans in the early 19th century.

Fig. 1.1 (opposite): Tartan cloak, late 18th or early 19th century

The cloak was donated to the Scottish Naval and Military Museum in 1930 by Belle Sutton, widow of artist and antiquarian William Skeoch Cumming. It is part of a large collection of artefacts, accumulated by Cumming throughout his career.

IN the historic collection of the National War Museum is a man's cloak; it is made from a hard worsted tartan, the particoloured check small and visually dense [Fig. 1.1]. The tartan has been woven in a close twill-weave, composed of four distinct coloured yarns: indigo, green, scarlet and azure. The resilient structure of the fabric would have made the cloak a sturdy piece of outerwear, keeping its owner relatively warm and dry when walking or riding in poor weather. The cloak is three-quarter length with a vent at the centre back, the cut suited to taking long strides or mounting a horse. The thick shoulder cape and high turned-down collar further underscore the garment's practical functions. A series of buttons can be employed to close the cloak at the neck, each one containing a wooden core covered by the same tartan used throughout the rest of the garment. This is a common stylistic feature of tartan clothing made and worn in the late eighteenth and early nineteenth centuries, its uniformity and neatness echoing the general move towards greater simplicity and less ornamentation in elite male clothing of the era [1.2]. Recent conservation saw the cloak washed, which released large quantities of acidic soiling from the fabric and restored some of the lightness of the original colours. This – combined with the ragged, stained hem of the cloak and the many visible repairs about the collar – implies that the garment once saw heavy use [1.3].[1]

Laying the cloak flat on a table and opening it up, we can get a better sense of its overall construction. The eye is immediately drawn to the inside of the collar, where two cotton tapes have been sewn into the neckline [1.4]. The newest and cleanest of the two is evidently a twenty-first century museum object label, secured delicately to the brittle cloth with a light tacking stitch. It carries the number used to identify the cloak to curators; this corresponds to the number entered against the object description in the museum register, on its physical object file and to its digital record on

Fig. 1.2 (above): Cloak buttons

The cloak buttons contain a wooden core, covered by the same tartan used to construct the main body of the garment. This technique can often be observed in men's tailored clothing dating from the 18th and 19th centuries.

Fig. 1.3 (opposite, above): Cloak collar

The cloak was evidently a practical and much favoured garment. The collar shows distinct signs of repair. A different coloured thread has been used to restitch loose seams and reinforce weakened areas, prolonging the life of the object.

Fig. 1.4 (opposite, below): Labels

Sewn inside the collar of the cloak are two labels. The first bears the name of the cloak's collector, 'W. S. Cumming'. Although it is not an original feature of the garment, the label is part of the object's history and will never be removed by curators. The second label carries the unique number used to record and identify the object by National Museums Scotland.

the museum catalogue. The number is prefixed by the letter 'M', classifying the object as belonging to the military collections of National Museums Scotland. The first half of the number contains a date – 1930 – which denotes the year that the object was accepted into the collection. The second half of the number – 272 – indicates that it was the 272nd military object collected that year.

For those familiar with the history of the National War Museum, sight of the label will tell them that it was among the first objects to be collected by what was then known as the Scottish Naval and Military Museum (SNMM). This organisation was established in the grounds of Edinburgh Castle in 1930, near the colossal structure of the Scottish National War Memorial. According to the former curator of military collections, Stuart Allan, the purpose of the new museum was to act as 'a place to record systematically Scotland's military history, with especial reference to the Scottish regiments'.[2] Naturally, uniform and weaponry were significant aspects of the museum's early collecting activities and remain important concerns to this day. It is possible that the cloak once served a military function; volunteer forces raised during the Napoleonic Wars, for example, were expected to provide their own kit, which included appropriate outerwear.[3]

After a period of closure during the Second World War, the SNMM reopened as the Scottish United Services Museum (SUSM) in 1949 and operated independently for several decades before eventually being absorbed into the Royal Scottish Museum (RSM) in 1970. When the RSM amalgamated with the National Museum of Antiquities of Scotland (NMAS) in 1985, the SUSM became part of the newly-established museum consortium, the National Museums of Scotland, and was rechristened the National War Museum following an extensive refurbishment in 2000. The bringing together of the disparate holdings of these separate heritage organisations laid the foundation for the collections of the present-day National Museums Scotland, so-called since 2006. The hierarchy of information displayed on the neatly penned label speaks to the cloak's journey as a collected object and its navigation through this complex institutional history. Understanding that journey is crucial to understanding the full biography of the object: from manufacture, to use, to the reasoning behind its preservation and occasional display.

The other, older label speaks to its life before the museum. The name 'W. S. Cumming' has been woven into the cotton tape, the red thread contrasting starkly against the white. This marker of ownership does not relate to the original wearer of the cloak, but to the man who collected it, William Skeoch Cumming. A celebrated scholar and artist, Cumming is best known for his watercolours depicting Scottish military and historical subjects, executing portraits in oil, and for designing the tapestry *The Lord of the Hunt* for the 4th Marquess of Bute, which was woven at Dovecot Studios in Edinburgh. Comprising some 178 objects, the Cumming donation was among the earliest and most substantial to be made to the SNMM upon its institution in 1930. It contains a varied selection of regimental uniform, arms and accoutrements, ranging in date from the late eighteenth to early twentieth century; its contents reflect Cumming's creative and intellectual interests, as well as his artistic method. Cumming habitually referenced extant examples of Scottish costume and weaponry in his historical compositions, drawing inspiration from his own personal collection of artefacts and from the copious notes, sketches and photographs made during a lifetime of visits to Scotland's ancestral houses [1.5].[4]

At the time of its accession into the museum collection, the cloak was said to date to *c*.1745, placing its period of initial use within the context of the last Jacobite Rising of 1745–46, when the exiled House of Stuart embarked on its final military effort to reclaim the British throne from the ruling

HIGHLAND DRESS CULTURE AND THE NATIONAL COLLECTIONS

Fig. 1.5: *Portrait of William Skeoch Cumming (1864–1929) in interior*, unknown artist, unknown date, photograph

Cumming is depicted in a studio, standing beside one of his own watercolours. He is surrounded by historical artefacts. Several of the objects displayed within this image have been identified in the Cumming donation at the National War Museum, including an 18th-century dirk [NMS M.1930.290] and a carved powder horn [NMS M.1930.300] mounted side by side above the mantlepiece on the far left.

(National Galleries of Scotland)

HIGHLAND STYLE

House of Hanover. During the campaign – which was initiated and relied heavily upon support from within Scotland – Highland dress and tartan clothing emerged as popular emblems of the Jacobite army and were widely adopted by advocates of the Stuart cause.[5] Following the failure of the Rising in 1746, Parliament introduced legislation that banned the use of 'the Clothes commonly called Highland Clothes' by Scottish civilian men and boys and stated that 'no Tartan, or party-coloured Plaid or Stuff shall be used for Great Coats, or for Upper Coats', upon penalty of imprisonment or transportation overseas to a British penal colony.[6] By highlighting 'Great Coats' and 'Upper Coats' made from tartan cloth as proscribed articles, the authors of the ban acknowledged the symbolic power of tartan in the context of Jacobite unrest and sought to curtail its use in forms of male outerwear readily associated with outdoor military activities, such as marching or the rallying of volunteers. An exception enshrined within the wording of the Dress Act meant that Scots serving in the British army could retain tartan as part of their uniform, effectively transforming a marker of rebellion into a martial icon of the state.[7] The ban on civilian use would last for almost forty years, and while tartan and Highland dress did not altogether disappear in Scotland during the era of proscription, this aspect of regional dress culture was irrevocably changed.

Dating the cloak to *c*.1745 situates it within a small yet significant group of rare material survivals from this period, when the ownership of such clothing carried with it an element of danger. However, Cumming provided no supporting evidence to suggest that the mid-eighteenth-century dating was accurate, presumably relying on his own expertise in historical artefacts to gauge its authenticity. Provenance unchallenged, it would later feature in an exhibit of Jacobite relics in the museum gallery, displayed alongside a tartan dressing gown and a mid-eighteenth-century tartan coat and trews, allegedly worn by Prince Charles Edward Stuart and collected by Augustine Earle of Heydon Hall, Norfolk in 1746 [1.6].[8]

More than twenty years after the Cumming donation entered the collection of the SNMM, the son of his erstwhile patron, Lord David Crichton-Stuart of Bute, made two substantial donations of early tartan fabrics, costume and documentary material to the National Museum of Antiquities of Scotland. These donations, made in 1952 and 1953, once belonged to John Crichton-Stuart, 4th Marquess of Bute, and are collectively referred to as 'The Bute Collection' by dint of provenance. De-

Fig. 1.6: Display of objects in the Scottish United Services Museum, 1958

An array of tartan clothing thought to be associated with the last Jacobite Rising of 1745–46, on display at the SUSM. The cloak collected by William Skeoch Cumming is visible on the far left.

(© Scotsman Publications Ltd / www.SCRAN.ac.uk)

spite the name, much of what The Bute Collection contains was originally collected and researched by beneficiaries of the Marquess of Bute's patronage – most notably by Cumming and the eminent Scottish sculptor James Pittendrigh MacGillivray.[9] Among the material formerly belonging to Cumming is a group of twenty tartans, checks and drugget, reputedly amassed by the folklorist and antiquarian Dr Alexander Carmichael during travels in the Outer Hebrides in the late nineteenth century [1.7].[10]

The age and quality of Carmichael's specimens vary considerably, but can be largely dated to the Georgian era. A keen collector of material and oral culture, Carmichael was the compiler and editor of *Carmina Gadelica*, a seminal work based on his own extensive research into and collection of Gaelic history, language and culture.[11] A portrait of Carmichael by Cumming was reproduced in the first volume of *Carmina Gadelica* in 1900, indicating that the pair enjoyed a professional relationship in the years immediately prior to its publication. Each fragment of textile attributed to Carmichael in The Bute Collection is glued to heavy sheets of paper, the edges perforated as if once bound into a book for easier perusal. One of the fragments is a rectangular swatch of twill-weave worsted tartan, the sett quite small and visually dense, composed of indigo, green, scarlet and azure coloured yarns [1.8].[12]

Fig. 1.7: Dr Alexander Carmichael (1832–1912)

Carmichael is pictured outside his home on the Isle of Lismore, Argyll, c.1900. He was a noted scholar, folklorist and collector of Gaelic literature and material culture.

The possibility that Carmichael's swatch and Cumming's cloak may have a shared history did not surface until 2018, when the survey of the tartan and Highland dress holdings of National Museums Scotland funded by the William Grant Foundation brought these two objects into conversation for the first time. Examining the interior construction of the cloak, it became apparent that a rectangular panel of cloth used to cover and reinforce the backside of the exterior buttons had been cut short [1.9]. This area of loss corresponded, both in pattern and size, to the textile fragment thought to have been collected by Carmichael in the Outer Hebrides. It therefore seems likely that the swatch was in fact harvested from the inside of the cloak in Cumming's possession, although exactly when this might have occurred is difficult to ascertain.

In addition to this intriguing discovery, the survey of the museum's

HIGHLAND STYLE

tartan and Highland dress holdings allowed for comparisons to be made between Cumming's cloak and other garments and textiles in the collection. This exercise illuminated stylistic and material qualities of the cloak that would more readily place it within the early nineteenth century, as opposed to the mid-eighteenth. Not only does this elicit important questions about the accepted dating and Jacobite era associations of the cloak – aspects which have historically been integral to its interpretation and display – it also prompts us to reassess the origins and character of the Carmichael textiles held by the museum. Always assumed to be separate to the well-known body of textiles and garments collected by Carmichael and deposited with the West Highland Museum at Fort William, it now appears probable that the twenty textile fragments held by National Museums Scotland date from Carmichael's days in Edinburgh and from his late-in-life collaborations with other antiquarians, such as Cumming. While we are left with more queries than answers, we know for certain that things we once accepted about these two objects hailing from the museum's historic collections require fundamental reassessment and reinterpretation.

Figs 1.8 and 1.9 (left and right): Swatch, and cloak interior

A swatch of tartan, thought to have been collected by Dr Alexander Carmichael in the late 19th century. Beside it is a view of the interior of the cloak from the collection of William Skeoch Cumming. It is probable that Carmichael harvested the swatch from Cumming's cloak, and not from the Outer Hebrides as was previously supposed.

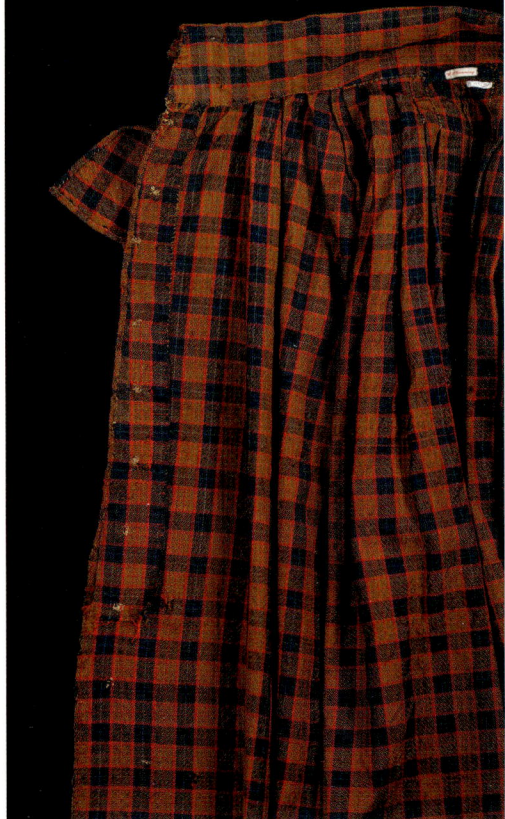

Old objects have the capacity to tell new stories, perhaps different to the ones they told before. Revisiting the history of a museum artefact can bring details to the fore that may have been unknown or gone unquestioned by an object's previous custodians. This is not a comment on the aptitude of curators past, but rather a reflection on how the world of museums – physically, organisationally and intellectually – has gradually changed with the passage of time. Museum collections are not static things. The information we hold about the objects in our care is always open to reinterpretation, informed by shifts in historical and curatorial perspectives and material discoveries about the objects themselves. Like any other aspect of the museum collection, tartan and Highland dress artefacts are subject to re-evaluation as fresh findings come to light and popularly accepted notions are tested.

In the current displays of the National Museum of Scotland on Chambers Street, Edinburgh, Highland dress artefacts and tartan costume do not loom large – but they are present, representing just one of the material manifestations of cultural identity that form part of Scotland's national story. As is the case for most museums, the objects that are selected for public exhibition represent only a small sliver of what is held behind the scenes. The museum's extensive holdings of Highland dress and tartan objects have a long and a multifaceted history, stretching back to the foundation of the Society of Antiquaries of Scotland in 1780. Focusing on a selection of these artefacts from the museum's stores and displays, this chapter will provide a brief overview of the major curatorial and cultural concerns which have guided the growth of the Highland dress and tartan collections since the late eighteenth century.

The Society of Antiquaries of Scotland

The Society of Antiquaries of Scotland (SAS) was formally instituted in Edinburgh on 18 December 1780 by David Erskine, 11th Earl of Buchan. Shortly thereafter, a museum was established to care for its burgeoning collections: books, manuscripts, objects of prehistoric, Roman, Viking and medieval origin, ethnographical artefacts, and objects of natural history.[13] The SAS characterised its museum as a museum of 'antiquities'. However, as noted by Hugh Cheape, it is important to recognise that this concept was widely interpreted by its members. Alongside the collection of artefacts that spoke to the history and pre-history of the nation, other objects were collected 'in the prevailing spirit that times were changing and that the familiar would soon be an irretrievable thing of the past'.[14] In this context, Highland dress artefacts emerged as a category of object that seemed to represent Scottish culture both past and present – a living tradition in need of preservation and cultivation. That being said, the antiquaries did not

HIGHLAND STYLE

value all aspects of Highland dress culture equally and were quite selective in what they chose to accumulate for study. This was not outside the ordinary for the Georgian curatorial tradition, which tended not to recognise dress as worthy of collection.

During the late eighteenth and early nineteenth centuries, garments were not typically considered the stuff of museums. The nascent study of dress was largely confined to the compilation of richly-illustrated costume books, which carried plates detailing regional style against discussion of local habits. Clothing was a resource; it was ephemeral and necessary. Rather than safeguarding costume as a historical artefact, it was common practice for dress of all ages and types to be passed down, cut up and reused, recycled into fancy or theatrical wear, or sold off on the second-hand market. Treasured pieces and relics sometimes found their way into early nineteenth-century waxwork exhibitions celebrating national culture, but for the most part the collection and preservation of dress was a private endeavour conducted by the interested few.[15] Such societal attitudes may explain the relative absence of Highland clothing in the earliest collections of the SAS and why other, hardier aspects of Highland dress culture were privileged in their stead. Whereas garments were treated as transitory and useful things, Highland weapons and accoutrements were increasingly regarded as talismanic and displayable objects, communicative of a bygone world still within living memory.

One of the first Highland dress objects to enter the collection of the SAS was a weaponised sporran cantle [1.10].[16] It was donated by Francis MacNab, the 12th Chief of Clan MacNab, around the time that the SAS was incorporated by Royal Charter in 1783. The earliest description of the cantle can be found in an inventory of the antiquities housed at the Society's first museum in Edinburgh, thought to have been taken around 1785.[17]

Fig. 1.10: Weaponised sporran cantle

This weaponised sporran cantle was among the earliest donations to the Society of Antiquaries of Scotland in the late 18th century. It was presented by Francis MacNab, the 12th Chief of Clan MacNab.

The Head of a Highland man's Purse, where in is concealed 4 Pistols, 2 pointed to the right & as many to the left side. Presented by Francis McNab of McNab, Esq. NB – They may be fired either singly, in pairs, or all at once. The materials are brass, steel, & silver.[18]

The original description accompanying the MacNab donation of the weaponised sporran cantle is replete with scrawled deletions and amendments – the compiler of the inventory evidently indecisive on how best to articulate the inner workings of such a peculiar thing. Although the cantle does host a firing mechanism – not dissimilar to that of a flintlock pistol – its design is less elaborate than its description in the inventory might suggest. When properly loaded and triggered, the device is theoretically capable of producing a shot explosive enough to injure the hands of the person holding it, though no record exists to suggest a curator ever tested this assumption. Comparable examples are scarce; the artefact is not representative of a popular style of sporran, rather a modish interpretation on the accepted form.

The archetypal Highland dress sporran evolved from the soft leather purses of the late medieval period, which were typically worn suspended from a waist belt and kept closed by way of leather thongs or drawstrings [1.11].[19] These purses were considered necessary accessories, useful for carrying money and other small, portable belongings close to the body. While their chief functions were to convey and conceal precious things, it was also common for them to be decorated in eye-catching ways. Fine materials were often incorporated into their manufacture to communicate

Fig. 1.11 (below, left): Buckskin sporran with plaited drawstrings, late 17th century

A belt would have been threaded through the loop sewn to the body of the purse, allowing the sporran to be securely suspended at the waist. The braided leather embellishing the purse flap was a popular form of sporran decoration prior to the introduction of metal clasps.

Fig. 1.12 (right): Doeskin sporran with brass cantle, early 18th century

The ring and dot motifs which adorn the metal clasp are typical forms of sporran decoration for the period. According to tradition, this particular sporran belonged to a cousin of Mackenzie of Caberfeidh, Piper Bhan, and was worn at the Battle of Culloden in 1746. The small cut visible at the top of the purse is said to have been made by a sword thrust. The Mackenzie crest, a stag head, is stitched into the leather front of the purse.

HIGHLAND STYLE

the social status and identity of the wearer, as well as advertise the skill of the maker.

From at least the late seventeenth century, it became more common for Highland purses to be closed by way of a metal clasp. Also known as cantles or 'locks', these clasps provided a plain surface into which devices and initials could be engraved or embossed by the maker, or scratched by the owner. Most surviving examples are made of brass or pewter and carry names, dates or simple emblems such as ring and dot motifs or interlocking triangles [1.12].[20] Some makers would cast the molten metal into protuberant shapes, such as human and animal heads. Ringing the top of the sporran and facing outward, these bestial faces were perhaps meant to signify the protectors of the purse and its contents [1.13, 1.14].[21] To connect the metal clasp to the body of the purse, the maker would typically stitch the two elements together using strong leather thread or catgut. When the purse became damaged or decayed, the decorative clasp could be removed and retained as an heirloom, or else reused to provide a top for a new sporran. This potential for generational refashioning and regifting – combined with the physical and emotional closeness that a wearer could develop for the object itself – transformed the cantle into an important, highly expressive aspect of Highland dress culture over the course of the long eighteenth century.

Incorporating an elaborate firing mechanism into the body of the cantle may be regarded as a logical progression of the integral functions and cultural meanings embodied by the design of a typical sporran clasp. It can also be interpreted as an example of how historical interest and the pursuit of novelty could converge within the styling of an elite commission. MacNab's unusual donation was manufactured during the later decades of the eighteenth century, at a time when complex mechanical objects were considered fashionable collectables and, in some cases, were specifically constructed to act as guards against theft.[22] It was also a period when, increasingly, people

Figs 1.13 and 1.14: Sealskin sporran with a brass cantle, early 18th century

The design of the cantle includes a series of human and animal faces, symbolically guarding the entrance to the purse. Although unusual, this style of decoration is not unique. National Museums Scotland holds similar examples, possibly by the same maker. The cantle has been mounted onto the purse backwards using string, implying it has been repurposed from a different sporran.

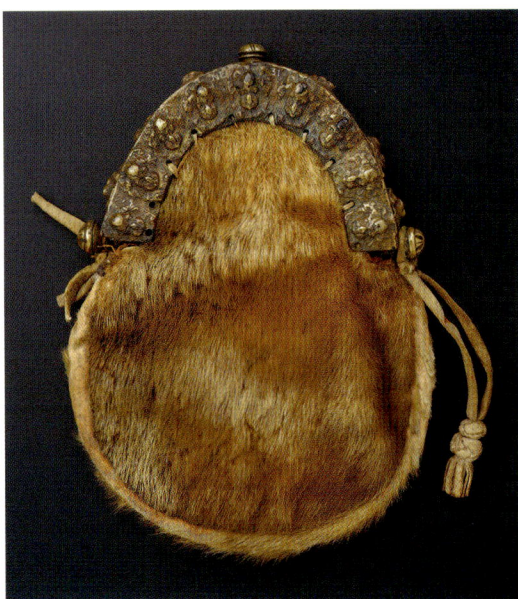

looked to material things, whether inherited or newly-forged – as a way of negotiating their relationship with the past.²³ MacNab's cantle, with its blending of ancient and contemporary features, represents an object straddling two eras.

It is now generally accepted that the weaponised sporran lock in the early collections of the SAS was the inspiring object for a passage in Sir Walter Scott's historical novel *Rob Roy* (1817). In this, the titular character produces 'a large leathern pouch, such as Highlanders of rank wear before them when in full dress, made of the skin of the sea otter, richly garnished with silver ornaments', and warns his surrounding kinsmen:

> 'I advise no man to attempt opening this sporran till he has my secret,' said Rob Roy, and then twisting one button in one direction, and another in another, pulling one stud upward, and pressing another downward, the mouth of the purse, which was bound with massive silver-plate, opened and gave admittance to his hand. He made me remark, as if to break short the subject on which Baillie Jarvie had spoken, that a small steel pistol was concealed within the purse, the trigger of which was connected with the mounting, and made part of the machinery, so that the weapon would certainly be discharged, and in all probability its contents lodged in the person of any one, who, being unacquainted with the secret, should tamper with the lock which secured his treasure. 'This,' said he, touching the pistol – 'this is the keeper of my privy purse.'²⁴

Fig. 1.15: *The MacNab*, by Sir Henry Raeburn (1756–1823), *c*.1810, oil on canvas

In this portrait by Sir Henry Raeburn, Francis MacNab's preoccupation with wealth, status and fashionable consumption is on full display. Although he projected an image of a secluded laird, he was thoroughly enmeshed in high society living and had a reputation for lavish spending. On his death in 1816, MacNab left an impoverished estate and debts in the region of £35,000.

(Photograph © CSG CIC Glasgow Museums Collection, reproduced by kind permission of Diageo)

For Sir Walter Scott, the cantle in the collection of the SAS represented an ingenious security measure, worthy of the canny mind and character of a legendary Highland folk hero. For MacNab, a notorious showman and spendthrift, it was an exercise in extravagance [1.15]. Whether the cantle was ever capable of firing a shot is debatable, yet its complex symbolisms endure in the eye of the beholder. This rare and perplexing artefact exemplifies the transformation in attitude towards Highland dress that occurred over the course of the long eighteenth century: a careful blending of material fact, conspicuous consumption, and a romanticised vision of Scottish history and culture. The method of the cantle's collection and its translation beyond the walls of the SAS museum into the literary landscape of Georgian society exemplifies how the materials of the past could shape popular perceptions of it.

As the nineteenth century progressed, the character and fortunes of the SAS underwent significant change. Its collection was continually on the move as the society struggled to find a permanent home, retain a sense of enthusiasm and commitment among its membership, and remain solvent.[25] Eventually, the SAS collection passed into public ownership in 1851, with the National Museum of Antiquities of Scotland opening on the Mound in 1858. A catalogue of the NMAS holdings, printed in 1865, records a slight increase in donations of Highland dress material associated with the Jacobite era of unrest, such as the engraved blade of a *sgian dubh* 'found on Culloden Moor' and a dagger with a wooden handle 'left by a Highlander in a farmhouse near Edinburgh, in 1745'.[26] A further catalogue was published in 1892, marking the removal of NMAS to its long-time home on Queen Street. This revised edition detailed how the national collections had grown and diversified by the close of the Victorian period, outlining landmark acquisitions, such as the iconic Lewis chess pieces and the Hunterston brooch.[27] Scottish weapons and jewellery are well represented within its pages, with many examples purporting to hail from the historic Highlands. Several of these pieces had once belonged to noted history painter and former curator of NMAS, James Drummond.

Drummond's curatorship in the mid-nineteenth century heralded a more focused approach to the collection and cataloguing of Scottish martial culture, with a noticeable inclination towards the accumulation of Highland arms and accoutrements. During his years at NMAS, Drummond created a series of watercolour drawings based on museum artefacts and objects in the possession of fellow artists and members of the Highland gentry. Several of the objects that he recorded were part of Drummond's personal collection, which he bequeathed to NMAS on his death in 1877. The drawings he created were eventually lithographed and published in the volume *Ancient Scottish Weapons* (1881), which included an introduction and descriptive notes provided by the Keeper of NMAS, Joseph Anderson [1.16, 1.17].[28] As noted by historian Anne MacLeod, the generic title of the volume belies its broadly Highland content.[29] Drummond's detailed depictions of targes, swords, dirks, powder horns, pistols, muskets, axes, sporrans and brooches were accompanied by illustrations of ancient pipes, harps, drinking vessels and agricultural implements. This accumulation reinforced the popular understanding of the Highland past as warlike, ritualistic, and indivisible from the harshness of the land. Drummond's style of visual cataloguing, replicated elsewhere by contemporaries, represented the material culture of the Highlands as an antique regional artform, with the artefacts themselves held up as emblematic repositories of generational memory and custom [1.18].[30]

In line with other museums in Britain, by the early twentieth century NMAS had begun to regard historic clothing and fabrics as collectable, displayable things. Archaeological textiles entered the museum as and when they were unearthed, imparting a sense of early weaving and dress

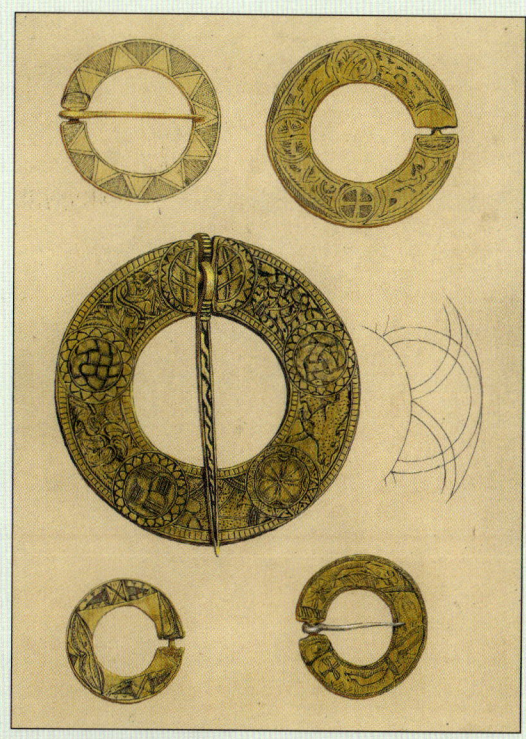
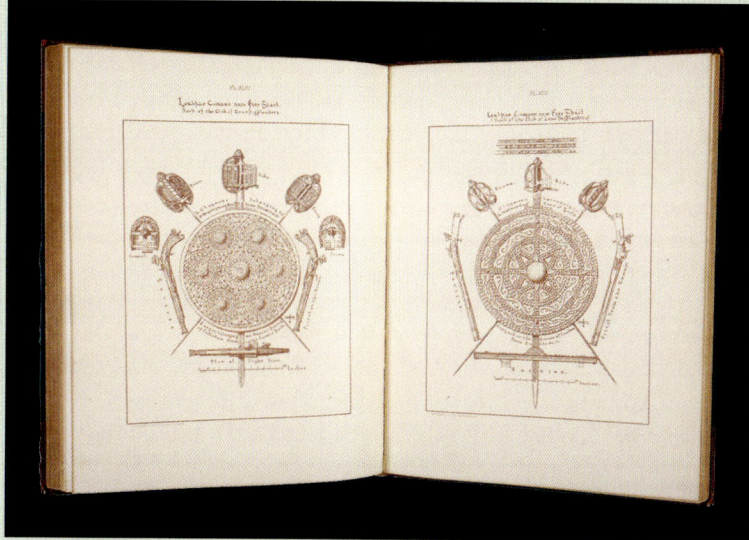

Figs 1.16 and 1.17 (above, left and right): *Ancient Scottish Weapons* (1881)

Illustrative plates from the book, based on original paintings and drawings made by James Drummond RSA. Several artefacts depicted in this publication are now in the care of National Museums Scotland.

Fig. 1.18 (left): *Leabhar Comunn nam Fior Ghael* (*Book of the Club of True Highlanders*), in 2 volumes (1880–81)

Artefact illustrations made by London architect and surveyor, Charles Niven MacIntyre North for *Leabhar Comunn nam Fior Ghael*. MacIntyre's study contains 340 detailed drawings based on Highland relics, encompassing traditional dress, accoutrements and musical instruments.

Fig. 1.19: Plaid, 17th century

Taken from the dressed skeleton of a man found preserved in peat at Quintfall Hill on the Barrock Estate, near Wick, Caithness, in 1920.

practices in Scotland that usefully augmented the fieldwork undertaken by Victorian ethnographers and folklorists, such as Dr Alexander Carmichael and John Francis Campbell of Islay.[31]

In 1920, the body of a man was found buried at Quintfall Hill on the Barrock Estate, near Wick, Caithness [1.19]. Although his linen undergarments had long since disintegrated, his woollen over and under breeches, two jackets, bonnet, plaid, leather purse and shoes had been preserved by the peat. A collection of coins found in the purse confirmed that he had lived during the late seventeenth century, making it one of the earliest surviving examples of quotidian Highland dress in public ownership.[32] The museum's collection of excavated apparel continued to grow over the course of the twentieth century, with comparable finds emerging in Morayshire, Ross-shire, the Isle of Lewis and Shetland.[33] Extremely fragile yet remarkably intact, these discoveries have enriched understanding of everyday wear within Highlands and Islands communities during the early modern period. As rare examples of common clothing, these objects provide a sobering counterbalance to the martial accoutrements of ceremonial Highland dress, which survive in relative abundance. The remains uncovered at Quintfall Hill in 1920 offer a glimpse of ordinary concerns, so often lost or difficult to discern within the historical record. The layering of rough woollen garments over homespun linen speaks to the challenges of travel and subsistence in the Highland landscape, and how an individual might come to rely upon the folds of a capacious plaid to trap warmth close to the skin and keep away damp. Once on display at NMAS, mounted onto a realistic mannequin of a standing man, the delicate garments are now stored in a facility where destructive handling can be kept to a minimum.[34]

Donations and purchases of historic cloth, attire and regional crafts became more numerous and varied in nature at NMAS. Suits of eighteenth and nineteenth-century Highland dress were acquired through loans, auctions and estate sales, most often tied to family stories of Jacobitism or to the visit of George IV to Edinburgh in 1822. Others were presented by members of the public, who had come to regard these outfits as an important part of Scotland's national culture and viewed NMAS as their natural home. However, despite this intuitional shift in attitude towards the social, cultural and economic significances of dress in historic and contemporary Scotland, this aspect of the NMAS collecting policy remained peripheral and piecemeal until at least the 1970s.

Preserving crafts and industry

Standing in the *Scotland Transformed* gallery of the present-day Museum of Scotland is an early nineteenth-century handloom, exhibiting a partially-woven length of Hunting Stewart tartan. The tableau of the loom is a striking one. The unfinished cloth, empty weaver's bench and scattered tools give the impression of a moment suspended in time – as if the weaver has simply stood up from his task and walked away [1.20]. It was acquired by the Keeper of the Technological Department of the Royal Scottish Museum in 1934 and today sits within the curatorial responsibility of the Department of Science and Technology at National Museums Scotland.[35]

Financed by the proceeds of the Great Exhibition of 1851, the RSM began life as the Industrial Museum of Scotland in 1854. When it was eventually opened to the public in 1866, it was rechristened the Edinburgh Museum of Science and Art before eventually becoming known as the Royal Scottish Museum from 1904. The RSM came into existence at a moment when museums started to embody civic values of education and progress; it was one of the many museums inaugurated during the mid- to late nineteenth century, with the primary function of recording and celebrating the rapidly evolving industrial landscape of Victorian Britain.[36]

HIGHLAND DRESS CULTURE AND THE NATIONAL COLLECTIONS

Fig. 1.20: Handloom, mid-19th century

A handloom dating from the middle decades of the 19th century, used by weavers in Kilbarchan until it was purchased by the Royal Scottish Museum in 1934. At the time of its acquisition, traditional hand skills were in decline and there was an institutional desire to preserve this aspect of textile culture in Scotland.

The handloom was sold to the RSM by a master winder and warper, John Houston, shortly after his retirement from the trade in 1934. Born in Port Glasgow in 1855, census records suggest that Houston had lived and worked in the same weaver's cottage in the small village of Kilbarchan, Renfrewshire, since the late nineteenth century. He would continue to reside there until his death in 1938 at the age of eighty-three. The sale of his loom to the RSM also included various tools used by Houston in his work, and two windows salvaged from the shop of a fellow retiring weaver, also from Kilbarchan.[37]

Following receipt of his loom by the RSM in July 1934, Houston travelled to Edinburgh to take part in its installation in the gallery. After the loom had been successfully reconstructed, the old man was photographed sitting at the weaver's bench, working a length of Hunting Stewart. The choice to weave a section of tartan reflected the usual output of the loom, illustrating the economic significance of the cloth to the cottage industry of the village. Perched expertly with both feet resting lightly on the treadles, Houston is shown raising the picking stick in one hand and grasping a loaded shuttle in the other [1.21]. The purpose of the image was to provide curators with a demonstrative pose, which could later be used to create a realistic human model to fill Houston's place. Whether such a plan ever came to fruition is unclear. However, the retention of the original photograph in the object file for the loom preserves Houston's practiced, instinctive motions in perpetuity. The scene it captures is a poignant one, recording the moment when the handloom ceased its active, creative function and became a museum artefact.

'It was an interesting experience for me,' reflected Houston, writing to curator Thomas Rowatt to acknowledge payment for the objects and for his time. 'I hope and trust when all the looms are erected and the scheme completed that it will prove as great a joy to those who promoted the idea as it was to me to have the distinction of being associated in a small way in providing an exhibit which will be interesting for future generations.'[38] Houston's words convey a tacit acceptance that he – and the loom he had given over into the care of the national collection – represented the last gasp of a bygone industry, fated to become a cultural curio.

The loom was positioned as the central object within a replica of a weaver's workroom, constructed to be representative of the year 1830. This date was chosen to reflect the probable decade of the loom's manufacture. In the same corridor stood a nineteenth-century silk loom with a Jacquard mechanism, once used in Stonehouse, Lanarkshire, and also collected by the RSM in 1934.[39] Interpretative boards positioned alongside the display informed visitors that handlooms had once occupied an essential role not only within the industrial landscape of Scotland, but also within the homes and lives of Scottish weavers working to contract in rural areas:

HIGHLAND DRESS
CULTURE AND THE
NATIONAL COLLECTIONS

Hand-loom weavers were a thoughtful and diligent class scattered throughout the length and breadth of the country and forming a large and important part of the industrial population. They mostly worked in their own homes, where a room, set apart for weaving, was equipped with one of perhaps two looms, together with pirn wheel and other necessary accessories. It is to the craftsmen who operated these looms that the originality of Scottish fabrics is largely due and many of the early tartan designs were first woven upon the cottage hand loom.

Fig. 1.21: John Houston (1855–1938)

Retired handloom weaver Houston at the Royal Scottish Museum in 1934, working the same length of Hunting Stewart tartan that remains in the loom to this day.

The label further asserted that with the invention and mass-adoption of the power loom and factory system, cottage handweavers had become a marginalised workforce in Scotland 'and by the late 19th century they had to be content with an occasional web when the productive capacity of their mechanical competitors was unduly taxed'.[40] The design and interpretation of the exhibit sought to underscore the importance of inherited skills within areas of specialised industry and hinted at the pangs of anxiety and loss felt within rural communities, like Kilbarchan, when such pathways to reliable employment and collective manufacturing identity broke down in the wake of increased mechanisation.

The accession and subsequent display of Houston's handloom in the RSM reflected a broader preoccupation with the decline of traditional handcrafts that marked the early decades of the twentieth century. Kilbarchan itself briefly emerged as a focal point within this discussion, brought to national attention by the activities of handloom weaver and contemporary of Houston, Willie Meikle. With his own inherited handloom – representing three generations of weaving skill – Meikle participated in numerous craft demonstrations in Britain and overseas, presenting himself as a living exhibit to raise awareness of the exodus of skilled workers in the trade with the passing of his generation.[41] Today Meikle's loom is housed at the Weaver's Cottage in Kilbarchan, a traditional eighteenth-century weaver's dwelling that passed into the care of the National Trust for Scotland in 1953. The loom still forms an active part of demonstrations and represents the last 'working' handloom in the village.

In the wake of the Second World War, museums began to take a more active role in preserving and promoting the tartan weaving industry in Scotland; some even instigated schemes aimed at fostering traditional hand skills among the younger generation of workers, offering their collections as teaching tools. In 1949, curator Margaret O. MacDougall and Captain Jack MacLeod of the Cuchullin Handloom Company set up a 'tartan room' at Inverness Museum and Art Gallery [1.22]. Their aim was to provide train-

Fig. 1.22: Margaret O. MacDougall

Margaret O. MacDougall was Inverness County and Burgh Librarian and the curator of Inverness Museum. She was an acknowledged expert in several areas of Scottish material culture and local history, including old Inverness silver and tartan.

(ANL / Shutterstock)

ing and follow-on employment for war veterans within their community, with original fabric samples from the museum's collection provided for consultation in a bid to ensure accuracy and historical authenticity in the tartans being produced locally.[42] Such regional efforts were complemented by schemes executed on a national scale.

As a Scottish counterpart to the *Britain Can Make It* exhibition staged at the Victoria and Albert Museum in London in 1946, the RSM hosted the *Enterprise Scotland* expo in August 1947. This was an enormous exhibition of post-war commodities made exclusively in Scotland and was composed of more than three thousand items – from stoneware jugs to toy elephants, barrel chairs to dress sporrans. Planned to coincide with the inaugural Edinburgh International Festival, the overarching goal of the event was to encourage commercial investment in Scottish industry from buyers at home and overseas. Like many expositions of the period, *Enterprise Scotland* was designed to champion technological innovation in established, as well as emerging, industries. Traditional Scottish textile crafts – such as tartan and Fair Isle – were presented with a 'modern twist' and characterised as responsive to the changing times and needs of consumers.[43]

In the centre of the Textile Hall, an eighteen-foot-high plaster figure of a woman, known as 'Jenny Weave' [1.23], was draped in swathes of Stewart tartan, specially woven for the occasion by a local Scottish maker. Jenny Weave held a bolt of the tartan in her left hand and, from her upraised right, threads of tartan stretched across the full forty feet of the exhibition hall and provided a particoloured canopy under which visitors could walk and engage with the products of Scotland's looms and workshops.[44] Although

Fig. 1.23: 'Jenny Weave' (1947)

The sculpture known popularly as 'Jenny Weave', installed in the Textile Hall of the *Enterprise Scotland* exhibition at the Royal Scottish Museum in 1947.

(© Design Council, DHRC / University of Brighton / www.SCRAN.ac.uk)

HIGHLAND STYLE

it is not currently known where Jenny Weave ended her days, her installation at the RSM represents a curious blending of the commercial and the curatorial in the post-war era of economic reconstruction. The use of the museum as a venue for *Enterprise Scotland* helped to imbue modern Scottish crafts with an attractive sense of historical and national significance in the eyes of the buying public, while also demonstrating the increasing convergence of the heritage and industrial spheres.

Makers and the museum world

In 1906, James Pittendrigh MacGillivray contacted the Head of the Department of Textile Industries at the University of Leeds, Professor Roberts Beaumont [1.24]. He wanted to procure a plaid of the MacGillivray clan tartan, but was dissatisfied with the quality of the fabric then being produced by commercial mills in Scotland. Before a meeting of the University of Leeds Textile Society in 1908, he described the difficulties that he had encountered and the high material quality he expected from the contemporary producers of historically-rich fabrics:

> *I could find nothing better than some thin, soft, flannel-like material, with the traditional stripes all out of proportion, crude, sharp colours, and the scale of the sett reduced to less than a quarter of what I deem proper size. To anyone acquainted with the artistic beauty and masculine character of the fabric known as old Highland hard tartan, made of hard hand-spun yarns, coloured with kindly vegetable dyes, and woven on the hand-loom – the modern product is far from being acceptable. There is a dignity of character about these old Highland, hand-craft fabrics which the best work of the machine – even with the most scientific care – can only emulate but not excel.*[45]

Fig. 1.24: *James Pittendrigh MacGillivray (1851–1938) with a Statuette of Lord Byron in the Background*, unknown artist, unknown date, silver gelatin print

Although he is best known as a sculptor, MacGillivray also possessed a rich knowledge of tartan. As well as building a collection of historic and contemporary tartans, he was responsible for transcribing 19th-century pattern books belonging to the celebrated tartan weaving firm Messrs Wilson of Bannockburn. Today, MacGillivray's transcriptions are part of the Society of Antiquaries of Scotland Numbered Manuscript Collection.

(National Galleries of Scotland)

He was determined to acquire a piece of modern MacGillivray that faithfully reflected the qualities he had observed in samples from his own personal collection of historic tartans. Professor Beaumont, with the resources and technical expertise of the Department of Textile Industries at his disposal, was well-positioned to help him achieve that goal.

Professor Beaumont and his cohort of students began MacGillivray's commission by consulting old specimens from the sculptor's personal collection of eighteenth and early nineteenth-century samples. They examined the tartan under a lens, and photographed the enlarged web for later reference when weaving; they noted its material characteristics, such as the coarseness of the wool, the twist of the yarn, and the twill structure of the cloth. In reproducing these integral elements in the finished textile, they hoped to match the 'handle' (essentially, the feel) of the historic fabric as closely as possible. However, despite the original aim of the project being to produce a length of cloth reminiscent of extant Georgian examples, Beaumont chose to employ thoroughly modern techniques and materials for the sake of cost and practicality. Although the pieces in MacGillivray's collection were all hand-woven, the college did not have a handloom of the requisite size to produce MacGillivray's desired fabric width. Instead, to MacGillivray's displeasure, Beaumont instructed his students to conduct the weaving on a mechanised dobby loom, of the type in use since the mid-nineteenth century.[46]

MacGillivray was unimpressed with their first attempt, sent to him in September 1906. The structure of the fabric was altogether too loosely woven when compared to the 'old fabrics' he had shown them, and 'the pattern was not square, and some of the stripes and setts which should have agreed were unequal in width'.[47] In defence of his student's work, Beaumont pointed out that the specimens in MacGillivray's collection were 'all differing in texture and materials' and there was a 'lack of symmetry in the dimensions of the checks'.[48] Nevertheless, they agreed to try again.

In addition to issues of texture, durability and pattern consistency, the question of authentic colouring was also raised. MacGillivray clearly believed that vegetable dyestuffs, such as heathers and lichens native to the Scottish Highlands, would produce the best effect. However, Beaumont was insistent that he could reproduce a Georgian colourway using twentieth-century chemical dyes, which he claimed would not degrade with age or exposure to the environment. He enlisted the help of a silk dyer in Yorkshire, who assembled a palette of chemically-derived shades in imitation of the 'soft tones' found in MacGillivray's historic samples. The result satisfied Beaumont's wish for permanence, while also catering to MacGillivray's desired aesthetic.[49]

While the first attempt sent for MacGillivray's inspection had proved unsatisfactory, the second met with his immediate approval. Writing to Beaumont on receipt of the new fabric in August 1907, MacGillivray congratulated him on the success of their experiment: 'I thank you for yesterday's letter covering sample of the new web of tartan, the texture of which seems to me very satisfactory – it has quite the character of an old bit.'[50] He promptly ordered four yards, with the promise of more. Upon examining the cloth at MacGillivray's home the following month, the 4th Marquess of Bute was impressed and observed that it was of a much 'finer appearance' than a plaid recently made for him by a mill in Aberfeldy.[51] Meanwhile, fellow collector and friend, Dr Seivwright Davies of Blackburn, Lancashire, upon receiving a sample of the cloth from MacGillivray, bemoaned the modern concessions made in its production: 'It is quite the best modern hard tartan I have seen, and is as you say nearly but not quite as good as the old, but we shall never have the same colours as formerly[,] now that they can make colours chemically and so cheap. I believe they are very permanent, but are more rank raw & impure than the old natural organic colours.' Criticisms notwithstanding, he asked MacGillivray whether Beaumont would produce a length for him. Davies was looking to have an eighteenth-century style tartan jacket made for a fancy dress ball and could not bear to cut up a surviving piece of historic fabric for the purpose.[52]

The surviving products of MacGillivray and Beaumont's collaboration are today held by National Museums Scotland, forming part of The Bute Collection donated to NMAS by Lord David Crichton-Stuart in 1952 and 1953 [1.25, 1.26].[53] They were purchased by the 4th Marquess of Bute when MacGillivray was obliged to sell his personal collection in 1930 due to financial hardship. The material collected by MacGillivray includes an array of textile samples and documents related to the tartan weaving company, Messrs Wilson of Bannockburn, which he purchased directly from the firm in the early 1900s shortly before their liquidation.

Founded in the mid-eighteenth century, Wilsons was a major supplier of tartan in Britain for much of the Georgian era. The firm is considered by many as responsible for the commercial development and success of clan tartans, and for the transformation of the cloth into a desirable fashion fabric with a life beyond the specialist spheres of Highland dress tailoring and military uniform. MacGillivray's collection includes tartans woven by the firm in the late eighteenth and early nineteenth centuries, an original account book containing tartan pattern tabulations, and transcriptions of dedicated pattern books made by the firm around 1819, which MacGillivray copied from the originals in 1907.[54] It seems probable that this was the body of historical material that Beaumont and his students consulted in the preparation of their replica fabrics. In embarking on a project to manufacture tartan that faithfully reflected the material qualities of the Georgian samples he treasured, MacGillivray was attempting to recapture elements of traditional tartan production that he regarded as lost to history with the passage of significant firms, such as Wilsons.

Although they did not know it at the time, MacGillivray and Beaumont's academic experiment anticipated an emergent material trend within modern tartan studies, manufacturing and curatorial practice. By the middle decades of the twentieth century, there had been a makers' turn within tartan and Highland dress scholarship; researchers embarked on projects to reconstruct the tartans of the past, hoping to gain an instinctual understanding of the fabric and its history via the manual labour involved in physically recreating it. Their varying successes or failures relied on their individual ability to attain the requisite knowledge and skill to manufacture cloth – from sourcing, handling and preparing the raw materials, to setting

Figs 1.25 and 1.26 (opposite): Tartan samples, *c.*1907–8

Surviving samples of the tartan woven for James Pittendrigh MacGillivray by Professor Roberts Beaumont of the Department of Textile Industries, University of Leeds.

up and working the loom, to mastering appropriate finishing techniques. Their conclusions drew upon the gains of embodied experience and were informed by their observations of surviving artefacts and documentary sources held in private hands and in public museum collections, such as those in the stores of National Museums Scotland. The innovative reconstructive work of these men and women created a significant bridge between the academic, curatorial world of Highland dress studies and the commercial, manufacturing world of contemporary tartan mills and Highland dress outfitters. While many participated in this community of research and remaking, it was the lifework of two individuals which truly formalised this practice-led area of scholarship and set the stage for those who came after – Donald Calder Stewart and James Scarlett.

D. C. Stewart inherited his interest in tartan from his father. Donald William Stewart had been a partner in the firm Romanes & Paterson, which had been retailing tartan in Edinburgh since the early decades of the nineteenth century. His *Old and Rare Scottish Tartans* (1893) was regarded as a respectable addition to the considerable body of work produced on the subject in the Victorian period. While authors such as William and Andrew Smith had received notable success with their 'machine painting' method of tartan reproduction in *Authenticated Tartans of the Clans and Families of Scotland* (1850), most scholars had struggled to successfully articulate the materiality of tartan through the medium of print, despite many having access to artefacts and commercial samples for reference. *Old and Rare* was remarkable for being the only publication so-far produced to illustrate the setts under discussion with actual pieces of tartan, woven in silk.[55]

The work of D. C. Stewart further pushed the boundaries of tartan reproduction in the world of print and, ultimately, provided curators of the cloth with a useful method of comparing patterns held by different collectors. Stewart took to the loom in the late 1940s, reassessing his father's work from the vantage point of a weaver's bench. His efforts resulted in *The Setts of the Scottish Tartans* (1950; 1974), the first publication devoted not only to exploring tartan's history but also to outlining the physical nature of its construction. Distinct from the works of his predecessors, Stewart assessed each piece of tartan he encountered as an individual object with its own material character and history. The innovative 'colour-strips' that accompany Stewart's notes on the various patterns he studied were designed to imitate the arrangement of the warp threads as they would appear on the loom before weaving, prompting the reader to visualise how the cloth would be formed with the introduction of the corresponding weft.[56] This approach fostered a greater appreciation for the cloth itself, drawing attention away from its inherited symbolisms of clanship and heraldry.

The primary research which underpinned Stewart's work on *The Setts* can now be perused at the Highland Archive Centre in Inverness. Chief among these working papers is SINDEX (shorthand for *Sett Index*); this is essentially a filing system of the threadcounts and scales of numerous historic and modern tartans, derived from the physical specimens consulted by Stewart in his fieldwork. It also contains instances of tartan setts taken directly from paintings from the eighteenth and early nineteenth centuries, which feature Highland dress and tartan costume. Each sett is given a card and each card is topped by a colour strip, allowing for cross-referencing against extant objects [1.27]. The cards also carry notes of any published works which mention these objects or paintings – an extremely useful feature when one considers the relative absence of formal referencing in nineteenth- and early twentieth-century texts. Upon his death in 1977, Stewart bequeathed his working papers to his friend and long-time collaborator, James Scarlett, whose continued work on and promotion of SINDEX fed directly into the creation of the present-day Scottish Register of Tartans, curated by the National Records of Scotland.[57]

James Scarlett came to the study of tartan later in life. From a chance visit to Scotland in the early 1960s, an observational interest in tartan quickly developed into an absorbing personal quest for the attainment of manual skill and understanding. By 1976, tartan weaving, study and design consultation had become his full-time occupation. Scarlett firmly believed that one's ability to conduct a serious study of tartan could only be enhanced by practical knowledge of the cloth and its construction, as well as an appreciation of its commercial history. Reflecting on the state of the field in 1987, Scarlett asserted:

> With such a quantity of tangible material and such a mass of myth to work on, tartan research has become a delicate mixture of detective work and experimental archaeology. Tartan is a textile owing its particular character to the crossing of coloured warp and weft threads, the full implication of which can only be fully understood by a practical weaver. This empiric approach is the key to tartan research, for the question 'What did the early Highland weavers do?' can often only be answered by 'What would I do in their place?'[58]

Throughout their respective careers, Stewart and Scarlett encouraged a craft-based approach to tartan research, shunning the popular preoccupation with clan tartan mythologies entertained by many of their contemporaries, in favour of studying the practical artistry involved in tartan design and execution. As colleagues with aligning mindsets and methodologies, their mutual desire to position tartan manufacturing in the public eye as a

HIGHLAND DRESS CULTURE AND THE NATIONAL COLLECTIONS

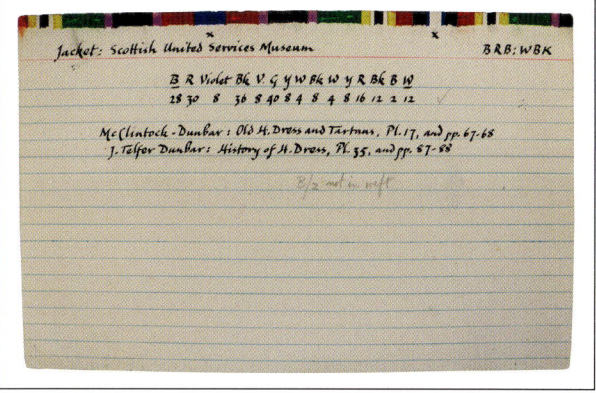

Fig. 1.27: SINDEX Tartan Index card, n.d.

SINDEX was a filing system of tartan patterns devised by the historian and handloom weaver D. C. Stewart as a method of recording the setts of tartan artefacts held across various public and private collections. This particular card records the sett of a tartan used in a mid-18th-century coat, formerly on loan to the Scottish United Services Museum.

GB0232/D108/1/4/1 [Papers of D. C. Stewart] (Highland Archive Centre)

Highland artform shaped by generations of inherited knowledge, fostered an entire school of thought within modern tartan scholarship. The interrogative object-based approach they championed has, over the past few decades, fed directly into the interpretation of objects in the care of the museum and continues to influence the work of contemporary scholars and makers to this day, such as the tartan historian and handloom weaver Peter Eslea MacDonald.[59]

Challenging myth and curatorial convention

Highland dress culture is characterised by the conflation of tradition and myth, of real and imagined objects. Since its emergence as an area of antiquarian interest in the late eighteenth century, scholars have explored how aspects of its historical authenticity have been complicated by its place within the commercial landscape of luxury goods and elite patterns of consumption. A major concern within these debates has been the system of clan tartans that emerged in the early decades of the nineteenth century; fuelled by the desires of contemporary Highlanders, manufacturers took inspiration from the ritualised heraldry practiced by Highlanders in the past to fashion an array of setts associated with specific clans. The extent to which this system can be considered a valid avenue of personal, familial and national expression remains a source of controversy and continues to attract derision within both scholarly and popular discourses. For some, the relative newness of clan tartans and their widespread adoption beyond the confines of Scotland itself makes them less worthy of serious study. For others, their rapid proliferation by the middle decades of the nineteenth century represents a single thread within multiple, interweaving narratives, that makes Highland dress culture what it is today. Encouraging a constructive dialogue between these two perspectives marked the curatorial approach to Highland dress collection and exhibition throughout the second half of the twentieth century.

Writing to fellow Highland dress historian and Honorary Curator of the Scottish United Services Museum, John Telfer Dunbar, in May 1948, H. F. McClintock voiced his scepticism of the 'debunking' tone levelled at historical fictions, such as the clan tartan system. For McClintock, clan tartans represented a bridging chapter within the continuing story of Highland dress. To ignore or dismiss them out of hand as outright fakery was not a useful exercise and would, he reasoned, stunt the pursuit of knowledge around the historical development of Highland dress more generally. '[T]he "heraldic" use of tartans seems to me to have been a natural and indeed a useful development', he noted. 'Highland dress is still very much a living thing. Nothing that lives stands still, and growth or change is a sign of life. I have no doubt that the adoption of family tartans has done much to keep alive interest in the dress and to promote its use.'[60] He did, however, urge the application of a critical eye. Like McClintock, Dunbar was wary of the dominating influence of clan tartan scholarship within the broader study of Highland dress and the impact of this on popular culture. In his dual capacity as a respected collector and professional curator, he sought to present a more nuanced interpretation of the historical significance of clan tartans to the wider public. As well as publishing what would come to be regarded as definitive revisionist histories of Scottish and Highland dress in the second half of the twentieth century, Dunbar's curatorial work marked a decisive shift in the presentation and interpretation of Highland dress culture within museum and gallery spaces.[61]

Exhibitions offer a unique staging ground for the presentation of new and emerging research. Designed as sites of discovery, they provide curators with the rare and valuable opportunity to highlight objects that challenge preconceived notions surrounding familiar topics. Until the middle decades of the twentieth century, the public exhibition of tartan and Highland dress objects had taken two distinct forms – commercially-centred efforts that positioned contemporary material alongside demonstrations of traditional skill, and the gathering together of historical relics that sought to explain the resonance of tartan within the political and dynastic histories of the nation. The latter invariably consisted of tartan remnants or costumes associated with exiled Stuart heirs and Jacobite adherents, sitting alongside examples of inherited Highland weaponry said to have been carried at one battle or another, denoting ancestral stories of victory and defeat. Reports that a tartan cloak worn by Prince Charles Edward Stuart in 1746 was on display in a tailor's shop window in Pitlochry, Perthshire, in 1902, represents a peculiar instance of these two worlds colliding.[62]

On 16 August 1949, Dunbar opened an exhibit titled *Old Highland Tartans* at Gladstone's Land, a seventeenth-century high-tenement house situated on the Lawnmarket in Edinburgh. Sponsored by The Saltire Society, the exhibition was drawn entirely from Dunbar's personal collection and displayed examples of eighteenth- and nineteenth-century rural and commercial tartans, spinning implements, dyestuffs, Georgian prints of Highland military and civilian costume, and manuscripts from Dunbar's own archive of Messrs Wilson of Bannockburn correspondence. That members of the royal family visited the exhibit during its run guaranteed it was well publicised by the Scottish press.[63] It was restaged in 1950 at Lady Stair's House with the support of Edinburgh council, to celebrate the gifting of Dunbar's extensive collection to the City. Retitled *Two Centuries of Tartan*, the interpretation and thematic arrangement of the material was much the same as in the previous year, but conducted on a grander scale.

The aim of the two exhibits was to document tartan and Highland dress culture prior to the popularisation of the clan tartan system in the mid-nineteenth century. Themes included tartan manufacture in rural communities, Highland dress as a regional and as an aristocratic costume, and the importance of the British military for the standardisation and promotion of Highland dress around the world. The commercial export of tartan was also explored, with one letter in particular catching the attention of journalists, causing a minor sensation in the press. Dated 25 May 1797, it was an order received by Wilsons that concerned the shipping of tartan to a plantation in America, for use in slave clothing.[64] This object unsettled traditional interpretations of the cloth by aligning it with Scotland's colonial legacy. Pointing to its use beyond the battlegrounds and ballrooms of Georgian Britain, the letter indicated how tartan had once been employed as a form of racial oppression.[65]

In each of the souvenir booklets made available for visitors to buy, Dunbar laid out his thesis for why a formalised system of clan tartans could not possibly have existed prior to the Battle of Culloden in 1746.[66] In particular, he decried the commercial influence of the *Vestiarium Scoticum*, published by the controversial Sobieski Stuart brothers in 1842. Purported to derive from a sixteenth-century manuscript that only the brothers had access to, the work assigned specific tartans to different Highland and Lowland families. Despite concerted scholarly efforts to debunk its contents, the *Vestiarium Scoticum*'s florid descriptions and pattern illustrations became standard references for Victorian manufacturers and fuelled the public perception of clan tartan as an ancient badge of Scottish identity for decades to come.[67] In curating a collection of costume, fabrics, domestic implements and makers' manuscripts that illuminated the craft and commercial histories of Georgian tartan, Dunbar hoped to cultivate a popular understanding of Highland dress that went beyond the familiar territories of Jacobitism and the romantic revival of clanship. Reception of the exhibits was divided, with some commentators deriding Dunbar's assertions as affronts to national pride.[68] However, the publication of D. C. Stewart's *The Setts of the Scottish Tartans* that same year reinforced the new direction modern tartan and Highland dress studies had taken: a greater emphasis on the cultural histories of makers and ordinary wearers, based on evidence gleaned from the physical and contextual study of individual artefacts. This in turn reflected a broader cultural shift within the work of curators and scholars by mid-century, who had begun to acknowledge dress as a viable area of historical enquiry.

Today the display of historic and contemporary fashion is an accepted part of the museum world. Most regional and national institutions will represent dress and textiles within their permanent galleries, even in some small way. Temporary fashion exhibitions prove extremely popular with visitors year-on-year, while re-enactment societies and historical reconstruction groups are thriving. The intimate nature of clothing is regarded as such a relatable and replicable experience, that seeing a costume on display is akin to stepping inside it, offering a sensory impression of the distant past that is difficult to achieve with other object types. However, this lauding of the fashion exhibit as an embodiment of historical and contemporary culture is a relatively recent phenomenon.[69]

The systematic collection and interpretation of dress only came to the fore in British museums during the second half of the twentieth century. Although dress had been collected before, it was very much a marginalised interest both curatorially and academically. For example, despite owning a large and diverse collection of ethnographical textiles and dress accumulated from various sources since its foundation, the RSM did not host a fashion display until the mid-1960s.[70] There were few heritage institutions or curatorial departments dedicated exclusively to the preservation and study of dress; and the skills to care for, research and interpret these objects was confined to a small network of individuals with emerging specialist knowledge. With the advent of clothing sales by British auction houses in the 1960s, a new appreciation of historical costume as a valuable and rare commodity became more prominent in the popular consciousness. Purchases and donations of such material increased as a result, accompanied by a growing public desire to see these things on display.[71]

In her capacity as Curator of Costume and Textiles, Naomi Tarrant was the guiding curatorial voice on dress history interpretation at National Museums Scotland until her retirement in 2002. Beginning her tenure at RSM, she was responsible for opening the National Museum of Costume at Shambellie House in 1982. Located in New Abbey, near Dumfries, this was the first museum devoted to the exhibition of costume in Scotland.[72] Between 1982 and its closure in 2013, this Victorian mansion in the Scottish Borders housed a permanent exhibition that spanned several rooms, populated by realistic fibreglass mannequins dressed in historic costumes [1.28]. Each room was themed to a different decade – 1882, 1895, 1905, 1913, 1945 and 1952 – with the figures inside dressed to reflect the social function of the space and the prevailing style of the moment. As discussed by Julia Petrov, this innovative arrangement allowed the visitor to navigate through the house, learn about the history of the family that had once inhabited it, and discover what fashion choices were available to successive generations, thus placing the exhibited costume firmly within a recognisable historical context.[73] This meant that a formal Highland dress suit once belonging to John Sutherland and manufactured in Glasgow by Hugh Morrison & Co., c.1890, could be installed within the drawing room at Shambellie House and be clearly identified by the roving visitor as an acceptable mode of late Victorian evening wear.[74]

Following the merger of the RSM and NMAS in 1985, Tarrant was responsible for devising a refurbished gallery of

HIGHLAND DRESS CULTURE AND THE NATIONAL COLLECTIONS

Fig. 1.28: Highland dress, c.1890

A formal suit of Highland dress once owned by John Sutherland, on display in the National Museum of Costume at Shambellie House. The suit was manufactured in Glasgow by Hugh Morrison & Co., a gentlemen's outfitter based on Jamaica Street that specialised in quality Highland costume for men and boys during the late 19th century.

HIGHLAND STYLE

Fig. 1.29: *Tartan* exhibition (1989)

A parade of historic tartan clothing, on display at the Talbot Rice Gallery as part of the Scottish iteration of the *Tartan* exhibition in 1989. By displaying the costumes uncased and in an elevated position, as if walking a catwalk, the fashion and design elements of tartan history were emphasised to visitors.

costume within the Chambers Street site. Open to the public from 5 April 1991, the overarching focus of Tarrant's new gallery was the physical making and structure of clothing. Themed largely on western European fashion, the displays also included comparative examples drawn from the museum's impressive collection of world dress and textiles accumulated since the 1860s. This approach saw a figure dressed in a modern sari placed alongside an eighteenth-century plaid, stitched with the date 1777, in a case dedicated to ethnographic material. The direct comparison between these two objects was meant to illustrate the commonplace use 'of a long length of cloth to make a complete garment', thereby placing this aspect of traditional Highland dress costume for women within a broader cultural and chronological perspective.[75]

From 1974 until his departure from the museum in 2007, Hugh Cheape was the resident expert on tartan and Highland dress culture at National Museums Scotland. In 1988, Cheape was closely involved with an exhibition staged at the Fashion Institute of Technology (FIT) in New York, to which National Museums Scotland lent a considerable amount of material. Responding to the enduring popularity of tartan as a fashion fabric, the *Tartan* exhibit at FIT was an extremely innovative show that presented a design history of tartan from the eighteenth through to the late twentieth century. The show was notable for its dynamic groupings of costumed figures, which were spaced throughout the exhibition to illustrate its major interpretative themes: the relationship between tartan and the military, the adoption of tartan in civilian dress, and the use of the fabric in modern and contemporary *haute couture*. These impressive tableaux were contextualised by a 'Tartan Library' and a 'Tartan Identification Gallery', where visitors could learn about the codification of clan tartans in the nineteenth century through the examination of portraits and cased displays of books and manuscripts. The press release for *Tartan* promised the public that they would be presented with a 'modern' and 'factual' history of the cloth, without losing any of the romantic intrigue ingrained within the subject matter, claiming, 'the Exhibition demonstrates that the colourful and rich features of tartan can be enjoyed even when presented analytically'.[76]

In the summer of 1989, *Tartan* came to Scotland [1.29]. Staged at the Talbot Rice Gallery in association with National Museums of Scotland, this version of the exhibition was timed to coincide with the Edinburgh International Festival and was meant to act as an appropriate accompaniment to *The Wealth of a Nation* exhibition then running at the Royal Museum of Scotland. Reflecting on the experience in 1993, Cheape noted how differently *Tartan* was received on either side of the Atlantic. While the audience in New York had been broadly enthusiastic, those who saw the show in Edinburgh were 'less accepting' of the style of presentation and mode of interpretation:

> *Critical comment at the time identified a failure to subscribe to orthodoxy or alternatively the neglect of a sometimes scholarly scepticism. For example, one body of opinion regretted that clan tartans were not paraded in the exhibitions and identified in their idiosyncratic detail, and another body of opinion searched for the explanation of tartan as a modern by-product of romanticism. A lively awareness of the various schools of thought contained between these polarities of the conservative and the revisionist prompted a thorough-going process of question and answer.*[77]

Cheape was acutely aware of the difficulties which attended the scholarly study of tartan in Scotland during the later twentieth century. Staged in the years following the publication of 'The Invention of Tradition: The Highland Tradition of Scotland' by Hugh Trevor-Roper (1983), it should perhaps have been expected that the Scottish incarnation of *Tartan* would divide opinion for evidencing a long and materially rich history of an apparent fabrication.[78] Trevor-Roper's essay remains an influential and much-cited text, despite its author's demonstrative lack of knowledge around important aspects of Scottish history and Gaelic scholarship.[79] However, work by specialists in Gaelic material culture, such as Cheape, have done much to lessen the academic framing of historic Highland dress culture as inherently inauthentic.[80]

Following the mixed critical reception of *Tartan*, the way that National Museums Scotland researched and exhibited its tartan and Highland dress collections underwent a period of sustained change. Hugh Cheape positioned himself at the vanguard of this endeavour, combining scientific analysis with historical research to test popularly-held assumptions about the stories these objects tell. In 1995, he curated a special exhibition titled *Prince Charlie's Tartan* at the Royal Museum of Scotland in commemoration of the 250th anniversary of the last Jacobite Rising of 1745–46. Several remnants of tartan were brought together in one place, their collective display meant to interrogate the emotive cult of textile relics associated with the exiled House of Stuart in Scotland. Among these pieces was a small fragment of tartan thought to have been cut from a kilt worn by Prince Charles Edward Stuart in 1746, purchased by the museum in 1993 [1.30].[81]

Following the defeat of the Jacobite army at the Battle of Culloden on

HIGHLAND DRESS CULTURE AND THE NATIONAL COLLECTIONS

Fig. 1.30: The Borrodale fragment

This small fragment of tartan is one of three belonging to a garment worn by Prince Charles Edward Stuart in 1746.

16 April 1746, the Prince had been forced to go into hiding. For several months, he relied on the protection and hospitality of his remaining supporters in Scotland before eventually making his escape to France in late September. Disguises were integral for ensuring safe passage, as he was hunted from place to place by British troops. This remnant is thought to be one of the few genuine textile relics associated with the Prince's flight across the Highlands, among a plethora of dubious examples in public and private collections. Two other fragments of the same tartan are held by the West Highland Museum in Fort William and at Stonyhurst College in Lancashire, with all three pieces believed to have come from a suit of Highland clothes given to the Prince by Catriona MacGregor, wife of Angus Macdonald of Borrodale, on 20 April 1746. Extensive historical research by Peter Eslea MacDonald, Tom Massey Lynch and Hugh Cheape on the different fragments appear to support this story.

Microscopic fibre and dye analysis of the fragments reinforced the suspicion that all three remnants had once belonged to the same historical garment. While the fibre analysis showed that the wool had likely come from a native breed of sheep, the presence of indigo and cochineal pointed towards the good availability of imported dyestuffs in the West Highlands during the early eighteenth century. These discoveries ran contrary to traditional interpretations of early tartan as a product of isolated labour reliant upon access to local stuffs, such as the heathers and lichens cited by James Pittendrigh MacGillivray in his reconstruction experiment with Professor Roberts Beaumont in 1906–8.

Between the years 1996 and 2007, Hugh Cheape was involved in an ambitious cross-institutional tartan dye analysis project which built upon the methodological approaches and initial findings of the Borrodale investigation. The project, which ran in three phases, drew on material held by National Museums Scotland, the West Highland Museum, Highland Folk Museum, and Inverness Museum and Art Gallery. Samples taken from eighteenth and early nineteenth-century specimens with reliable Highlands and Islands provenance corroborated the findings of the Borrodale analysis, evidencing the habitual use of imported stuffs in early Highland dress culture: indigo created brilliant blue, cochineal a blazing scarlet, and old fustic a gleaming yellow. The impression of the Highland economy that emerged from this project was of a society well-integrated into the networks of international trade, despite its apparent remoteness. It was also evident that, contrary to long held assumptions regarding a preference for muted palettes, bright colours abounded in tartan clothing of the era. This scientific data was corroborated by analysis of Gaelic sources, such as praise poetry, which celebrated scarlet as a key colour in Highland displays of social and political power.[82]

In 2007, the year Hugh Cheape stepped away from his curatorial role, a special exhibition on tartan fashion was staged at the National Museum of

Costume at Shambellie House. Titled *Fabric of a Nation*, the presentation and interpretation of the clothing on display echoed that advanced by the *Tartan* exhibitions of 1988–89. However, much of what was on show had been acquired for the national collection in the late twentieth and early twenty-first centuries. Historical tartan clothing and Highland dress costume were displayed alongside examples of contemporary British fashion; eighteenth-century arisaids once worn by Highland women and formal kilt suits intended for Victorian men and boys were contrasted against outfits from notable designers such as Vivienne Westwood, Jean Paul Gaultier, Sir Edwin Hardy Amies and Tommy Nutter.[83] Like *Tartan*, the exhibit proved popular with visitors. Unlike *Tartan*, it did not elicit negative criticism for dwelling on the long design history of the fabric. Rather, what had once been considered 'revisionist' now appeared almost conventional.

Highland dress and the Museum of Scotland

On St Andrew's Day 1998, the doors of the Museum of Scotland were officially opened by Queen Elizabeth II. This moment was the result of a sustained campaign to inaugurate a site dedicated to the display and interpretation of the combined Scottish collections of the NMAS and RSM, amassed over two centuries. The new building was designed by architects Benson & Forsyth, whose plan was inspired by Scotland's distinctive history and landscape. The exterior of the building is clad in Morayshire sandstone, while the shape and interior echo the feel of medieval Scottish castles with their spiral staircases, towers and narrow slit windows. Adjoining the grand Victorian building of the RSM, the Museum of Scotland is physically connected yet stylistically and conceptually separate.[84]

The question of how best to articulate the historical and contemporary relevance of tartan within the Museum of Scotland – a site dedicated to the exploration and presentation of Scottish culture – proved complex. The new museum was regarded as a valuable opportunity to address preconceived notions of what constituted the material culture of Scottish identity, past and present. Audience research conducted during the early planning stages had suggested that visitors expected to see stereotypically 'Scottish' emblems on display, such as 'quaichs, thistle cups, tartan and claymores'. However, respondents also indicated that such inclusions should not define the presentation of Scotland or come at the expense of telling lesser-known stories. The desire to celebrate tartan as a cultural symbol of the nation, while also suppressing connotations of kitsch and controversy, extended beyond the plan of museum exhibits and impacted the design of corporate branding. Members of the public wanted to see just 'a touch of tartan' in the uniforms of gallery attendants, and for 'tacky tartan' to be banished from the shelves of the giftshop. It was clear that the presence of tartan in the new museum, whether it be behind glass or behind the ticket counter, needed to be handled sensitively. In 2000, Mary Bryden, Head of Public Affairs at National Museums Scotland, reflected on the ensuing balancing act of showcasing familiar interpretations of Scotland alongside the unexpected:

> *Most people we were aware of had enjoyed the myths of Scottish history, but with the arrival of the Museum of Scotland it was literally 'time to get real'. A central element in our visitor campaigns was based on using stereotypes to attract attention, followed immediately by the strong message that the new Museum was going to knock them on the head. […] The response of some visitors is 'I never realised …'. Others do ask where the tartan and the bagpipes are. Of course they are there in the displays, taking their place alongside other objects in a wider context.*[85]

Historian Charles McKean noted that the Museum of Scotland project was significant for seeking 'a new relationship between architecture and artefact', at a time when the extremes of museum design tended towards the isolation of objects within neutral gallery spaces. Such spaces sought to remove architectural interference and provide curators with the freedom and flexibility to display objects like 'iconic artworks' detached from all exterior distraction.[86] Anyone who has visited the Museum of Scotland will have seen how the objects arranged across its several floors appear almost nestled into the fabric of the building itself. Many of its cases and installations are physically integrated into the walls and floors with different finishes applied to different areas, imparting a sense of fluidity and progression. These were quite deliberate choices, requiring close collaboration between curators and designers to make the space work for the objects and the objects work for the space. The chronological arrangement of the material works its way up the building, beginning with the prehistoric in the basement and culminating with the presentation of the modern and contemporary on the upper floors. The objective was not to give a thoroughly comprehensive overview of Scotland's past – though diverse and extensive, the combined Scottish collections of the RSM and the NMAS would not allow for something so ambitious – but to exhibit a thematic history of the nation, which drew upon the strengths of the museum's holdings.

The material culture of tartan and Highland dress is threaded throughout the displays of the Museum of Scotland, yet at no point does is overwhelm or obscure. Like the rest of the objects selected for display within the Scotland Galleries, the intension was to place this aspect of Scottish identity within a broader national context. Its appearance across a multitude of spaces is illustrative of the disparate aspects of Scottish life that Highland dress culture has touched, and at which points throughout Scottish history it has been most visible.

In the displays of *Scotland Transformed*, a gallery dedicated to the emergence of Enlightenment culture and the industrialising nature of late eighteenth- and nineteenth-century Scots, tartan is at its most prevalent. In the shadow of the towering Newcomen atmospheric engine, visitors are invited to explore the powerful material legacy of 'The Jacobite Challenge' within this age of great social and economic transition. A prominent theme in the display is Prince Charles Edward's assumption of Highland dress, which fixed the iconic persona of 'Bonnie Prince Charlie' in the popular imagination. Born and raised in exile, it was important for the younger members of the House of Stuart publicly to emphasise their Scottish roots in their fight to oust the ruling House of Hanover from the British throne. By donning tartan and carrying weapons associated with the historic warrior culture of the Highlands, they hoped to project a sense of dynastic legitimacy and strength. A key object in this story is an elaborate dress targe, sent to the Stuart court in Rome around 1740 by James Drummond, 3rd Duke of Perth. It is traditionally believed to have been part of a lavish commission of Highland dress and accoutrements, destined for Prince Charles Edward and his brother, Henry Benedict, and carried by the former during the ill-fated Jacobite Rising of 1745–46. Abandoned with the Prince's baggage train in the aftermath of the Battle of Culloden, it was rescued by a Jacobite officer, Ewen McPherson of Cluny, and remained in the family until 1928 when it was sold to John G. Murray of Clava. The targe is constructed in the typical Highland fashion, with over-lapping wooden boards covered by tooled leather made from pigskin. However, in place of

HIGHLAND DRESS CULTURE AND THE NATIONAL COLLECTIONS

Fig. 1.31: Dress targe, c.1739–41

A dress targe with elaborate silver mounts, associated with Prince Charles Edward Stuart. Although the front of the targe is covered by leather, it is backed with jaguar skin. This is a significant departure from the materials commonly found in Highland targes of the era and may be taken as a signifier of status.

HIGHLAND STYLE

the brass studs and plates which would customarily decorate the surface of a traditional targe, is an array of finely cast silver mounts coded with the iconic visual language of Jacobite loyalty [1.31].[87] The object entered the collection of NMAS in 1945 and remains one of the most significant Jacobite relics collected by the museum to date.[88]

At the opposite end of the gallery, around the corner from John Houston's handloom with its abandoned length of Hunting Stewart, the post-proscription history of tartan is presented in the 'Textile Trades' corridor. In a discrete display, documents from the Messrs Wilson of Bannockburn archive, a bound collection of clan tartan samples amassed by the Highland Society of London, a presentation copy of *The Clans of the Scottish Highlands* by James Logan and R. R. McIan (1845–47), and an array of Mauchline-ware trinkets collectively illustrate how tartan became a commodified emblem of the nation over the course of the nineteenth century. Surrounded by cases that are dedicated to knitting, lacemaking and cotton printing, tartan is interpreted as just one aspect of Scotland's rich textile heritage. Here its cultural significance is couched in commercial terms, with the cloth positioned as an influential product whose global success was hastened by the coming of the industrial age.[89]

Fig. 1.32: Highland dress suit

This suit of Highland dress was worn during the visit of George IV to Edinburgh in 1822 and was later taken to Australia by Donald Munro Ross in 1864.

Travelling to the floor above, the international resonance of Highland dress culture is addressed in an area of *Industry and Empire* dedicated to the experiences of the Scottish diaspora. Forming part of a display on 'Scotland and the World' is a Highland dress costume tailored in the Georgian style. It consists of a short tartan coat with a high collar, military braiding and domed metal buttons, a little kilt and plaid, and a taxidermy sporran. The Royal Stewart rosettes that adorn the front apron of the kilt and the epaulette of the coat are probably later nineteenth-century additions. According to family provenance, it was first worn during the visit of George IV to Edinburgh in 1822 and later taken to Australia by Donald Munro Ross when he emigrated there in 1864 [1.32].[90] The material additions to the costume imply that Ross incorporated the suit into his new life abroad, possibly as part of the thriving associational culture of Highland clubs and societies which had been established around the world by Scottish migrants by the close of the century.[91] The suit was gifted to National Museums Scotland by an Australian descendant of Donald Munro Ross in 1992, who wished to see it returned to the ancestral homeland of its erstwhile owner.

The historical roots of the Highland image can be found two floors down in the *Kingdom of the Scots* gallery, where the cultures of the different peoples and places that forged medieval Scotland are systematically explored. In an area titled 'Na Gaidheil', the material culture of the Gaels is presented to the visitor in thematic object groupings: weaponry, musical instruments, oral and literary traditions, and personal adornment, including plaid brooches, dirks, and sporrans dating from the seventeenth and eighteenth centuries [1.33].

Until recently, these displays were overlooked by a large portrait of the Piper to the Laird of Grant, William Cumming. Painted by Richard Waitt in 1714, the portrait is not a romanticised depiction of an imagined Highland past [1.34].[92] Rather, Waitt's work is a faithful document of the clothing and accoutrements that Cumming was expected to wear as a ceremonial figure within the household of the Chief of Clan Grant. Pipers were an important part of the retinue of retainers meant to communicate the status of a clan within a region. Taking their place alongside an array of storytellers, harpists, historians and fighting men, pipers were often rewarded for their fealty to the chief with gifts of hereditary land rights.[93] Cumming was in such a favoured position, as part of a family of trained musicians who had been in the service of the Lairds of Grant through multiple generations. With Castle Grant positioned prominently in the background, Cumming is shown flying the heraldic banner of the Grants from the drones of his bagpipe, the white silk painted with the clan motto of 'Stand Fast'. Much like the red ribbon cockade sewn to the brim of his broad bonnet, the tartan girded about his waist can be regarded as a form of livery, denoting Cumming's affiliation to the Grants. The luxurious fabrics used to fashion the belted plaid and heavily decorated coat would have been part of Cumming's wages. The dirk, basket-hilted broadsword, pistol and targe that hang about his person further underscore his dedication to the clan, as weapons he could draw upon in its defence. This portrait was one of many commissioned to impress visitors to Castle Grant with a sense of the Laird of Grant's wealth and authority as a Highland chieftain. However, at the time Cumming's portrait was made, clan society was in a state of transition and such displays of feudal power were fast becoming relics of history.[94] It was paintings such as this, hung in the ancestral houses of Highland families, which provided inspiration for later generations in their quest to 'revive' traditional Highland culture at the turn of the nineteenth century.

Over twenty years have passed since the opening of the Museum of Scotland in 1998, and little has changed regarding the interpretation of tartan and Highland dress culture within its displays. However, the same

Fig. 1.33: Highland flat ring brooch, 17th century

An archetypal Highland flat ring brooch of brass from Tomintoul, Banffshire. Such brooches were commonly worn by women throughout the late medieval and early modern periods. However, by the 19th century the plaid brooch had become a highly decorative piece worn by both men and women.

Fig. 1.34 (overleaf): *Piper to the Laird of Grant, William Cumming*, by Richard Waitt (d.1732), 1714, oil on canvas

Waitt's painting shows Cumming in the full Highland regalia of a loyal retainer. His costume is replete with markers of fealty to the clan, including a belted plaid of livery tartan, a red ribbon cockade, and a heraldic pipe banner.

41

cannot be said for the National Museum of Scotland as a whole. Significant financial investment in the site on Chambers Street brought with it the opening of ten new galleries in 2016, dedicated to the exploration of science, technology, art, design and fashion. In the *Fashion and Style* gallery, located on the ground floor off the grand Victorian atrium, visitors are invited to browse walls of cased displays containing historical dress, textiles, accessories and design ephemera. In the centre of the gallery a dramatically underlit catwalk showcases an array of posed mannequins dressed in contemporary fashion. Arranged in a broadly chronological narrative, the sections are themed to give an impression of how clothing and textiles have evolved with the passage of time. Changes in shape, texture, pattern and colour are contextualised against the cultural sensibilities and new technologies of different eras. The development of European style is implicit throughout, but with an eye towards the Scottish experience and the telling of individual stories. As in the 1998 displays of the Museum of Scotland, tartan is addressed in this space as a single element within the multifaceted cultural landscape of Scottish style [1.35].[95] Contemporary tartan fashion has occasionally made an appearance on the central catwalk, when gallery rotation and popular interest allow.[96]

Fig. 1.35: Tunic top, Turkish hareem trousers and headscarf, 1950s

Made from Farquharson tartan, this unusual ensemble belonged to Frances Strickland Lovell Oldham, also known as Frances Farquharson of Invercauld. Born in Seattle, Washington, in 1903, she travelled to Europe in the 1920s to pursue a career in journalism and became fashion editor for *Vogue* and *Harper's Bazaar*. On her marriage to Captain Alwyne Compton Farquharson, 16th Laird of Invercauld, in 1949 she embraced clan tartan as part of her new identity as a Highland society hostess. This unique outfit is currently on display in the *Fashion and Style* gallery.

Looking ahead

In 2018, a new object was purchased for the fashion and textiles collection at National Museums Scotland: a woman's tiered tartan cloak, fully lined with a bright, printed cotton and fastened at the neck by way of two yellow metal clasps, cast in the shape of lion's paws. The tartan used for the outer fabric is a large setting of the Royal Stewart, believed to date to *c.*1810–20 [1.36]. Due to its high-profile adoption by members of the British royal family and Scottish regiments since the early decades of the nineteenth century, the Royal Stewart has become one of the most popular and widely recognised tartans in the world and remains a common reference point within contemporary fashion to this day. Its dominance in the material construction of the cloak speaks to the emerging popularity of the sett during the era of Scottish Romanticism, while the presence of the printed cotton lining speaks to tartan's place within a broader culture of fashionable consumption.[97]

The newly-acquired cloak was selected for inclusion in the major summer exhibition *Wild and Majestic: Romantic Visions of Scotland*, which ran at the National Museum of Scotland from 26 June to 10 November 2019.[98] This exhibition interrogated Scotland's place within the European Romantic movement of the late eighteenth and early nineteenth centuries, a period when the cultural traditions of the Scottish Highlands and Islands were transformed into enduring symbols of wider Scottish identity. The cloak was displayed alongside three other tartan outfits from the museum's collection, set against a wall of customer letters and fabric samples selected from the Messrs Wilson of Bannockburn archive. This grouping of objects and documentary material collectively illustrated the rise of tartan as a popular fashion fabric within Georgian society and demonstrated to visitors how it was incorporated into ordinary clothing, as well as Highland dress costume. The juxtaposition of garments and manuscripts conveyed the importance of consumer choice in shaping the physical and ideological legacies of tartan in the nineteenth century, contextualising the symbolic resonance of the cloth by examining the material preferences of purchasers [1.37].

In conserving and mounting the cloak for display in the exhibition *Wild and Majestic: Romantic Visions of Scotland*, it became apparent that at some point in its long history the garment had been altered. Museum conservators unearthed details of the cloak's original construction that are, by now, difficult to discern with the naked eye. Formerly, the tiers of the cloak had been edged with pink silk ribbon. This was either removed – a

Fig. 1.36 (opposite): Cloak

A cloak of Royal Stewart tartan, lined with a bright printed cotton and fastened at the neck by two gold clasps in the shape of lion's paws, *c.*1810–20.

Fig. 1.37: Display of tartan costume in the *Wild and Majestic: Romantic Visions of Scotland* exhibition (2019)

common occurrence when refashioning a garment in the Georgian era – or else the fragile silk had perished with the passage of time. Without its gaudy trim, the visual and material impact of the cloak is somewhat diminished. When the garment was newly made, the lustre of the silk fibres would have caught the light and shone with the movement of the wearer, acting as points of brightness that accentuated the shape of the individual tiers as they cascaded down the body from the curve of the shoulder to the waist. Small scraps of rose-coloured silk can still be seen clinging to the stitch lines that border each tier, their relative lightness contrasting against the rougher texture of the worsted tartan beneath. The collar, now flattened against the shoulders of the mannequin, would once have sat much higher on the neck of the woman who owned it, affording her greater warmth and comfort as she went about her tasks. Present along the interior seam that joins the collar to the garment below is a ragged edge, composed of torn, undyed wool and fragments of red silk velvet. These remnants indicate the earlier presence of an interlined, quilted collar that was cut away by later hands. Uncovering and interpreting these details was only possible because time and money were invested in preparing the object for exhibition to the public; had it not been selected for display, the story of the cloak's remaking would have lain dormant in the storeroom, encased in tissue paper. The museum collection is full of such stories, waiting patiently to be told.[99]

As a living tradition, tartan is forever changing. As cultural perspectives, consumer habits and technologies shift, the meaning and the material scope of Highland dress will respond accordingly. As National Museums Scotland moves further into the twenty-first century, it is important that we continue to re-evaluate our relationship with tartan and Highland dress culture and assess its influence within historic and contemporary society. This is significant both for the objects we hold and for those that we may one day seek to acquire. What tartan means to different people at different points in time will continue to generate a rich vein of material culture, in need of careful reflection and interpretation by the curators of Scotland's material heritage.

Notes

1. NMS M.1930.272.
2. Allan 2012, 787.
3. See in particular: Gee 2003.
4. Dunbar 1981, 19.
5. There is a wide and varied literature on the complex relationship between tartan, Jacobitism, and the expression of Scottish cultural identity. See in particular: Nicholson 2005; Tuckett 2009; Pittock 2009; Coltman 2010; Pittock 2013.
6. 19 George II, Chap. 39, Sec. 17 (1746).
7. Clyde 1995; Mackillop 2000; Dziennik 2012.
8. These pieces of costume were on long term loan to the Scottish United Services Museum until the late twentieth century, when they were returned to the lender. They are not in the collection of National Museums Scotland.
9. The material donated to the National Museum of Antiquities of Scotland by Lord David Crichton-Stuart in 1952 and 1953 was originally housed in The Bute Collection at Mount Stuart, Isle of Bute.
10. NMS H.TTB 18.1–20.
11. See in particular: Stiùbhart 2008.
12. NMS H.TTB 18.14
13. Anderson 1989, 2.
14. Cheape 2000, 65.
15. Cumming 2004, 50.
16. NMS H.NE 12.
17. See inventory held by National Museums Scotland.
18. *Ibid.*
19. NMS H.NE 44.
20. NMS H.NE 43.
21. NMS H.NE 31.
22. There was a vogue for hidden mechanisms in furniture and personal adornment during the later decades of the eighteenth century, leading to the creation of myriad objects aimed at satisfying the twinned consumer desire for security and novelty. See in particular: Sargentson 2007.
23. Campbell 2016.
24. Scott 1818, vol. III, 209–10.
25. Bell (ed) 1981.
26. National Museum of Antiquities of Scotland 1865, 131.
27. National Museum of Antiquities of Scotland 1892.
28. Drummond 1881.
29. MacLeod 2012, 85.
30. McIntyre North 1881, 2 vols.
31. On the ethnographical approach to the study of dress that emerged in the later nineteenth century, see Taylor 2002, 193–236.
32. NMS H.NA 408–16; Orr 1921.
33. NMS H.NA 477.1; NMS H.NA 477.2; NMS H.NA 477.3–33; NMS H.NA 478; NMS H.NA 1037–1050; K.1997.36 A–B; K.19997.1115 A–H; M.1935.208.
34. See in particular: Wilcox 2016; 2017.
35. NMS T.1934.171.
36. Anderson 1989, 6–16.
37. Although the tools – comprising a pirn winding wheel and a yarn winder – have been retained, the two shop windows have been deaccessioned.
38. See correspondence retained in object file for NMS T.1934.171.
39. NMS T.1934.241.
40. See copies of old object labels retained in object file for NMS T.1934.171.
41. Meikle continued to appear at fairs and expositions right up to his death in July 1951, at the age of seventy.
42. *The Highland Herald* (15 September 1949).
43. Buckley 2007, 119.
44. *The Scotsman* (12 July 1947), 3.
45. National Library of Scotland (NLS) Dep. 349/15 (Copy of lecture on 'Scottish Clan Tartans' delivered by James Pittendrigh MacGillivray before the University of Leeds Textile Society, 21 February 1908).
46. NLS Dep. 348/2 (Professor Roberts Beaumont to James Pittendrigh MacGillivray, 29 September 1906); NLS Dep. 348/2 (Professor Roberts Beaumont to James Pittendrigh MacGillivray, 19 November 1907). The loom was constructed by Messrs Hutchinson, Hollingworth & Co. Ltd of Dobcross, Yorkshire.
47. NLS Dep. 349/15 (Copy of lecture on 'Scottish Clan Tartans' delivered by James Pittendrigh MacGillivray before the University of Leeds Textile Society, 21 February 1908).
48. NLS Dep. 348/2 (Professor Roberts Beaumont to James Pittendrigh MacGillivray, 6 September 1906); NLS Dep. 348/2 (Professor Roberts Beaumont to James Pittendrigh MacGillivray, 29 September 1906).
49. NLS Dep. 348/2 (Report by Professor Roberts Beaumont titled 'Clan MacGillivray Tartan – Produced by the Textile Industries Department of the University, Leeds, under the direction of Professor Roberts Beaumont, M.Sc., Chief of the Department', 1907).
50. NLS Dep. 348/2 (James Pittendrigh MacGillivray to Professor Roberts Beaumont, 15 August 1907).
51. NLS Dep. 348/2 (James Pittendrigh MacGillivray to Professor Roberts Beaumont, 18 September 1907).
52. NLS Dep. 348/2 (Dr Seivwright Davies to James Pittendrigh MacGillivray, 1 December 1907); NLS Dep. 348/2 (Dr Seivwright Davies to James Pittendrigh Mac-Gillivray, 3 January 1908).
53. NMS H.TTB 14.1–2; Stewart 1893; Smith and Smith 1850.
54. An inventory of James Pittendrigh MacGillivray's collection was prepared in 1930, when financial difficulties pushed him to sell it. See copy of inventory in NLS Dep. 348/2. The account book and transcriptions can be accessed through the Research Library at National

Museums Scotland, where they form part of the Society of Antiquaries of Scotland Numbered Manuscript Collection, SAS Mss No. 609–613. See also: NMS H.TTB 12.
55. K.2006.301.1–2.
56. Stewart 1974, 5.
57. The working papers of D. C. Stewart and James Scarlett may be consulted at the Highland Archive Centre, reference HCA/D108.
58. Scarlett 1987, 67; Scarlett 1990.
59. MacDonald 2012.
60. NLS Acc. 12251/33 (H. F. McClintock to John Telfer Dunbar, 17 May 1948); McClintock 1943.
61. Dunbar 1962; Dunbar 1981.
62. *Sheffield Evening Telegraph* (17 July 1902), 7.
63. *The Scotsman* (7 September 1949), 6.
64. *The Daily Record* (15 August 1950), 6.
65. Faiers 2008, 270–72.
66. Dunbar 1949, 1950.
67. Sobieski Stuart 1842; Dunbar 1962, 112–43.
68. *Old Highland Tartans* led to the publication of several opinion columns in Scottish newspapers during its run. Correspondents seldom agreed with Dunbar's revisionist stance, with one contributor branding his interpretation of Highland dress history as 'anti-traditional'. See in particular: *The Scotsman* (27 August 1949), 9.
69. Petrov 2019, 1.
70. Taylor 2004, 131.
71. Tarrant 1999, 12.
72. Tarrant 1982.
73. Petrov 2019, 86.
74. NMS A.1987.258 A–T.
75. Tarrant 1996, 159.
76. The press release was reprinted in a review article for the FIT exhibition, which featured in *Scottish Quest Magazine*, see: Martin, 1988.
77. Cheape 1993, 35.
78. Trevor-Roper 1983. It is also worth noting that the *Tartan* exhibitions appeared in the wake of the highly influential *Scotch Myths* exhibition (1981), devised by Murray and Barbara Grigor. This show brought significant critical attention to caricatures of Scottish culture, prompting a national debate around the role of 'tartanry' in contemporary Scotland.
79. Pittock 2010, 32.
80. Cheape 2006; Cheape 2010; Dziennik 2012.
81. NMS H.1993.86.
82. See in particular: Quye, Cheape, Burnett, Ferreria, Hulme and McNab 2003; Cheape 2006, 85–87.
83. The *Fabric of a Nation* exhibition ran at Shambellie House between 1 April to 31 October 2007 and encompassed the following objects, the majority of which were collected in the wake of the Tartan exhibitions of 1988–89: NMS H.SMA 32; NMS A.1990.27; NMS A.1993.63 A; NMS A.1987.20; NMS A.1994.102 A–C; NMS A.1988.47 A–B; NMS A.1987.358 A–T; NMS K.1997.1034 A–C; NMS K.2005.28.1; NMS A.1990.231 A–C; NMS A.1989.228; NMS K.2004.286.1; NMS K.2005.70.1–2; NMS K.2007.27; NMS K.2007.37. Christened the Museum of Scotland when it first opened in 1998, today this area of the National Museum of Scotland site on Chambers Street is more commonly referred to as the 'Scotland Galleries'.
84. McKean 2000; Fladmark (ed) 2000; Bucciantini 2018.
85. Bryden 2000, 36.
86. McKean 2000, xii.
87. Dalgleish 2000, 98–99; Wyld and Dalgleish 2017, 87–89.
88. NMS H.LN 49.
89. It is significant that the central objects in this display are the ledgers of clan tartans assembled by members of the Highland Society of London in the nineteenth and twentieth centuries, thus presenting the antiquarian and the industrial histories of the cloth as if these two aspects of tartan interpretation are indivisible. See: NMS IL.2018.93.1 and NMS IL.2018.93.2.
90. NMS H.1992.1829.1–9.
91. Bueltmann 2014.
92. NMS H.OD 69.
93. Dodgshon 1998, 88–89.
94. Watt and Waine 2019, 12; Cheape, 1995.
95. NMS A.1994.1036 A–C.
96. Until recently, a tartan suit from Vivienne Westwood's *Anglomania* collection (Autumn–Winter 1993/4) occupied one of the cases on the central catwalk. It was tailored using a Bruce of Kinnaird sett woven for Westwood by Lochcarron of Scotland. The jacket can be worn with bondage trousers or a kilt (NMS K.2005.319. 1–3).
97. NMS K.2018.87.
98. Watt and Waine 2019, 44–47.
99. These discoveries were made and recorded by textile conservator Rosie Nuttall.

Highland targe

Made of wood and covered by tooled leather, the surface of this traditional Highland targe is studded with brass nail heads. The center of the targe is occupied by a double-headed eagle, the heraldic badge of the MacDonalds, Lords of the Isles. The targe was bequeathed to the National Museum of Antiquities of Scotland in 1877 by former curator, James Drummond, and was illustrated in his posthumous work *Ancient Scottish Weapons* (1881).

CHAPTER 2

The rise and influence of the Highland societies

'Now I will allow you to call me your Chief. Send that box with my kilt and plaid to Lady Lovat, Edin[burgh]. *I must get my dress complished there.'*

Archibald Fraser of Lovat to Simon Fraser of Boblainy (1 July 1782)

Pages 50–51: Kilt suit belonging to Andrew Clark, *c.*1815 (detail)

The early 19th century brought clan tartans and Scottish insignias to the forefront of Highland dress tailoring. Gentlemen who commissioned such outfits often belonged to a convivial Highland club or society, where the costume was regarded as a kind of patriotic uniform.

(See Fig. 4.3)

AT mid-day on 12 July 1828, one hundred members of the Highland Club of Scotland boarded a steamer at Newhaven harbour and made the crossing to the island of Inchkeith. They were accompanied by a crowd of guests and a regimental pipe band, which broke into a rendition of 'The Highland Laddie' as the party set off.[1] The club had been instituted in Edinburgh three years prior to this for the preservation and promotion of 'Manly National Games and Exercises', 'the Gaelic Language' and 'the Ancient Poetry and Music of the Highlands and Borders of Scotland'.[2] Their journey across the Firth of Forth on that afternoon would culminate in the staging of the club's annual competition of Highland sports, which was set to include demonstrations of rifle shooting, putting the stone and throwing the sledge-hammer, and the hop, step and jump. So far, it had proven to be a popular affair with locals and usually drew a large audience from both sides of the Forth. At the games in 1827, so many uninvited guests had descended upon the island to watch the event that 'at one time its population must have exceeded five hundred souls'.[3]

When the company landed on the south side of Inchkeith, it proceeded towards the site of the old military fort, where an awning had been set up for club members and their guests to watch the games, dance, and take refreshment. The structure had been erected to shelter participants from the ravages of the sea wind and summer sun. Throughout the day, however, heavy rain had battered the roof of the tent. As the company sat down for dinner, water broke through the canvas and began to drip steadily upon the ladies, gentlemen and musicians assembled beneath. Pressing on despite the discomfort, a round of patriotic toasts was made by various club members: to the King, to the patron of the society, Lord Glenorchy, and to glorious Caledonia 'with all her mountains and glens – with all her lochs and her rivers – with all her Countesses in their Castles, and her bonny lasses in their cottages; and might he who would not drink that toast never drink whisky-punch again!' The proposal of the latter by Dr Alexander Stewart of Bonskeid was delivered to great applause from the company.[4]

Disappointed by the inclement weather, the party was soon obliged to return to the steamer for the presentation of the prizes. These were awarded by Ranald George Macdonald of Clanranald, President of the Highland Club of Scotland and the Captain and Chief of Clanranald. In its report of the games, the *Edinburgh Evening Courant* noted that Clanranald wore a basket-hilted broadsword as part of his Highland costume. This illustrious weapon had once belonged to Princes Charles Edward Stuart and had been gifted to the chief by King George IV in 1820. Today this same sword forms a significant part of the Clanranald collection of Jacobite and family relics, donated to the National Museum of Antiquities of Scotland by a direct descendant in 1944.[5] The newspaper claimed that upon learning of the sword's association with the long-dead heir of the exiled House of Stuart, a Highlander in attendance at the games held the sword by the blade and reverently kissed the hilt, informing Clanranald that 'this sword should never be touched but with an ungloved hand'. The exchange, reported the paper, was 'highly indicative of national feeling'.[6]

Of the three silver medals known to have been presented by Clanranald that day, one survives in the collection of National Museums Scotland [Fig. 2.1]. According to its inscription, it was won by William Dickson for his demonstration of the hop, step and jump. The scene engraved into the surface of the medal speaks to the patriotic character of the club that awarded it: a man in Highland dress stands in a mountainous landscape with blade drawn, holding a shield emblazoned with a lion rampant. The three eagle feathers in his bonnet indicate that he is a clan chief, likely the master of the ancient castle depicted behind him. At the man's feet is the inscription '*AMOR PATRIÆ*', meaning love of one's country. The flowering thistle at the base of the medal further underscores the national dimension of the chosen iconography.

The Highland Club of Scotland was one of many such societies founded in Britain during the late eighteenth and early nineteenth centuries. Inspired by the Romantic movement then gathering apace in Europe, their collective aim was to preserve and promote aspects of Gaelic culture they deemed in danger of disappearing amid rapid modernisation and a perceived loss of regional distinctiveness.[7] These various clubs and societies were responsible for fashioning a standard style of formal Highland dress costume and for encouraging its wider adoption within spaces of elite sociability in Britain, such as the theatre, the coffee-

THE RISE AND INFLUENCE OF THE HIGHLAND SOCIETIES

Fig. 2.1: **Sporting medal**

This silver athletics medal was awarded to William Dickson by the Highland Club of Scotland at their annual competition of Highland sports on 12 July 1828, for his demonstration of the hop, step and jump.

house and the royal court. In refining their vision of what modern Highland dress costume should be, they looked towards the material and performative cultures of the Highland past for inspiration, incorporating what they observed in extant artefacts, surviving portraiture and oral tradition into the luxurious trappings of Georgian high society.

The 'revival' of Highland dress culture occasioned by these clubs and societies was not without controversy. There was disagreement on what constituted an authentic Highland costume and who had the ancestral right to wear it. What one deemed accurate, others saw as a series of embellishments that wilfully burlesqued the character and habits of a region. It also proved increasingly difficult to ignore the paradox created by Scottish aristocrats outwardly celebrating the clan society of earlier generations, while also enacting schemes of economic and agricultural improvement on their lands that irrevocably altered the lives of their tenants. In this fraught context, the elaborate costumes commissioned and worn by members of Highland clubs and societies during the closing decades of the Georgian era came to represent an uneasy meeting of excess and loss, of material fact and historical fiction.[8] The surviving sartorial culture of these Highland clubs and societies has seldom been the subject of serious academic enquiry.[9] In this chapter, we will examine an array of objects from the national collection and seek to understand their place within the creation of the archetypal Highland dress silhouette we recognise today.

Repeal and revive

The associational origins of the Highland dress revival can be traced to the foundation of one society in particular: the Highland Society of London (HSL), a private gentlemen's club established in the nation's capital on 28 May 1778. Originally meeting at the Spring Gardens Coffee House in St James, it was composed of influential Scots drawn from across the landowning, political and military classes of British society. According to histories published by its own members, the founding ambition of the club was to halt the perceived decline of traditional Highland culture in Scotland and to promote the interests of their countrymen at home and abroad through charitable giving and representation in the city. Over the late eighteenth and early nineteenth centuries, this mandate would inspire schemes to preserve the Gaelic language, investigate the authenticity of Ossianic literature, celebrate Scottish martial achievements in the service of the British army [2.2], and promote regional styles of music and dress as popular, patriotic emblems of a pro-Union, pan-Scottish national identity. One of their first public initiatives in this vein was to secure a repeal of the Dress Act in the summer of 1782, which they achieved by lobbying a sitting Member of Parliament within their ranks, the Marquess of Graham.

When the House of Commons convened on 17 June 1782, Graham moved for the Dress Act to be repealed, on the grounds that the original circumstances prompting the British government to ban the use of Highland dress in Scotland no longer applied.[10] He argued that since the defeat of the last Jacobite Rising of 1745–46, the three main reasons for passing the Act had been answered: the Scottish Highlands and its people had received sufficient 'punishment' for their rebellious behaviour against George II in their support of the exiled Stuart dynasty; their 'attachment' to clanship had been broken; and their 'disloyalty' to the British state had been effectively curtailed.[11] He stressed that he represented the interests of 'an obedient and a loyal people'. If his fellow MPs could agree that one of the first and leading principles of all good governments was to 'conciliate the affections of the people, and to win their confidence and esteem', he perceived no obstacle in relaxing the decades-old restrictions imposed upon the regional dress of civilian Highland men. Aspects of the garb had, after all, been retained as a form of Highland regimental uniform for almost forty years without prompting unrest. If anything, the costume had come to be regarded as an emblem of British martial power.[12]

Fig. 2.2: Commemorative medal

Following the Battle of Alexandria in 1801, the Highland Society of London decided to honour the 42nd Regiment of Foot (Black Watch) with the presentation of commemorative medals in recognition of the conspicuous role the regiment had played in the conflict. The design – which centres on the moment Major James Stirling captured the standard of Napoleon's Invincibles – was engraved by George Frederick Pidgeon, after a drawing by Benjamin West.

His compatriot and fellow HSL member, Archibald Fraser of Lovat, duly arose and seconded the motion. Addressing the chamber, he declared that he saw no reason why Highland men, who had 'bled so freely, so loyally, and so usefully to this empire', should not be afforded the legal right to wear 'the striped party-coloured woollen manufactures of their own country, cut in the fashion the best suited to their fancy and predilection'. He then drew the attention of the assembled MPs to his own clothing – a three-piece suit of the sort that defined British menswear of the period – and explained that unless an act 'could be made to level the hills', such garments would forever be incompatible with the practicalities of life in the rugged Highland landscape. In closing, he reminded the Commons that the time had come to look towards the end of the current war with America, when economic migration between the two countries might once again become an attractive prospect for British subjects. In lifting the ban on Highland dress, perhaps the government might ensure Highlanders were kept 'happy at home'.[13]

Graham's motion, though seconded by Fraser of Lovat, did not go unchallenged. The MP for Totnes, Sir Philip Jennings-Clerke, argued strongly against the use of the garb in England, citing the supposed sexual impropriety of Highland soldiers serving in the British army and the corrupting influence of the regimental kilt upon English women. He would come to revise his position in a later debate, explaining that he had not realised that the ban on Highland dress applied to Scotland alone, thereby making his objection legislatively invalid. However, he maintained that the costume should be restricted in England for the sake of wives and daughters vulnerable to 'attack' from Highland men.[14] Jennings-Clerke's comments immediately attracted the attention of London satirists, who issued a number of prints throughout that summer characterising the Repeal movement as an insidious example of the growing political influence of Scots in Westminster.[15] One such print, published by William Humphrey of the Strand on 1 August 1782, depicts the interior of a Hampshire tavern in which two Highland soldiers are being waited on by three women and a disgruntled male host. The women fawn over their Highland patrons, one staring pointedly at a large dirk resting suggestively in the soldier's lap. Both men's legs are exposed to mid-thigh, revealing brawny knees and well-turned, muscular calves. Their obvious athleticism and natural charm is intimately connected to the swathes of tartan that envelop their bodies, the bright chequered fabric lending them an air of exoticism with which their English host cannot possibly compete. A further print, published anonymously in 1782, plays with similar themes of impropriety and corruption. The scene centres on sixteen men, signifying the sixteen Scottish representative peers elected to sit in the House of Lords after the Union of 1707. The peers are in varying stages of undress, discarding their English breeches in favour of the philabeg and shoulder plaid. They are watched by a crowd of women, who peek at them from behind a folding screen. Another man has gathered the scorned breeches into a sack, the side of which reads, 'They Have use for Monies But none for Breeches Now' [2.3].[16]

Fig. 2.3: *The Scotch made happy by a late Act of Parliament*, unknown artist, 1782, etching on paper

Bonnets, tartan coats and plaids often appear in prints that negatively stereotype the role of Scots in Georgian Britain. Even after the success of the Repeal movement in 1782, Highland dress continued to be freighted with the legacy of rebellious Jacobitism. However, as the century progressed, the Highland elite sought to reclaim these emblems as a source of cultural pride and fortitude.

(© The Trustees of the British Museum)

The Marquess of Graham's motion ultimately passed without issue on 19 June and was given royal ascent on 1 July 1782.[17] From that moment on, freedom to wear Highland dress without fear of fine, imprisonment, military impressment, or transportation to a British penal colony, was restored across Scotland. In the following months, Gaelic poets such as Donnchadh Bàn Mac an t-Saoir composed verses lauding the return of the kilt, and grateful communities published letters in Scottish newspapers, thanking the Marquess – and by extension, the HSL – for re-establishing their ancestral right to don the plaid.[18] 'Now I will allow you to call me your Chief,' wrote Fraser of Lovat triumphantly to his kinsman, Simon Fraser of Boblainy. 'Send that box with my kilt and plaid to Lady Lovat, Edin[burgh]. I must get my dress complished there.'[19]

In their efforts to vindicate Highland dress before Parliament, Graham and Fraser of Lovat both drew upon the dramatic transformation of the Highlands that had taken place within the popular imagination in the years since the defeat of the Jacobite army at Culloden. With the publication and international success of James Macpherson's Ossianic poetry in the 1760s, the region had become characterised as historically rich and picturesque, as opposed to desolate and threatening. This mode of thought extended beyond sublime perceptions of the landscape, to encapsulate those who inhabited it, their past and their cultural habits. At the same time, mass military recruitment in the region had cemented the image of the Highlander as a natural warrior, whose abilities could be actively channelled into the defence and enrichment of the British empire [2.4]. However, the crude remarks and negative stereotypes confidently proclaimed by Sir Philip Jennings-Clerke indicate that while public hostility towards the Highlands had begun to shift with the extirpation of Jacobitism, there remained a level of animosity regarding the increased visibility of Scots within British society and government.

It was during this period of tension that the HSL began seriously to court royal patronage as a form of social rehabilitation, seeking to transform Highland dress from an emblem of erstwhile rebellion into a badge of loyalty to the Union and to the Hanoverian monarchy.

Fig. 2.4: *Colonel William Gordon of Fyvie*, by Pompeo Batoni (1708–87), 1766, oil on canvas

When visiting Rome while on the Grand Tour in 1766, Gordon was painted by Italian artist Pompeo Batoni. Swathed in luxurious plaid and sporting the regimental coat of the 105th Highlanders, Gordon's exotic appearance reflects the European Romantic perception of the Scottish Highlander as a heroic figure steeped in a rich yet turbulent history.

(National Trust for Scotland)

HIGHLAND STYLE

Fig. 2.5 (opposite, above):
Prince Augustus Frederick, Duke of Sussex and Earl of Inverness, by Sir William Beechey (1753–1839), 1816, oil on canvas

Prince Augustus Frederick was a leading member and vocal patron of the Highland Society of London. Throughout his lifetime, he accumulated an impressive collection of Highland costume and weaponry, much of which still survives. By publicly adopting the revivalist style of Highland dress, the Duke contributed towards its transformation into a patriotic icon of the British state.

(Reproduced with the kind permission of the Fishmongers' Company)

Fig. 2.6 (opposite, below):
Sporran, *c.*1805 and kilt, *c.*1815

This jaguar skin dress sporran is among the earliest objects in the collection of Highland dress amassed by the Duke of Sussex. It was probably commissioned in celebration of his election to the Highland Society of London and worn at his first meeting in March 1805. The front of the sporran carries the jewelled badge of the Order of the Thistle, while the gold cantle bears the royal insignia. It sits atop a kilt of Earl of Inverness tartan. Both objects are clearly identifiable in the portrait of Prince Augustus Frederick, painted by Sir William Beechey in 1816 [see 2.5].

(On loan from The Scottish Tartans Authority. Image © National Museums Scotland)

Courting royal patronage

The successful repeal of the Dress Act in 1782 not only rehabilitated tartan in the eyes of the British state; it also ushered in a period when the fabric was considered extremely fashionable with the aristocracy beyond the confines of Scotland. The growing popularity of this once regional textile and its associated costume can be explained, at least in part, by the social connections forged between members of the HSL and the sons of George III during the final decades of the eighteenth century.

The timing of club events was planned to take strategic advantage of the London season, when Parliament was in session and the city became a hub of upper-class activity. These months were crucial for sowing alliances and reinforcing one's social ties through house calls, attendance at balls and assemblies, and presentation at court. They also represented a valuable opportunity for those who normally resided in the country to access the latest forms of stylish entertainment across the city's many pleasure gardens, theatres and concert venues.[20] Being a gentlemen's club based in the capital, the elite membership of the HSL regularly appeared both at court and at aristocratic functions attended by the royal princes. Such occasions lent themselves well to the public promotion of Highland costume, bringing the ethos and aims of the club directly to the heart of British cultural and political life.

Military Scot and founder member of the HSL, Colonel John Small, was instrumental in stoking the interest of the elder brothers in Highland dress culture and the related weaponry. He instructed them on how best to wear 'the tartan plaid, philabeg, purse and other appendages', and it was due to his influence that George, Prince of Wales, and his brothers Prince Frederick and Prince William, acquired complete suits of Highland dress in 1789. The future George IV wore his suit to a masquerade ball in London that same year, demonstrating that his interest in the aristocratic revival of Highland dress culture originated well before his infamous state visit to Edinburgh in 1822.[21] By carefully cultivating such convivial relationships between the club and the royal family, the HSL was able to persuade many of the princes to become fully-fledged members of their association and to directly patronise their various causes.

At a general meeting of the HSL at the Crown & Anchor Tavern in February 1805 – at the suggestion of the Marquis of Douglas and Duke of Atholl – HRH Prince Augustus Frederick, Duke of Sussex and Earl of Inverness, was officially elected a member of the club. Learning of the success of his candidacy, the Duke of Sussex communicated to the society that he would appear at their next meeting in March wearing a complete Highland dress outfit as a mark of 'respect' for his hosts and a symbol of his great 'Attachment for Highlanders'.[22] Word was swiftly circulated that all who wished to attend the meeting should do so in Highland dress, as a compliment to their royal sponsor. A sumptuous dinner was called for and the patriotic pledge made by the club to forgo drinking French wines during wartime was relaxed. When the appointed day arrived, the Duke of Sussex was welcomed into the society's midst by a deputation of the Highland aristocracy, suitably attired, and the society's contracted piper playing 'The Prince's Salute'. He was elected President of the HSL in 1806, and his brothers, the Dukes of York, Clarence, and Kent, soon consented to join.[23]

The Duke of Sussex proved to be a significant royal patron of romanticised Highland culture within late Georgian society. Between the years 1806 and 1825, he was elected President of the HSL on at least three separate occasions. During this period he amassed an impressive collection of Highland costume and weaponry, influenced in no small part by the dress codes of the club he presided over. The earliest pieces of the collection are meticulously recorded in a portrait by Sir William Beechey, painted in 1816 [2.5]. In the painting, the Duke stands in a Highland landscape, with windswept mountains in the far distance and a thriving thistle bush to the fore. He is dressed in an immaculate suit of Earl of Inverness hard tartan, a sett designed specifically for him to celebrate his acquisition of that title in 1801. The coat is cut in the characteristic revival style, the high-standing collar decorated with thistle emblems and gold bullion ribbon visible at the shoulders and cuffs. The capacious folds of both the tailored kilt and plaid combine to give the illusion of a *feileadh mòr*, although they are in fact two separate pieces. The outfit is completed by a set of formal Highland dress accoutrements, namely an elaborate dress sword, two engraved percussion dress pistols, a black velvet cross belt decorated with silver mounts in the shape of thistles and lion heads, and a large jaguar-skin sporran topped with a gold cantle inlaid with precious Scottish stones [2.6].

When the Duke of Sussex died in 1843, his

59

Fig. 2.7: Dress sword, c.1805

Prince Augustus Frederick commissioned this sword on his election to the Highland Society of London. Its design is closely modelled on a Jacobite relic associated with Prince Charles Edward Stuart, which was stored at Carlton House until 1820.

(On loan from The Scottish Tartans Authority. Image © National Museums Scotland)

Highland dress collection was included in an auction of his personal effects retrieved from Kensington Palace, managed by Messrs Christie & Manson. Placed within a sale of trinkets, jewellery, historical relics and modern fowling pieces, it was purchased by a member of the Glennie family of Aberdeenshire.[24] While the Glennie family made material additions to the collection during the later nineteenth century, the core objects once owned and worn by the Duke of Sussex remain distinct and identifiable.

The collection remained in private hands until the late twentieth century, when it was sold at auction by Sotheby's. It has been on loan to National Museums Scotland from The Scottish Tartans Authority since 2015, during which time it has been the subject of ongoing research. It is now possible to make quite definitive connections between pieces in the Duke of Sussex collection and Highland dress objects in the permanent collection of the museum.[25]

The Duke of Sussex collection is a remarkable assemblage – an overt, material demonstration of royal patronage for Scottish Romantic aesthetics. In terms of its importance and completeness, it may be favourably compared to the Highland dress outfit commissioned by George IV from army clothier and tartan retailer George Hunter of Edinburgh in 1822, which remains in the Royal Collection to this day.[26] Individual pieces from the Duke of Sussex collection are fascinating objects in their own right, revealing much about the mindset of the man who purchased and wore them. However, it is the dress sword which is of particular interest to the present study; not only because of its striking material qualities, but because of the high esteem in which it was held by its owner. While the Duke of Sussex collection evidently expanded multiple times over the course of his life, the dress sword appears to be among the earliest and most cherished of the Highland dress accessories he had specially commissioned to celebrate his election to the Highland Society of London. As well as appearing in the portrait by Beechey in 1816, it can also be clearly seen in a painting of the Duke of Sussex made by Sir David Wilkie in 1833 and gifted to Queen Victoria in 1838.[27]

The Duke's dress sword was commissioned from London-based jewellers T. & L. Tuck of Haymarket in the year 1805 and features a silver basket-hilt and a blued and gilt single-edged blade [2.7]. The gilt decoration on the blade includes a beautiful array of foliate motifs, royal cyphers and insignia, and a Gaelic motto that spans the front and back of the blade: 'Na taric mi gun gliachús' / 'Sna chriss mi gun chliú'. The design of the chased silver hilt showcases an intricate grouping of allegorical figures and the pommel is cast in the shape of a thistle, topped with a citrine quartz jewel. While the style of the dress sword is certainly distinctive, it is not in fact unique. It is evident that the Duke of Sussex based the design of his own ceremonial weapon on a mid-eighteenth-century backsword, thought to have been in the possession of Prince Charles Edward Stuart during the

Jacobite Rising of 1745–46 – the same Jacobite relic proudly carried by Macdonald of Clanranald on that wet and windy day in 1828, in his capacity as President of the Highland Club of Scotland [2.8].

According to tradition, the backsword was once part of a costly present of Highland dress and weaponry given by James Drummond, 3rd Duke of Perth, to Prince Charles Edward and his brother Henry Benedict at the exiled Stuart court in Rome. This gift of tartan clothing, sword, targe, pistols and dirk has long been viewed as a significant moment in the making of the 'Bonnie Prince Charlie' image, which would come to dominate popular remembrances of the Stuart claimant in the aftermath of the last Jacobite Rising of 1745–46 [2.9].[28] The backsword bears the mark of the silversmith Charles Frederick Kandler and is believed to have been made in London at some point between 1740 and 1741. The solid silver basket-hilt displays a curious interlocking design of allegorical figures, while either side of the blade carries an engraved and gilt cartouche, bearing the inscriptions *'Ne me tire jamis sans raison'* / *'Ne me remette point sans honneur'*. Seized by Prince William, Duke of Cumberland, following the defeat of the Jacobite army at the Battle of Culloden in 1746, the backsword subsequently entered the Royal Collection. It was first recorded in a catalogue of arms and armaments stored at Carlton House, before it was gifted to Macdonald of Clanranald by the Prince of Wales in June 1820. It became part of the permanent collection of the National Museum of Antiquities of Scotland in 1944 and is commonly referred to as the 'Clanranald sword' by dint of provenance. The sword was donated by Angus Roderick Macdonald, the 23rd Chief of Clanranald, within a large group of Jacobite and family relics. Although questions have circulated in recent years regarding the validity of the direct connection between the object and Prince Charles Edward Stuart, there is no doubt that at the time the Duke of Sussex commissioned his own blade from T. & L. Tuck in 1805 the Jacobite heritage of the Clanranald sword was regarded as genuine.[29]

Comparing the two weapons side by side, it is evident that the Duke of Sussex enjoyed direct access to the Clanranald sword when it was in his older brother's possession at Carlton House. Comparing the hilt of the original sword with that of the early nineteenth-century adaptation, it is clear that the distinctive allegorical design of the former has been almost entirely duplicated in the making of the latter. There are only a small number of stylistic changes, the most significant of these being the discarding of the eagle pommel seen in the Clanranald sword in favour of a wrought thistle. This was perhaps deemed a more appropriate icon of Scottishness, befitting the status of a Highland dress object executed in the revivalist

Fig. 2.8: Backsword

According to tradition, this elaborate backsword was among the objects seized from the abandoned baggage train of Prince Charles Edward Stuart in the aftermath of the Battle of Culloden in 1746. In the late Georgian era, the sword was regarded as a genuine relic of the exiled House of Stuart and was thus heavily romanticised as a remnant of the 'lost' Jacobite Cause.

HIGHLAND STYLE

Fig. 2.9: *Prince Charles Edward Stuart* (1720–88). *Eldest son of Prince James Francis Edward Stuart*, by William Mosman (c.1700–771), c.1737–50, oil on canvas

The heir of the exiled Stuart dynasty famously adopted Highland dress during the last Jacobite Rising of 1745–46. Likely painted in the aftermath of the failed campaign, this portrait by William Mosman exemplifies the potent legacy of his 'Bonnie Prince Charlie' persona.

(National Galleries of Scotland)

style. Similarly, in the course of replication the French inscription etched into the blade of the Clanranald sword has, on the Duke's iteration, been translated into Gaelic. Although the chivalric sentiment expressed on each blade remains the same – 'Draw me not without reason' / 'Sheath me not without honour' – the language preferred by the Duke of Sussex is the one that the HSL was actively working to preserve and promote through their investigation of the authenticity of James Macpherson's Ossianic literature, and which he himself was privately attempting to learn.[30]

Made on the eve of his acceptance into the ranks of the HSL, the choice of the Duke of Sussex to commission a Highland dress sword in imitation of a prestigious Jacobite relic does not seem so surprising. The stylistic changes he imposed upon the design of the replica object align perfectly with the ethos of historical and cultural revivalism toted by the club during the Duke's premiership. This episode of duplication and conscious re-fashioning is not an isolated incident; it is emblematic of a broader trend within Highland dress culture of the era. Inherited objects with Highland origins were often incorporated into the formalised style of Highland dress that emerged in the Georgian era, forging material connections between the past and the present and conflating history with the pursuit of novelty.

Designing a uniform

In the wake of the Repeal movement, leading members of the HSL sought to encourage the general adoption of Highland dress at its meetings and public events. As early as 1784 it was resolved that Queen Charlotte's birthday would be nominated as an occasion when all members were expected to don the costume as a 'mark of respect to the garb of their ancestors'.[31] However, it was not until the presidency of politician and agricultural improver Sir John Sinclair of Ulbster that a prolonged and concerted effort was made to fashion and integrate a formal style of Highland dress uniform into the official structure of the club [2.10].

When Sinclair was elected president of the HSL in 1796, one of his first acts in the Chair was to propose that members of the governing committee adopt a Highland dress uniform at all future meetings. Though such mandates had been previously proposed, there is little evidence to suggest they had been met with widespread enthusiasm. By insisting on the wearing of the dress in their formal capacity as elected directors, Sinclair hoped that the governing committee would lead by example and inspire the general membership to follow suit.

Desirous that any costume adopted by the committee be a unified expression of association with the club, Sinclair suggested the commissioning of a button bearing the Gaelic motto *'Clán na Gael'* (meaning 'children' or 'family of the Gael'), for use as a common decorative emblem. The committee appears to have acquiesced to Sinclair's recommendation – at least in principle – as no objections were noted in the official minutes of the meeting.[32] However, perusal of the surviving papers of the HSL deposited with the National Library of Scotland reveals that Sinclair's proposed button was never financed out of the club's own coffers. This absence is illustrative of a broader trend within the society's accounts, which show that funds were seldom directed towards the purchase of clothing for use by individual members. Rather, expenditure on dress was directed towards clothing the society's contracted musicians, its charitable dependants, and for prizes of tartan cloth and Highland costume awarded at the HSL's annual piping competitions at Falkirk and, later, Edinburgh.

Seniority within the club clearly did not come with material incentives, meaning that

Fig. 2.10: *Sir John Sinclair, 1st Bart of Ulbster* (1754–1835), by Sir Henry Raeburn (1756–1823), *c.*1794–99, oil on canvas

Sinclair served as President of the Highland Society of London in 1796. He continued to exert considerable influence over the cultural activities of the club in later years, including its investigation into the authenticity of James Macpherson's Ossian poetry and the administration of its annual bagpiping competitions in Edinburgh. Sinclair was a firm believer in the ancient origins of Highland dress culture and advocated for its adoption as the uniform garb of Highland clubs and societies in Britain and abroad.

(National Galleries of Scotland)

Fig. 2.11: Uniform coat, *c*.1713

The Royal Company of Archers was founded in Edinburgh during the late 17th century as a private archery club. It successfully petitioned Queen Anne for a royal charter in 1704 and adopted tartan uniforms in 1713. By the early 18th century, tartan had become a widely recognised symbol of Jacobite sympathy. With the succession of the House of Hanover to the British throne in 1714, the distinctive dress of the RCA was treated with suspicion.

supporters of Sinclair's scheme would need to dip a hand into their own pockets to see it realised. The only recorded exception appears to be a receipt dated 22 February 1819, in which senior member the Hon. Sir Archibald Macdonald charged the committee £1-17s for altering an existing short coat, kilt, plaid, hose and waistcoat, which included the purchase of silk rosettes to decorate the outer edge of the kilt's front apron, in accordance with the latest fashion.[33] As a senior member of the HSL, it is likely that Macdonald had performed some ceremonial duty on behalf of the club. In such circumstances it would be reasonable for Macdonald to recoup monies spent on his making a good appearance.

Sinclair's desire to impose a club uniform on the membership of the HSL is indicative of a general tendency within British associational culture of the period. Clubs and societies would often nominate a preferred form of dress or emblem as it instilled a sense of togetherness among its members, lent proceedings a more officious air and projected a distinctive image that the public would recognise and respond to. This could be as simple as a meaningfully coloured cockade or lapel badge, but could also encompass the design of an entire outfit. When a committee was formed in 1788 to govern the annual Northern Meeting at Inverness, for example, one of its earliest resolutions was to impose a distinguishing dress code:

> *… against next meeting, it is expected every Member shall appear in an Uniform which is to be a Grass Green Coat, with a Buff-Edging, a White Metal Button, Black Velvet Cape, with four Silver Embroidered or Yellow Button-Holes. Buff or Fancy Waistcoat, and Buff, or Black Silk Breeches. The Buttons to have the Letters N. M. in Cypher.*[34]

The style and material components of associational dress typically reflected the aims and the ideals of an organisation, adjusted to fit the social dimension of club activities and events. A well-known instance of this within the Scottish context would be the early tartan uniforms of the Royal Company of Archers, of which National Museums Scotland holds many surviving examples [2.11].[35]

It was not until 1804 that Sinclair formalised his request to the HSL to adopt an official Highland dress uniform, in the form of a targeted publication titled *Observations on the Propriety of*

Preserving the Dress, the Language, the Poetry, the Music, and the Customs, of the Ancient Inhabitants of Scotland. He later expanded upon this request in *An Account of the Highland Society of London, From its Establishment in May 1778, to the Commencement of the Year 1813*, a short treatise published in 1813 which outlined the founding aims and ambitions of the society and the progress it had so far made in achieving them. These two publications offer a rare glimpse into the practicalities and rules of etiquette that dictated the formalised style of Highland dress adopted by society members during the early nineteenth century. As much as Sinclair was a firm believer in the ancient roots of the garb, what he described as suitable attire for attendees is more in line with contemporary male fashions and the silhouette of Scottish military uniforms. This, one assumes, was because he wanted the dress to be as accessible as possible and to feel less like an affectation or fancy dress costume. The accommodation of personal preference is a significant theme which runs throughout Sinclair's lengthy description of what the dress should be:

> *It would not be proper to tie down every individual who may attend […] to one uniform, as persons in an advanced period of life, or who are engaged in grave professions, may not think it proper to appear wholly in so unusual a dress, though they may have no objection to wear some particular parts of it; but the generality of the Members, must feel a peculiar satisfaction in putting on that garb, as it recalls to their remembrance, the high character, and renowned atchievements of their ancestors, and must inspire those who wear, or even see, the dress, with an anxious wish to preserve and perpetuate the glory of former times.*
>
> *In regard to any dress to be fixed upon as a Uniform, to be worn at any Meeting of the Highland Society, more especially on great occasions, the following might be adopted: A Bonnet adorned with the plumes of the eagle, or any feathers of the same sort; the Coat or Jacket to be either of tartan, or of dark blue, or dark grass green cloth, with silver or gold buttons, and other ornaments, fitted close to the body and without skirts; either the Trews, or the Belted-plaid, to be worn, as might be most agreeable; also Hose, Shoes tied with thongs, like the ancient Brogues; a Dirk, a Purse, and a Plaid. Persons who might not be inclined to go the whole length, to wear such parts of the above dress as they may prefer.*[36]

Shortly after its publication, Sinclair's *Account* was circulated to branches of the HSL based across Scotland and in British colonies overseas. The first of these to appear was the Highland Society of Madras, established in September 1814 by Lieutenant General John Abercromby, son of the military celebrity Sir Ralph Abercromby. The new club, composed of the Scottish military, mercantile and administrative elite in the region, was issued with 25 copies of Sinclair's *Account*, with the intention that it would

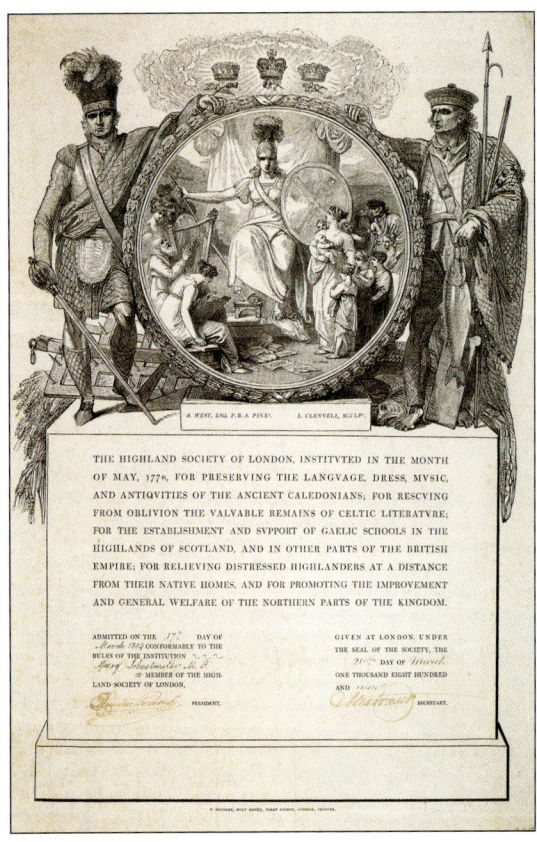

Fig. 2.12: *Diploma of the Highland Society*, by Luke Clennell (1781–1840), after Benjamin West (1738–1820), unknown date, wood engraving on paper

The diploma of membership designed by Benjamin West encapsulates Highland dress in its varying forms, from its rural origins to its military applications.

(National Galleries of Scotland)

act as a guide in the creation of club rules and etiquette. The expectation was that all members of the Highland Society of Madras would appear at meetings arrayed in appropriate Highland costume or, as was more likely, their regimental uniforms.[37] Newly-elected members were also sent engraved diplomas, based on a drawing commissioned from Benjamin West in 1805. The design reinforces Sinclair's observation, that the style of Highland dress should be adapted to suit the wearer's individual circumstances and concerns regarding historical authenticity [2.12].[38]

Until recently, there was no surviving sartorial evidence to substantiate Sinclair's desire for a Highland Society dress code, first proposed in *Observations* (1804) and reinforced in *Account* (1813). However, the survey of the tartan and Highland dress holdings of National Museums Scotland that took place in 2018 revealed an extant garment that fulfils all of Sinclair's requirements, while at the same time conforming to the qualities most often seen in examples of associational wear of the era: a hard tartan jacket in the Royal Stewart sett, featuring a high-standing military inspired collar with thistle insignia, decorated with 26 yellow metal buttons marked with a Gaelic motto, dating to approximately 1816 [2.13].[39] The jacket was purchased by the Society of Antiquaries of Scotland from Glasgow-based antique dealer Muirhead Moffat & Co. in November 1953 and formed part of the collection of the National Museum of Antiquities of Scotland. The minutes of the Society of Antiquaries of Scotland Purchasing Committee describe the garment, inaccurately, as a 'tartan waistcoat', with no indication given of date or previous ownership.[40] On its entry into the NMAS accession register, a dubious provenance was attached to it, for which no

---

Fig. 2.13 (opposite): Tartan coat, c.1816

The royal patronage of the Highland Society of London by the sons of George III may explain why the Royal Stewart emerged as a favoured sett among HSL members during the early 19th century. The cloth used to tailor this coat is extremely fine, incorporating both silk and worsted. The high collar is lined with brown velvet, and the thistle insignia has been worked in metal thread. The shoulder seams are slightly ruched and the chest is padded, creating a fashionable full breast and trim-looking waist.

HIGHLAND STYLE

supporting documentary evidence can be found: 'Said to have been worn during the visit of George IV to Edinburgh in 1822.'[41] This unsubstantiated association has, over the course of almost seventy years, come to obscure the true nature of the jacket from curatorial eyes. However, through a process of material reassessment and contextual research, it has been possible to unearth the hidden history of this institutionally misunderstood garment.

The design emblazoned on each of the jacket's 26 yellow metal buttons underscores its historic association with the Highland Society of London. The motto '*CLAN NA'N GAEL LUNNINN*' can be seen engraved along the inner band of a clasped strap and buckle, with a flourishing thistle bush occupying the centre [2.14]. This national symbol of Scotland, contained within an unbroken circle, alludes to a sense of timelessness and tradition, while also echoing the configuration of early nineteenth-century heraldic crest badges worn as part of formal Highland dress. The motto that appears on each button is an imprecise form of written Gaelic, which can be interpreted to mean the 'Highland Society of London', with '*LUNNINN*' – now more commonly spelt *Lunnainn* – signifying 'London'.[42] It should be noted that by the early decades of the nineteenth century there were multiple branches of the HSL operating in different towns across Scotland and in British colonial outposts around the world, so the addition of '*LUNNINN*' or 'London' would not be an unreasonable method of differentiation in forming the design.

Fig. 2.14: Coat buttons

Members of Highland clubs and societies often commissioned dress buttons to adorn the clothing worn at meetings. These buttons typically carried a Gaelic motto or bore symbols of Scottish significance, such as the thistle. The chosen design was meant to communicate the patriotism of the wearer, as well as their affiliation to a specific organisation.

While not the precise motto that was specified by Sinclair in his proposal to the governing committee to strike an official HSL button in 1796, in every other respect the jacket itself strongly adheres to the style suggested by him as most appropriate for adoption by club members, first in *Observations* (1804) and later in *Account* (1813): 'the Coat or Jacket to be either of tartan, or of dark blue, or dark grass green cloth, with silver or gold buttons, and other ornaments, fitted close to the body and without skirts.'[43] The jacket is indeed 'fitted close' and 'without skirts', while also employing the tartan cloth and 'gold' button options that was suggested by Sinclair. The matching and manipulation of the tartan along the outer seams of the jacket is notably immaculate, making it a suitable candidate for associational wear. The cloth has been cut and pieced in such a way as to create a close-fitting, flexible garment, which showcases a striking kaleidoscopic pattern of colliding scarlet, azure, green, and black worsted, with the lighter yellow and white stripes woven in silk; this interweaving of different textile fibres within the cloth creates an additional dimension of visual and material richness. Considering the observation of tartan historian Donald C. Stewart, that each colour used within a tartan webb 'appears not only in its pure or solid form, but also in an equal blend with each other colour' at the intersection of warp and weft, one can appreciate the textured depth of colour achieved within this single garment as well as the overall quality of the textile itself.[44] When the jacket is fully fastened, the tartan sett becomes mirrored along the centre-front, converging on the vertical line created by the positioning of the collar hooks and buttons. On the centre-back, meanwhile, the tartan has been cut and joined to produce a series of bright, interlocking diamonds. This method of tailoring – explored further in Chapter 4 – is an inventive and sophisticated way of employing the characteristic grid of a tartan sett, allowing the maker to indulge in the beauty of the original pattern while also transforming it into something entirely new [2.15]. While not unique to this jacket, this innovative and well-executed detail of construction speaks to the expense of the finished garment, the obvious skill of the person who made it, and the fashionable context in which it would undoubtedly have been worn.

Sinclair's *Account* does not specify a particular tartan for the universal use of HSL members. However, evidence from surviving correspondence held by the National Library of Scotland and by National Museums Scotland strongly suggests that by the year 1816 the Royal Stewart had become a preferred pattern for attendance at meetings. For some members, the gatherings of the HSL represented an opportunity to be seen at their best in the company of like-minded peers. Admiring and commenting on the dress of others, as well as parading the superiority of one's own costume, contributed to the enjoyment of the event and was often reflected on in letters between friends. Secretary to the society, James Hamilton, for example, took evident pleasure in procuring tartan of the best possible quality for his associational wear. In a letter to Major-General David Stewart of Garth in February 1816, he wrote effusively about his latest purchase from the army clothier and purveyor of clan tartans, George Hunter & Co.: 'Hunter in Edinburgh sent a Pattern of the Stewart Tartan on an enlarged Ground [Royal Stewart]; certainly the most beautiful thing I ever saw. I have got a complete Dress of it for the next Meeting.'[45] Hamilton later informed his friend that his costume had been 'universally admired' and urged Stewart of Garth to

THE RISE AND INFLUENCE OF THE HIGHLAND SOCIETIES

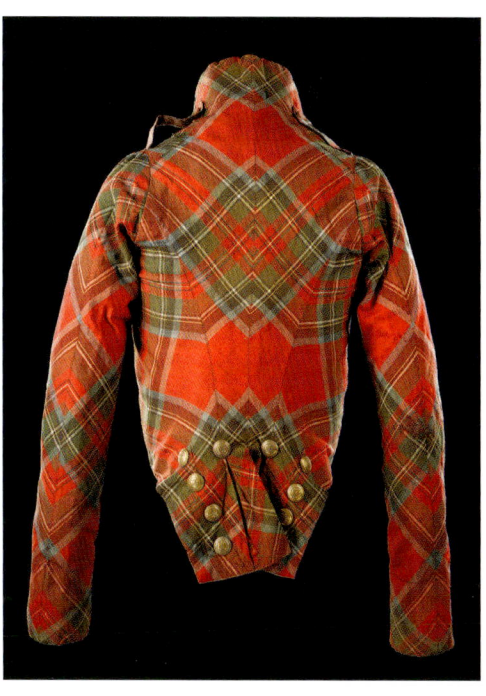

Fig. 2.15: Back of tartan coat, c.1816

Tailoring with tartan is notoriously difficult. Georgian makers had to learn how to cut and piece the fabric in such a way as to turn the characteristic grid to their advantage. The individual who made this coat was clearly creative and highly skilled at their craft.

appear in his own suit of George Hunter & Co. tartan when he was next able to travel to London.[46] Indeed, Hamilton's new clothes had made such a positive impression on fellow members of the HSL committee that he was asked to procure more of the same fabric for their use. Having sent an order to Hunter & Co. on their behalf, Hamilton later complained to Stewart of Garth that the clothier had not yet responded:

> *I wrote Hunter and Comp some time ago to send me up a whole piece of the Royal Stewart Tartan, large pattern, and on Receipt the account would be paid immediately to their correspondent here. Will you be so kind as to see them on the subject, as they have taken no notice of my Letter? McGillivray and the others for whom it is intended are anxiously expecting it.*[47]

The significance of the Royal Stewart tartan to the membership of the HSL extends beyond this brief exchange. An order made in November 1816 to tartan manufacturers Messrs Wilson of Bannockburn by Sir Augustus Frederick d'Este, for 'two yards of the grand set of the Royal Stuart Tartan', further highlights a preoccupation with the pattern among the senior members of HSL at this time. The son of Prince Augustus Frederick and Lady Augusta Murray, d'Este had been made an Honorary member of the club in 1813 during his father's second term as President.[48] His order stated that if Wilsons could guarantee delivery of a quality product for a reasonable price, d'Este would gladly recommend the firm to the HSL, 'which has chosen that set'.[49]

Perusal of customer letters received by Messrs Wilson of Bannockburn in the early decades of the nineteenth century indicates that many Highland clubs and societies made similar efforts during this period to adopt a consistent approach to their dress. A common element in this endeavour was the designation of a society tartan, for use by members at meetings as a unifying associational emblem.

The Glasgow Highland Society assumed the Abercromby sett as early as 1813 for 'use in Jackets'.[50] The Abercromby is thought to have been in production since the later eighteenth century, gaining its current name in the 1800s in deference to the military memory of Sir Ralph Abercromby, who became a heroic figure in British popular culture following his death in March 1801 from wounds sustained at the Battle of Alexandria [2.16].[51] Stories of Abercromby's bravery and commitment to duty as the commanding officer of the British expeditionary corps in the Egyptian campaign came to dominate perceptions of Scottish military involvement in the ongoing fight against the ambitions of Napoleonic France.[52] The Strathbogie Ploughmen Society also adopted a tartan with martial significance, perhaps to achieve the same patriotic ends as the Glasgow club. In 1819, the society's clerk, George Maitland, ordered 125 yards of the '92nd Tartan' for sashes. The order was patently made with a specific event in mind, as reflected in Maitland's anxious tone: 'I hope you will not disappoint us, but will forward it as soon as it can be got ready. It is entirely at the risk of the Committee if not ready to be delivered to the members some weeks before Whitsunday.'[53]

The Caithness and Sutherland Friendly Highland Society, founded in 1821, wrote to Wilsons in March that year requesting 'a few samples of the best Patterns of Tartan, not of any distinct clan, as a choice is to be made to suit for a full dress to a Society now forming in this place'. It was requested that the order be made ready for an event scheduled in June. The society's preference was for the firm to design 'a new Pattern to please', somewhat based on the existing Macdonald sett, but with the addition of a white or a yellow stripe 'all worsted & the best quality'.[54] Possibly due to the time restrictions involved or the prohibitive cost of such a request, the society ultimately chose from Wilsons' stock of existing patterns, samples of which had been provided by the weavers for the customer's perusal. By late April, the club had made their choice: '200 yards of McKays Tartan. Eighty yards Prince Charles Edward. Let them be as Bright as possible and quality of the same as the Swatches. We will likely request more soon.'[55]

There are several reasons why the year 1816 might have been especially significant for the HSL, thereby prompting its members to adopt a consistent approach to Highland dress as a gesture of associational solidarity, when Sinclair's earlier attempts to institute a uniform had fallen upon deaf ears. Royal patronage of the club had reached its zenith by 1815–16, with several members of the royal family having served as President or attended events held in their honour.[56] In 1815, at the suggestion of then President Prince Frederick Augustus, Duke of York and Albany, the HSL created an honorary position titled 'Chief to the Highland Society'. This was dutifully bestowed upon the Prince of Wales, later George IV, although there is no evidence to suggest that he ever personally attended a meeting.[57] The governing committee also circulated a Loyal Address throughout the Highlands in 1815–16, prompting members and non-members alike to pledge their allegiance to the heir of the British throne.[58] Finally, and perhaps most significantly, 21 May 1816 saw the realisation of a long-held ambition of the club to become incorporated by Act of Parliament – a milestone worthy of material commemoration.[59]

Fig. 2.16: Cutting of Abercromby tartan, c.1822

The Abercromby (also spelt Abercrombie) was a popular pattern during the early 19th century. It was incorporated into suits of Highland dress, as well as everyday tartan fashion. This example is from a collection of commercially retailed tartans, compiled by Sir Samuel Rush Meyrick in 1822 with the help of Miller & Ewing, cloth merchants of Glasgow.

Disseminating the image

In January 1784, the governing committee of the HSL was approached by Mr Gwyne – 'a distinguished Welsh performer on the triple harp' – who pledged to instruct a native, Gaelic-speaking Highlander on their behalf.[60] The suggestion appealed to the club, who appreciated both the cultural and the reputational benefits implied by such a scheme.

Gwyne's proposal aligned with its long-term ambition to preserve and promote the Celtic arts in Britain, which included the championing of Gaelic music and language. The scheme also promised future advantage to its benefactors, whose protégé would be duty bound to use their skills in the interests of the society. It was decided by the committee that following Gwyne's tutelage the chosen student would serve as the society's resident harpist in London for the space of five years. At the termination of their contract, they were to return to Scotland for a minimum of two years and ply their trade as a 'Professor of the Harp', thus ensuring a new generation of trained musicians in the region.[61] On the strength of HSL's promise of patronage and steady follow-on employment, a young man named Christopher Macrae left his parent's home in Kintail, Ross-shire, and made the journey to London to begin instruction on the harp.

Shortly after Macrae's arrival in the capital in May 1784, Gwyne backed out of the arrangement – it would take well over a year for the society to make good on their intention to secure him a tutor. In the intervening months, Macrae was entirely dependent on the HSL for his subsistence. The duty of care proved to be an unexpectedly heavy burden for the society, who had not anticipated the true cost of supporting its charge in the city for such an extended period. Nevertheless, the society's accounts attest to their unwillingness to renege on their promise to train and maintain the boy. As well as providing him with an allowance and engaging the musician John Gow to instruct him on the violin – both expenses the committee could ill-afford, being on the verge of bankruptcy – the society also took it upon themselves to clothe Macrae. When a position was finally secured for him in Wales, what had begun as the fulfilment of a basic necessity soon escalated into a promotional exercise to boost the HSL's patriotic credentials.

In late September 1785, the HSL sent Macrae to study under the harpist of Sir Watkin Williams-Wynn, 4th Baronet, at the Wynnstay estate near Wrexham. As well as paying for the boy's travel to Wales via stagecoach, the committee also invested £17-2s-10d in a wardrobe of new clothes befitting the status of a Highland Society musician-in-training. This substantial outlay was in addition to £8-15s-8d spent on altering to fit several coats, waistcoats and breeches donated to Macrae 'from the Treasurer's own things'. 'It became necessary,' explained said-treasurer James Mackenzie, 'to fit him out with fit articles for a decent appearance on that occasion.'[62]

Of chief importance within this ample gift was a suit of 'Highland Dress', which included a feathered bonnet of the type habitually worn by pipers, and a handsome plaid and pair of hose obtained direct from an Edinburgh tailor.[63] Evidently the HSL regarded the boy as their representative in Wales, and his manner of dress – in addition to the core object of his studies – was a significant aspect of that representation.

Alas, in March 1786 – less than six months into his tutelage at Wynnstay – the society's struggling finances forced them to withdraw their patronage from Macrae. Clearly hoping that he would be able to make something of himself without any further assistance from them, the committee paid for Macrae's return to London and ongoing passage to Jamaica, promising to 'recommend him to the protection of their friends in that Island under whose patronage there is no doubt of his success fully proportioned to his own deserving'.[64] The committee allowed Macrae to keep the suit of Highland dress they had purchased for him the previous year, despite the considerable upfront expense. They also authorised an additional £16-17s expenditure 'to furnish him in Cloths for the West India climate' before sending him reluctantly on his way.[65]

The unfortunate case of Christopher Macrae, while a failed experiment in the annals of the HSL's charitable history, nevertheless reflects the attitude of the governing committee towards objects of its philanthropy and patronage. Through their efforts to support Macrae, the committee evidently hoped to establish the society as a national authority on the music of the *clàrsach*. And through their distinctive clothing choices for the young harpist, it is also clear they regarded Macrae as the embodiment of that anticipated acclaim. This desire to sartorially transform beneficiaries of their support into the outward symbols of their cultural ambitions can be observed across various aspects of the HSL's sponsorship during the late eighteenth and early nineteenth centuries, most notably in their sponsorship of Highland piping.

The HSL approached the patronage of piping via two main avenues. First, they retained a professional piper to perform at their general assemblies and paid towards the fashioning of their outfits. Second, they financed a competition of pipers that annually encouraged participants to travel from across Scotland to play for prizes. These exhibitions were run by the club's sister society in Edinburgh, the Highland Society of Scotland.

The first piper formally engaged by the society was Neil MacLean. His clothing, provided by the HSL, can be seen in a late eighteenth-century engraving by the artist William Satchwell Leney [2.17]. MacLean had competed at the first piping competition patronised by the HSL held at Falkirk in 1781, which resulted in his formal engagement as club piper. His uniform of Highland dress, including sundry weaponry, was paid for out of the society's own coffers and was kept in a special deal box when not in use. The credit and debit book of the society, covering the years 1784 to 1815,

Fig. 2.17: *Neil MacLean, Piper to the Highland Society*, by William Satchwell Leney (1769–1831), unknown date, stipple engraving on paper

By the late 18th century, the Great Highland Bagpipe had come to be regarded as the quintessential Highland instrument. Highland costume was deemed its natural accompaniment. MacLean was awarded first prize in the Highland Society of London's piping competition at Falkirk in 1781 and was subsequently engaged as the club's official piper. In addition to his wages, the HSL provided him with a full suit of Highland dress to wear when performing his duties.

reveals that supplying, maintaining and safely storing the dress was a frequent expenditure.[66] As new pipers came and went, fresh articles would be purchased, or old ones reworked. In 1797, tailor John Campbell was paid £3-13s-6d for 'furnishing a bonnet […] elegantly trimm'd with best foxtail & flat feathers and a handsome scarlet military plume'.[67] In 1801, the same tailor supplied the incoming piper, Charles MacArthur, with jacket, waistcoat and hose. The jacket was of scarlet and green superfine broadcloth, with 'chain plated shoulder wings' and 'two thistles & crowns embroidered with spangles for the turn out of the Jacket'. Both the jacket and waistcoat were to be trimmed with silver lace and sewn with silver-plated buttons, decorated with a thistle and crown motif.[68]

The HSL piping competitions were held at the Theatre Royal in Edinburgh during the early decades of the nineteenth century [2.18]. These annual occasions in the Scottish capital would prove to be instrumental in promoting the society's vision of Highland dress costume to the general public, and for inspiring the spread of similar events around the country. The competitions were opulent affairs, drawing accomplished pipers from across the Highlands and Lowlands to compete for medals, money, and national recognition. The surviving papers of the HSL outline the form and function of the competition year on year, and the measures taken by the club to formalise the presentation of professional piping. Their accounts demonstrate a substantial level of financial investment, from securing the location, hiring attendants and reimbursing players, to commissioning awards, set dressing, and promotional materials. The latter included posting advertisements in the national press and printing handbills for distribution throughout the major towns in Scotland. This was all done with the intention of attracting as wide a selection of competitors and attendees as possible.

In the early years of the competition, Highland dress had been encouraged but was not considered mandatory. However, by the 1810s it was annually stressed that anyone wishing to perform for prizes in piping had to do so arrayed in the full costume, including the accessories and weaponry traditionally associated with the martial character of the garb. Prizes began to be offered to those piping and dancing competitors who performed wearing the best interpretation of the dress, with special prizes awarded to young children who attended the event wearing tartan outfits,

and public acclamations given to competitors who made their own clothing. The event itself took place during the summer season in Edinburgh and was timed to coincide with the arrival of the elite crowds drawn to the yearly spectacle of the Musselburgh races. It was most numerously attended during the first quarter of the century, when the literary and theatrical culture of Scottish Romanticism was most heavily ingrained in the fabric of urban living. The peak of its popularity coincided with an endorsement by the popular Scottish actress and manager of the Theatre Royal, Harriet Siddons [2.19].

Siddons had been involved with the running of the theatre alongside her husband, Henry Siddons, since 1809. However, it was not until his death in 1815 that she became proprietor, with the support of her brother William Henry Murray. In June 1820, Siddons wrote to the committee of the HSL and offered to waive the fee usually charged for the use of the theatre.[69] This gesture of goodwill came in the wake of a hugely successful stage adaptation of Sir Walter Scott's *Rob Roy*, whose run had righted the theatre's shaky finances and created a vogue for 'the national dramas' in playhouses across the country.[70] No doubt hoping to ride the wave of cosmopolitan enthusiasm for all things Scottish, Siddons' offer ensured that the national competition of pipers, by now an Edinburgh institution, remained tied to her establishment for the foreseeable future. Moreover, it was her wish that the value of her fee be applied to a new prize presented at the competition in her name. The new prize, awarded each year between 1820–24, was a public advertisement of her support for the patriotic objects of the Highland societies. The governing committee, which was given free rein over what form the prize should take, fixed on awarding traditional Highland dress accoutrements worth £10-10s. These were an elegant

Fig. 2.18 (left): *Theatre Royal, Edinburgh*, by Thomas Hosmer Shepherd (1793–1864), 1829, engraving on paper

The Theatre Royal was built in 1767 in Shakespeare Square, at the east end of Princes Street. Situated in the heart of the metropolis, it swiftly became a thriving hub of Scottish cultural life. It was the obvious host for the annual piping competitions patronised by the Highland Society of London.

(City of Edinburgh Council – Libraries / www.capitalcollections.org.uk)

Fig. 2.19 (right): *Harriet Murray, Mrs Henry Siddons* (1783–1844), *actress and theatrical manager*, by John Wood (1801–70), unknown date, oil on canvas

During her tenure at the Theatre Royal, Harriet Siddons encouraged the rise of the 'national dramas'. Siddons was a close friend and colleague of Sir Walter Scott, who wrote many pieces for her stage. When George IV visited Edinburgh in 1822, she played the role of Diana Vernon in a command performance of Scott's *Rob Roy*.

(National Galleries of Scotland)

sporran in 1820, a silver-mounted dirk in 1821, a brace of handsome pistols in 1822, a claymore in 1823, and a silver-mounted powder horn in 1824.[71] The awarding of Highland dress accoutrements at piping competitions and athletic games was swiftly emulated by other clubs and societies throughout Scotland, until by the mid-nineteenth century the practice had become customary. There are numerous such pieces held in the national collection, with examples tending to conform to a particular style: foregrounding national iconographies and incorporating native materials such as silver and gemstones, evoking a sense of inheritance, landscape and ancestry [2.20, 2.21].[72]

By 1826, public interest in the Edinburgh competition was beginning to wane and ticket sales slumped. Members of the Highland Society of Scotland, who were responsible for adjudicating the event on behalf of the HSL, wrote to their patrons and explained that the event had lost its novelty: the competition had scarcely changed for years, fewer fashionables came to the city specifically to attend the races at Musselburgh, and 'the number and frequency of such Competitions now established in various districts of the Country' made the event a less appealing spectacle.[73] It was decided that the annual event should be abandoned in favour of a triennial model, in the hopes that a longer gap between exhibitions would encourage greater interest and improve the quality and uniqueness of the performances on show. The return of the competition in 1829 was marked by the largest array of prizes ever offered by the club, with a collective value of £73-10s.[74] In its report of the event, the *Caledonian Mercury* noted that the number of competitors across the piping, dancing, and 'best dressed' categories was much larger than in previous years. Improvements had also been made to the set decoration:

> *The rising of the curtain displayed a sight of high interest to those warmed by national feeling; between sixty and seventy competitors, all attired in the full Highland Costume, ranged on the stage, together with the different prizes laid*

Fig. 2.20 (above): Prize brooch, 1847

This chased silver plaid brooch set with a facetted crystal was awarded to Donald MacKenzie at the Northern Meeting in 1847, for the second best performance on the Great Highland Bagpipe.

Fig. 2.21 (below): Prize dirk, 1826

This silver mounted dirk was presented to piper Charles Duff at a competition organised by a Highland Friendly Society in 1826.

out before them, to which their earnest gaze was directed. The house being brilliantly illuminated with gas, and embellished with mountain scenery, heightened the truth of the representation, and rendered it of a dramatic character, altogether indescribable.[75]

In addition to the usual prize pipe, presented each year to the best player, other prizes across the three categories included a dirk, sporran, snuff mull, plaid brooch, and numerous sums of money. The best dancer, John Grant of Strathspey, was awarded 'a Highland Dress of the Royal Tartan'; and Donald MacInnes of Lochaber, in second place, won 'a Plaid of the Royal Tartan, with such farther quantity as will make a useful plain dress'. The cloth was sourced from Messrs Cameron and Nicholson, a tailors and clothiers based on North Bridge, Edinburgh.[76] The accounts of the society also note a special payment of £2 to John Paterson from Doune, a competitor for best dressed, who 'appeared Dressed with Sword, Pistols, Dirk, [etc] of his own manufacture'.[77]

Collecting tartan

Since their establishment in 1778, the HSL had sought to position itself as the national authority on the history of tartan and Highland dress culture. Its members published essays on the topic and, when approached, the club would answer petitions from individuals wanting a ruling on elements of the garb.[78] The most noteworthy of their efforts to preserve and promote the antiquarian study of Highland dress came in the form of an ambitious project, begun in 1815, to collect samples of the setts then in use by the clan chiefs of the Highlands and Islands. The collection they would ultimately form is significant for being the earliest known attempt by a Scottish association to amass and categorise tartans based on their supposed clan affiliations. As such, it represents a pivotal shift in the formation of tartan as we understand it today, documenting how the symbolic qualities of the cloth were harnessed to create a codified system of Highland heraldry.

The scheme was first proposed in a letter received by the governing committee on 16 June 1815 from portrait miniaturist Andrew Robertson, on behalf of himself and fellow club member Major-General David Stewart of Garth [2.22, 2.23]. Having consulted one another privately on the advantages of beginning a collection of clan tartan, they had concluded that without a curated material record 'all trace of their authentic costume' would be irrevocably lost. Furthermore, they hoped that by appealing to the chiefs directly for specimens of their ancestral patterns they could rekindle a sense of 'feudal feeling' in the Highlands and remind the chiefs:

THE RISE AND INFLUENCE OF THE HIGHLAND SOCIETIES

Fig. 2.22 (above): *Andrew Robertson (1777–1845), miniature painter (self portrait)*, 1811, watercolour on ivory set in octagonal brooch

Born in Aberdeen, Andrew Robertson studied under Alexander Nasmyth and Sir Henry Raeburn. He painted himself wearing tartan on several occasions, both as an advertisement of his Scottishness and of his ability to successfully render the intricacies of plaid. Having joined the Highland Society of London to cultivate a network of elite clients in 1806, he was the first to suggest that the club begin a collection of clan tartans in 1815.

(National Galleries of Scotland)

Fig. 2.23 (right): *Major-General David Stewart of Garth*, by Samuel William Reynolds (1773–1835), after James M. Scrymgeour, unknown date, mezzotint on paper

David Stewart of Garth was born in Perthshire into a Gaelic-speaking family which had supported the Jacobites in the Rising of 1745–46. Like many sons of the Highland gentry, he pursued a successful career in the British army. He belonged to several Highland clubs and societies in Britain, but was most active in the Highland Society of London and the Celtic Society of Edinburgh. In 1829, he became the colonial governor of St Lucia.

… of who they are and what their forefathers were and did. It may induce them to hold in greater estimation that costume which has been so long laid aside that even now perhaps few of them can ascertain with any degree of accuracy the pattern of their Tartan. It is even now almost too late, but never altogether so.

Robertson and Stewart of Garth's appeal met with enthusiasm from the committee and it was swiftly resolved to send out official requests to the heads of Highland families 'to furnish the Society with as much of the Tartan of their respective Clans as will serve to show the Pattern'. At Robertson's insistence, all copies of the application were to be written in Gaelic and signed by the President, HRH the Duke of Kent and Strathearn, with the rationale: 'A Royal signature may do as much to restore the Highland Dress in 1815 as a Royal Decree did in destroying it in 1746.'[79]

Over the coming months, administration of the tartan collection fell largely to Stewart of Garth and secretary to the society, James Hamilton. Much of the surviving correspondence related to the chiefs' submissions can be found in the personal papers of Stewart of Garth, now held by the National Library of Scotland.[80] Together, these letters provide remarkable insight into the attitudes and convictions of the various chiefs who chose to participate in the scheme, as well as the largely commercial origins of the specimens they authenticated with their seal. Reaction to the scheme was mixed; while most responded eagerly and lauded the patriotic aim of the project, others either did not know whether their clan had a specific tartan or else expressed irritation with the request. That being said, seldom did a respondent refuse to participate.

Helen Cumming Gordon and Donald Macleod sent their apologies, as they had no knowledge of their sett or a material specimen to impart. However, they promised to send on what they could after researching the topic themselves. 'It will be very interesting to collect them all', wrote Gordon, '& the Clans are very much obliged to you for suggesting it.'[81] Hamilton communicated his disappointment to Stewart of Garth in February 1816, after the project had been running for several months, that so many of the samples they had received reflected an absence of knowledge on the topic. 'Lady Stafford sent me part of that worn by the 42^d as the Sutherland,' he complained, 'in which I have every Reason to believe she is mistaken.'[82]

When approached by Andrew Robertson in December 1815, his kinsman Alexander Robertson of Struan immediately cast aspersions on the project and questioned its historical credentials. 'It does not appear to be apertained, either by tradition or authentick history that the different Clans, in the Highlands of Scotland, wore any particular distinctive pattern of Tartan', he wrote. Although he acknowledged his belief in a system of heraldry used by clans based on 'particular Colours or Standards, emblematical of some of their most honorable atchievments', he flatly maintained that 'they wore no uniform Garb'. Despite his adamant refusal to endorse the emergent concept of clan tartans, Robertson of Struan did consent to submit a specimen of Atholl tartan to Stewart of Garth, explaining that he wore it because his ancestors had once laid claim to:

> … the whole of Atholl, excepting a small space surrounding the Castle of Blair, and were occasionally stiled Earls of Atholl, and when that title was omitted, were at all times stiled of Atholl, I look upon it as my right to adopt the Atholl Tartan of which I inclose a Patern with my Seal affixed to it.[83]

By comparison, Duncan Macpherson of Cluny and his friend Sir Ewen Cameron of Fassifern – both proud 'old members' of the HSL – congratulated Stewart of Garth on the scheme, confessing themselves 'surprised that the idea never struck anyone before'.[84] Macpherson's enthusiasm for the project is reflected in the lengths he went to between December 1815 and April 1816 to secure his tartan a place in the HSL's collection. Having written to his family seat at Badenoch and finding 'none of it ready',[85] he sent to the tartan manufacturers of Bannockburn to have a piece made up for the purpose:

> *You'll be surprised at not having as yet received the pattern of the Macpherson Tartan, but the truth of the Matter is that I could only find one piece of it in the Country, which I have sent to Bannockburn to have a Plaid made from it, and how soon it is finished, I shall have the pleasure to send you a piece of it, as directed.*[86]

Macpherson's anxiety to preserve his sett in the HSL collection is echoed elsewhere in Stewart of Garth's correspondence with members of the Highland gentry. Lord Ogilvie, having forwarded a specimen in January 1816 under the cover of George Hunter, was dismayed to hear that it was 'not sufficient for the purpose'.[87] Simply put, there was too little of it to convey the full complexity of the pattern or to gauge successfully how it was to repeat across a full length. Attempting to rectify his mistake, Ogilvie commissioned Hunter to make two new pieces, one destined for the HSL collection and a further yard as a present for Stewart of Garth himself. 'I hope,' Ogilvie wrote apologetically, 'that as soon as the Tartan is ready [Hunter] will not delay in sending you the piece for the Highland Society, as well as that for yourself.'[88] For Ogilvie, the desire to physically preserve his pattern in the HSL collection was coupled with an impulse to impart his views upon its history. In his first letter to Stewart of Garth regarding the subject, he attempted to impress upon the collector the clan lore associated with the chosen colours of the Ogilvie sett:

> *The Tartan is remarkable in not having any Green in it which is a colour the name* [Ogilvie] *have a particular aversion to, being once dressed in that in some battle where they were <u>unfortunate</u>.*[89]

Highland patriotism frequently rears its head from the pages of Stewart of Garth's correspondence. On sending his specimen, William Farquharson informed Stewart of Garth in no uncertain terms that '[t]here is no person whatever more proud of being a Highlander than I have always been, since ever I remember anything'. He also described upholstering the furniture in his writing room with the Farquharson tartan and pledged that members of his masonic lodge, St Nathalan of Tullich-in-Mar, would be outfitted with the same.[90] In his response, Sir John MacGregor-Murray described himself 'radically & from the very deepest root an aboriginal Highlander', and earnestly suggested that Stewart of Garth expand his efforts to include information regarding the plant badges and war cries of the Highland clans. He also advised the collector that distinctions should be made between different branches of a clan that might wear different patterns, 'for instance in the case of the Earl of Breadalbane the request should be not for the Tartan of "your Clan" but for that of the Breadalbane Campbells if it differs from that of the Family of Argyle'.[91]

Despite its initial success, associational interest in building and maintaining the HSL collection soon reached a low ebb. The last identifiable submissions from this period appear to have been received in June 1822, when several samples were given into the possession of secretary John Wedderburn. So fragmentary had the administration of the HSL collection become, however, that these samples were never added to those initially gathered by Stewart of Garth and Hamilton. They eventually found their way into the permanent collection of National Museums Scotland through the historian W. F. Skene, the paper labels affixed to them the only indication they were ever associated with the HSL's early collecting activities.[92] By the 1820s, poor health and financial uncertainty had drawn Stewart of Garth away from London and vested his interests more firmly in the establishment and support of Highland clubs and societies in Scotland. Without his guiding hand and motivating presence, the scheme to collect and authenticate the tartans of the clans was quietly lain aside and seemingly forgotten.

In the early months of 1827, HSL clerk Martin Smith Metcalfe inventoried the office of the outgoing secretary, John Wedderburn. His chief concern was investigating the contents of a deal box belonging to the society, which had been in Wedderburn's possession for some years. In his report to the governing committee, Metcalfe detailed the recovery of approximately eighty tartan samples from the box. The samples were in varying states of decay, having fallen victim to pests while in Wedderburn's care. Over half the samples carried a wax seal and a note of provenance, indicating connections between specific patterns and members of the Highland gentry: these included 'Glengarry – as worn by the Chief', 'MacKenzie – Mr Mackenzie of Seaforth', and 'McGregor for Dress, [*ditto*] for Undress'. Metcalfe composed a list, outlining the scope of the collection before him and ticking off each specimen as he sorted through it. Multiple ticks appear beside selected names – such as 'McNab', 'Murray' and 'McIntosh' – indicating the presence of more than one sample attributed to that name. All other names which appear on the list have a single tick, indicating the presence of a single specimen. The remainder of the samples in the box bore no seal or explanatory missive, or else their marks of attribution had become illegible with the passage of time. Metcalfe fretted over his findings, dismayed by the neglected state of so grand a collection of ancestral textiles. As clerk to the HSL, he made a recommendation:

> *Many of the pieces are damaged by Moths and I beg to suggest in order to preserve the patterns that a piece be cut off each of the certified Tartans sufficient to shew the pattern and pasted in the pages of a Book, with the name of the Clan and by whom authenticated written on the top of the Page.*[93]

The accounts of the HSL show that Metcalfe's concern was upheld by the governing committee, who authorised £8-1s to mount and bind the

HIGHLAND STYLE

samples for posterity. The commission was given to Harper, Pearce & Co., stationers and account book manufacturers of Gracechurch Street, London, in November 1827. The best surviving tartans were cut down and stitched onto 48 Bristol boards, which were then bound together to form a ledger. A red Morocco label was affixed to the front of the volume and stamped with the title 'Highland Society of London Certified Tartans' in neat, gilt lettering [2.24].[94]

The current form of the HSL tartan collection was assembled in several stages throughout the nineteenth and twentieth centuries, prior to being placed on loan to National Museums Scotland in 1983. Awareness of the collection among the general membership of the HSL appears to have waxed and waned throughout the early decades of its existence. Just as M. S. Metcalfe unearthed a decaying collection of textiles in Wedderburn's office in 1827, successive generations of HSL members would periodically remember the story of the collection and seek it out, only for interest to once again flicker and die. This continual cycle of loss and rediscovery resulted in the degradation of institutional knowledge surrounding the contents of the collection and its foundational history, leading to myth-making and misapprehensions about its origins. It was not until 1887 that a committee, headed by Duncan Stewart, was formed specifically to address this reoccurring issue.[95] The committee produced a report, which explained how the collection began under the auspices of Major-General David Stewart of Garth, although Hamilton's substantial administrative efforts went unrecorded. The report also contained a survey of the collection's physical condition at the time of writing and outlined a set of recommendations for its continued preservation and improvement. An inventory of the named clan tartans in the collection was appended to the report, with remarks on the material quality, provenance and accuracy of pattern attributions entered against the name of each specimen. After deliberating the merits and the deficiencies of the collection as a whole, the committee concluded:

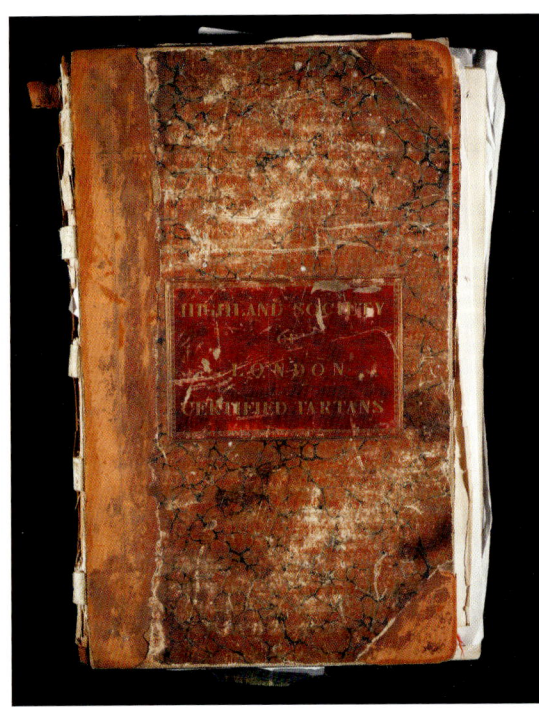

Fig. 2.24: Ledger of 'certified' clan tartans, c.1827

The collection of clan tartans amassed by Major-General David Stewart of Garth and James Hamilton on behalf of the Highland Society of London was rediscovered by Martin Smith Metcalfe in 1827. Shortly thereafter, the collection was bound into this presentation ledger by stationers and account book makers Harper, Pearce & Co.

(On loan from the Highland Society of London. Image © National Museums Scotland)

Many of the patterns are authenticated by the signature and seals of arms of the donors, but even among these all are not of undoubted accuracy. It is not proposed to tamper in any way with this Book but to retain it in its existing condition as a record of what was collected at that time, but it is recommended that application be again made in the name of the Society to persons who can be relied upon to furnish true specimens, (which shall be as far as possible of uniform size). The pattern would be most effectively shewn by a piece of Tartan extending the whole width of the web and about 18 inches long – and after being duly authenticated and verified that these samples shall remain in the possession of the Highland Society of London as the standard and authoritative patterns of such Tartans. Lists of these with descriptive tables on a fixed scale (such as are given in Logan's Scottish Gaël*) should be printed and issued to the members of the Society and others interested in the subject, including manufacturers of tartan stuffs, so that all doubts as to the true setts may be obviated for the future.*[96]

An inventory of property belonging to the HSL made in 1916 indicates that the collection was indeed enlarged by an influx of new specimens. However, this additional material remained largely unbound and uncategorised.[97] It was not until the interwar period the collection underwent the expansion and fundamental restructuring that resulted in its current condition. Against the recommendations made by the 1887 committee, in the 1930s the tartans amassed by Stewart of Garth and Hamilton were harvested from the pages of the old ledger and rebound into a new set of presentation volumes, sitting alongside more recently collected material. Behind the decision to deconstruct and reform the collection was a desire to render it more 'complete' – representing the full range of clan, family and regimental tartans then commercially available [2.25].[98] Today it spans over several volumes, box files and folders and comprises specimens from the late eighteenth, nineteenth and twentieth centuries; much of it can be seen on display in the 'Textile Trades' corridor of the *Scotland Transformed* gallery of the present-day Museum of Scotland.

As an artefact, the HSL tartan collection reveals much about the intersection of antiquarian interest and romantic consumerism that underpinned the success of clan tartan as a popular commodity in Georgian Britain. Meanwhile, the complex story of its compilation, deconstruction and material transformation, points to the importance of the collection within the early curatorial history of tartan. In binding and presenting the samples for scrutiny and allowing different hands to cut, arrange and annotate individual pieces, we get a sense of how tartan was regarded as an evolving historical curiosity by successive generations of wearers, collectors and interpreters. As the first collection of its kind, its influence can be clearly felt in the physical and ideological parameters of other tartan collections compiled in the nineteenth and twentieth centuries [2.26].[99]

Fig. 2.25 (above): Interior of ledger of 'certified' clan tartans, *c*.1827

In the early 20th century, the Highland Society of London cut samples of clan tartan from the 'certified' ledger to form the basis of a new tartan collection. On this page, only half of the Royal Stewart sample collected by Stewart of Garth and Hamilton in 1816 remains *in situ*. Below it, the specimen of Campbell of Breadalbane has been removed completely.

Fig. 2.26 (left): Tartan sample book

This sample of Cameron hard tartan is part of a bound collection of 58 clan setts, originally in the possession of Francis William Garden-Campbell of Troup (1840–95). The folio of patterns was purchased by clan and tartan historian David Prentice Menzies (1851–1927), who eventually sold it to John Crichton-Stuart, 4th Marquess of Bute (1881–1947). A piece of card has been sewn into the top corner of each sample, carrying the inked name of the sett with additional historical information over-written in pencil. Despite Menzies claiming that the collection was over two hundred years old, the swatches all date from the first half of the 19th century. The layout and alphabetical presentation of the collection strongly suggests that it once belonged to a textile merchant or manufacturer.

(Both images: On loan from the Highland Society of London. Image © National Museums Scotland)

Harnessing icons

In 2018, the Department of Scottish History and Archaeology at National Museums Scotland acquired a pair of emblematic steel cufflinks. The raised design featured on each cufflink showcases miniature representations of objects typically associated with the martial culture of the Scottish Highlands: a flintlock pistol, an axe, a basket-hilted broadsword, dirk, and a studded targe. Occupying the four corners of the squared ornament, these icons surround the central motto *'Fior Gaidel'* (meaning 'True Highlander') and the date '1815' [2.27]. The latter is a direct reference to the inaugural year of the Society of True Highlanders (STH), a convivial society of Highland gentlemen that first met at Inverlochy under the auspices of Alasdair Ranaldson MacDonell of Glengarry, 15th Chief of Glengarry, in June 1815. Though the cufflinks do not carry a maker's mark, other examples with this insignia held in private hands are known to have been manufactured by J. Nutting & Co. of Covent Garden during the first half of the nineteenth century.[100]

Like many of the individuals discussed in this chapter, Glengarry held memberships in several Highland clubs and societies across both Scotland and England. However, as such clubs began to proliferate in the early decades of the nineteenth century, he grew increasingly concerned that they were too accessible to outsiders. It was his belief that the cultivation of Highland culture should be the preserve of Highlanders alone, which prompted his decision to inaugurate his own association and restrict entry to those he considered 'genuine descendants' of the Gael.

The design emblazoned on the cufflinks held by National Museums Scotland is an indication of the differing sartorial and ideological emphasis of the STH, in comparison to its sister societies. Whereas the HSL allowed its members a degree of preference and individual interpretation in their Highland attire, Glengarry's guidelines for the construction of a proper Highland uniform were more exacting. Writing in 1822, he listed the full kit which he expected members of the STH to wear:

THE RISE AND INFLUENCE OF THE HIGHLAND SOCIETIES

Fig. 2.27: Cufflinks

The design of these steel cufflinks incorporates an array of martial icons, traditionally associated with the warrior culture of Gaelic society. Carrying such weapons had been proscribed in the aftermath of the last Jacobite Rising of 1745–46, thus embuing them with an almost talismanic quality.

HIGHLAND STYLE

> *A belted plaid and waist Belt, a Tartan Jacket with T.H. buttons & Shoulder buckles, a scarlet coat THrs Cut with THrs Buttons, A cocked bonnet with Clan Badge and Cockade, A Purse and belt, A Pair of Highland Garters, A Pair of Hose, A pair of Highland Brogues (with whangs) and A Pair of Clasps to Do for Court use.*

He also specified,

> *A Gun (or Fusee) with a sling, A Brace of Highland Pistols and a belt, A 'core Dubh' or Hoc knife called the 'Skian', a powder Horn with Chain or Card, a short Pouch and cross shoulder belt.*[101]

These specifications were geared less towards the urban spaces of elite sociability, such as Edinburgh and London, and emphasised instead the practical roots of the costume in the hunting and martial traditions of the Highland landscape.

Glengarry was a controversial figure within Highland society. In the view of Sir Walter Scott, he seemed to have lived 'a century too late', preferring the lifestyle of a Highland chieftain of old to that of a nineteenth-century landowner. As discussed by Stana Nenadic, he was 'a romantic consumer in spectacular and eccentric style', who spent lavish amounts of money on clothing and hunting paraphernalia, maintained a retinue of pipers, bards and foresters, and regularly hosted Highland balls and games on the Glengarry estate.[102] His portrait by Angelica Kauffman is an early testament to his love of Scottish Romantic aesthetics. Painted in Rome during his Grand Tour of Europe in 1799–1800, Kauffman's depiction of Glengarry emphasises his identity as a young Chief, newly-invested of his inheritance and fresh from military service as Colonel of the Glengarry Fencibles. The elaborate costume recorded by Kauffman's brush reflects the style habitually worn by Glengarry as a matter of native pride, even in the sweltering Italian heat [2.28].

Glengarry's overt patronage of Highland revival culture sat in sharp contrast to the policies of sheep farming and clearance he operated on his lands. Though by no means the only club member to embody such contradictions, his ostentatiousness and seeming lack of self-reflection put him – and the club over which he presided – increasingly at odds with others in his circle.

Hunter's Highlanders

On 14 June 1821, a curious article – appearing under the *nom de plume* 'PHILO-PHILABEGUS' – made its way into the pages of the *Inverness Courier*.[103] The anonymous piece attacked a club newly instituted in Edinburgh, known as the Celtic Society. While it is difficult to ascertain the identity of the author, it is likely the article was penned by a follower of the Society of True Highlanders.

The Celtic Society of Edinburgh first met on 7 January 1820 at Oman's Hotel on Charlotte Square, the former residence of Sir John Sinclair of Ulbster. The meeting was orchestrated by Captain William Mackenzie of Gruinard, 72nd Regiment of Foot, with the support of Major-General David Stewart of Garth. In his address to the company, Mackenzie stated 'that a National Society should be established in the Metropolis of Scotland for the purpose of encouraging a return to the Ancient Dress in the Highland Districts of the Country'.[104] This was a significant deviation from the foundational ethos of previous societies, such as the HSL and the STH, the aims of which had been more generally directed towards the preservation and the promotion of Highland cultural pursuits in general.

The centrality of dress to the culture of this fledgling association became more apparent as its inaugural year progressed. In addition to the usual appointments of a governing committee and a contracted piper, the Celtic Society also nominated a 'Garb Furnisher' and 'Dirk Maker' to advise and supply its members with appropriate clothing and accoutrements. John MacLeod, an armourer and cutler in College Street, was recommended as 'Dirk Maker' by John Norman MacLeod, 24th Chief of Clan MacLeod. The role of 'Garb Furnisher', meanwhile, was given to army clothier, weaver and well-respected retailer of quality tartans, George Hunter. Wearing formal Highland dress at meetings and public events was also enshrined in the rules of the Celtic Society from the outset, with emphasis continually placed on the importance of individual members appearing 'in the Tartan of his own particular Clan, so far as ascertained'.[105] In a statement made at a general meeting on 26 May 1820, all members were reminded that their 'private influence' and 'persuasive talents' mattered more than any recommendation the Celtic Society might make regarding the preservation of Highland dress to the public. 'It was not enough that the object of the Society was approved', read the statement, 'it required further to be actively supported.' In particular, it was deemed the responsibility of 'Highland Proprietors' to see such habits cultivated on their estates. As for the governing committee, they planned to develop a system of premiums that could be distributed to old Highlanders who

Fig. 2.28: *Alasdair Ranaldson MacDonell (1773–1828), 15th Chief of Glengarry*, by Angelica Kauffman (1741–1807), c.1799–1800, oil on canvas

Glengarry founded the Society of True Highlanders in 1815. He was also a regular member of the Highland Society of London and the Celtic Society of Edinburgh. He set himself against the latter following the visit of King George IV to Edinburgh in 1822, claiming in the *Edinburgh Observer* that 'their general appearance is assumed and fictitious, and they have no right to burlesque the national character or dress of Highlanders'.

(Armadale Castle, Gardens and Museum of the Isles)

'habitually' wore tartan, so as to encourage the adoption of the dress by a younger generation of native wearers.[106]

The satirical piece printed in the *Inverness Courier* in 1821 attacked the Celtic Society's plans to hold a summer meeting in the Highland capital. Adopting the persona of a helpful club member, the anonymous author sought to clarify the Celtic Society's position on Highland dress etiquette for the benefit of all prospective attendees, particularly addressing those who might feel 'discouraged' by the club's strict laws on the wearing of authentic costume.

'We are by no means so superstitious as they may imagine,' Philo-Philabegus reassured readers. 'Indeed the local regulations and bye laws of the Inverness Branch are wonderfully lax and accommodating to young beginners.' Flesh-coloured, knitted drawers were to be permitted beneath the kilts of 'more delicate juveniles', while 'elderly burgher gentlemen' possessing a doctor's note 'for gout, rheumatism, sciatica, luxations, or affections of the hip-joint' could don drab breeches or long gaiters under specially lengthened philabegs. Any doubts regarding such matters could be directed to the club secretary, who had a pattern card on hand detailing the most acceptable configuration of the garb. Elements of the costume could certainly vary, however, depending on one's occupation and social standing within the club. While a chieftain may be obliged to wear a single eagle plume in their bonnet, as per tradition, writers, clerks, poets, schoolmasters, excisemen, custom-house officers and members of the press could substitute a 'single grey goose quill'. The latter was a not so subtle gibe to the Vice Presidency of Sir Walter Scott, whose lack of Highland blood was seen by some as antithetical to the leading role he held in the governance of Celtic Society members. 'Any dandies,' meanwhile, 'are to be allowed the peacock's feather, like dignitaries of the Chinese empire.' As long as one avoided the ultimate *faux pas* – apparently already seen at club gatherings in the Lowland capital – of 'appearing with the fore-parts of their philabegs turned behind', all would be well.

Gentlemen wishing to avail themselves of local vendors could repair to 'ALLAN's Masquerade Warehouse', where 'silver mounted pistols, warranted not to go off' and 'sham dirks, – and real dirks well fenced with cork upon the points' were available to rent [2.29]. The author guaranteed that Allan's stock was entirely appropriate for the occasion, as it was approved of by that most fashionable purveyor of clan tartans in Edinburgh and sartorial consultant to the Celtic Society, Mr George Hunter. Allan had already outfitted several gentlemen in 'the uniform of "Hunter's Highlanders"', in a manner befitting the pages of ladies' fashion periodical *La Belle Assemblée*. And as for any women wishing to join the festivities, they were not to be excluded. Should the gentleman of the Celtic Society condescend to host a ball, hinted the author, a local wigmaker had already been approached to provide the ladies of Inverness with modish 'Malvina wigs', designed to complement the Ossianic spirit of the occasion. Philo-Philabegus also sought to address concerns raised by fledgling kilt-wearers, in two minds about parading openly in the streets of Inverness lest 'disagreeable comparisons' be made between themselves and the seasoned kilt-wearers of nearby Kintail, Strathglass and Lochaber, who might cross their path in the marketplace. But they need not worry, soothed Philo-Philabegus. On the day of the proposed meeting, the club had promised to station men on the bridge leading into town, turning away 'those swaggering, wild, six feet three inch fellows' and thereby neatly avoiding the threat of embarrassment altogether.[107]

By 1821, associational tensions had begun to circulate around the Celtic Society's efforts to preserve and promote the revivalist style of Highland dress, despite an apparent lack of Highland pedigree within its metropolitan membership. The satirical tone of the article printed in the *Inverness Courier* is reflected in other prose and poetry published throughout the 1810s–30s in newspapers and periodicals, which sought to characterise Highland men as ultra-masculine, martial figures, imbued with an inherently ancient grace and rural sensibility. Within such works, Highland costume was positioned as a means by which that identity could be accessed by anyone – Highlander or no – with the means to purchase it. Such pieces reflected a broader debate over what constituted authentic Highland culture, as well as who had the right to make those decisions. The formalised Highland dress silhouette promoted and refined by various Highland societies throughout the late Georgian era sat at the very heart of this debate, causing divisions even between the members of the societies themselves. This tension would come to national prominence in 1822, with the arrival of King George IV in Edinburgh.

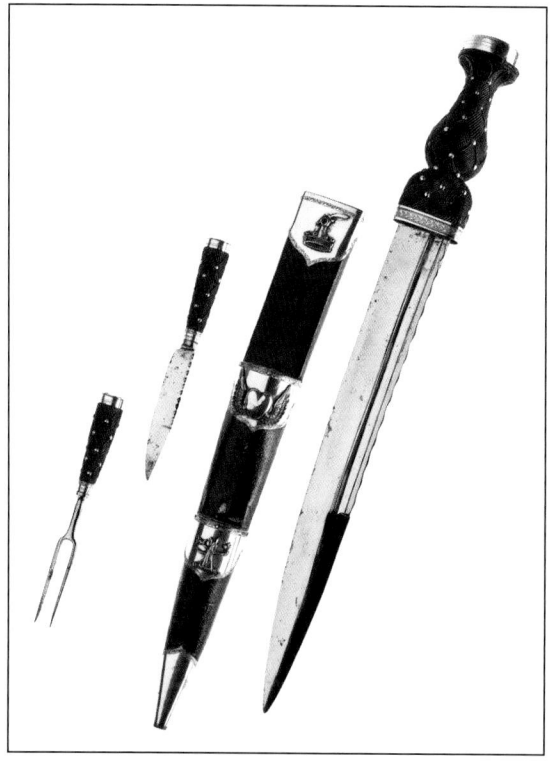

Fig. 2.29: Dress dirk

By the early 19th century, dirks were no longer considered practical weapons. They remained an essential element of Highland dress culture, but were increasingly worn for show as opposed to defence. Dress dirks were available for purchase or hire at varying price points, ranging widely in quality and workmanship. This example was retailed by the Albion Cloth Company in Edinburgh, a gentlemen's outfitter that specialised in military uniform and fancy dress.

The road to 1822

The famous visit of the King to Edinburgh in August 1822 launched tartan onto the national stage, leaving a controversial legacy in its wake [2.30]. It was the first time that a ruling monarch had visited Scotland since the coronation of Charles II and, as such, it was billed as a moment of high pageantry and political symbolism. Anticipating the King's desire for a great

Fig. 2.30: *George IV* (1762–1830), by Sir David Wilkie (1785–1841), 1829, oil on canvas

The Highland clothes and accoutrements worn by George IV during his visit to Edinburgh in 1822 were supplied by George Hunter, army clothier, clan tartan retailer, and 'Garb Furnisher' to the Celtic Society. According to the royal accounts, the costume cost £1354-18s. The appearance of the monarch in Highland dress elicited a mixed response from the public, with many mocking his choice to wear flesh-coloured stockings beneath his kilt.

(Royal Collection Trust / Her Majesty Queen Elizabeth II 2022)

Highland spectacle, the nominated organisers of the visit, Sir Walter Scott and Major-General David Stewart of Garth, devised a programme of patriotic events that was designed to showcase Scotland's distinct place within the British union, while also emphasising its loyalty to the Crown. The plaid, with its rehabilitated Jacobite past, ties to romantic clanship and arresting appearance, was deemed the perfect fabric with which to capture the popular imagination of the city and to garner enthusiasm for the event.

The Celtic Society, of which Sir Walter Scott and Stewart of Garth were proud founder members, played a pivotal role in the celebrations as the official guards of the ancient regalia of Scotland on its procession from Edinburgh Castle to the Palace of Holyrood. Glengarry's Society of True Highlanders was notably excluded, much to the consternation of the chief. Despite his lack of an official role, Glengarry successfully inserted himself into the parade by riding forward, unannounced, to greet the monarch. In the aftermath of the visit, he was among the most vociferous of critics of the Celtic Society's involvement and of Scott's inauthentic 'kiltification' of the Lowlander.

The material impact of George IV's visit on Highland dress culture can be observed in public museum and private collections across Scotland. In the same way that remnants of tartan fabric have periodically become associated with the Highland clothes of Prince Charles Edward Stuart and his flight from Culloden in 1746, tartan costumes dating from the late Georgian period are often said to have been 'worn at 1822'. The validity of such claims can be difficult to substantiate. However, among the many Highland dress outfits held by National Museums Scotland, a handful of them can be reasonably associated with the pageantry of the Royal Visit – either because they can be tied to individuals thought to have been in attendance, or their material qualities allow for such a connection to be made.

Shortly before the visit commenced, Scott published *Hints Addressed to the Inhabitants of Edinburgh, and others, in Prospect of His Majesty's visit. By an Old Citizen.* This pamphlet contained exacting instructions on how attendees should behave and, significantly, how they should dress to welcome the monarch to Scotland. 'We are THE CLAN,' he extolled, 'and the King is THE CHIEF.' At public processions, spectators were encouraged to wear blue and white ribbon cockades, the emblematical colours of St Andrew. For gentlemen in attendance at the Holyrood *levee*, military uniforms or suits of Highland dress were to be the order of the day. However, it was stressed that those who planned to wear Highland costume should only do so 'in the proper Highland fashion', accessorising the garb with 'steel-wrought pistols, broadsword, and dirk'. Elite women, meanwhile, were urged to show restraint when it came to national badges. Scott disparaged ladies from adopting tartan trains when being presented to the King at Holyrood, stating that these were too easily tripped over when walking backwards out of the monarch's presence. 'A scarf of tartan may do very well' as a substitute, wrote Scott, 'but four or five yards of tartan satin sweeping the ground must produce an effect, to say the least, of rather a novel character.'[108]

Merchants in the city did not hesitate to turn the visit to their commercial advantage. Edinburgh retailers, such as Romanes & Paterson, placed advertisements in London newspapers to capture the attention of English elites planning to travel to Scotland to attend the festivities. Directing potential customers towards their warehouse on North Bridge, the firm promised to provide 'a large choice of TARTANS of the SCOTTISH HIGHLAND CHIEFTAINS, in Worsted, Silk and Worsted, Poplins, Tabinets, Satin, Sarsnet, and Velvet', alongside a wide variety of tartan scarves, cloaks and 'Scottish Highland Bonnets' designed specifically for the use of women and children.[109] On North Bridge, William Steven & Co. boasted their connection to 'an experienced Tradesmen from London' who could provide gentlemen with 'TARTAN DRESSES, and every Article in the line', with commemorative 'WELCOME BUTTONS to match'.[110] By early August such advertisements were appearing alongside reports of shortages in the supply chain, suggesting manufacturers were struggling to keep up with demand. According to several papers, merchants from Edinburgh had flocked to Glasgow following the announcement of the King's visit and cleared the wholesalers and retailers of all their ready tartan goods; even 'remnants of silk tartan, however small, were bought up with the greatest avidity'.[111] John Duff, a merchant in Dunkeld, was so anxious about the status of his order for 1500 yards of Atholl tartan that he wrote to tartan weavers Messrs Wilson of Bannockburn on 24 July 1822 and asked them to send it off 'piece by piece as they come out of the loom'.[112]

This combination of commercial opportunism and material scarcity can be read in the construction of a tartan coat, gifted to the national collection in 1987 [2.31].[113] Although the identity of the original wearer is unknown, there can be little doubt that the coat was commissioned for use during the 1822 festivities. It is also apparent that the maker faced certain challenges in fulfilling the order. The prevailing fashion of the early nineteenth century was to employ a smaller setting of tartan in coats, waistcoats and kilts, and to reserve larger versions for plaids, as smaller setts were

THE RISE AND INFLUENCE OF THE HIGHLAND SOCIETIES

Figs 2.31 and 2.32 (above, left and right): Tartan coat, c.1822

Immediately prior to the visit of George IV to Edinburgh in 1822, tailors rushed to acquire the requisite tartan to clothe attendees. The large sett used in this coat belongs to a family of variations with its origin in the 18th century, which includes the Dalziel, Lochiel, Munro and a commemorative sett known as 'King George IV'. There was not quite enough material to finish the commission, leading to the incorporation of a different pattern in the construction of the right sleeve.

Fig 2.33 (left): Commemorative buttons

Several advertisements published in Scottish newspapers during the summer of 1822 list the sale of 'welcome' buttons, intended to decorate the garments being prepared for the arrival of the monarch.

easier to work with when it came to cutting and piecing. It is thus unusual to see such a large-scale tartan used in a tailored garment of this period. This, combined with the insertion of a panel of different tartan on the inside of the right sleeve, suggests that the coat was constructed from whatever material was available, irrespective of its suitability for the task. The fact that the tartan is not well-matched along the seams is a further indication that the garment was put together in haste [2.32]. The 16 buttons visible at the front closure, cuffs, and at the centre back, all carry the same motto, 'THIS I'LL DEFEND GIIIIR 1822', accompanied by a crown and thistle motif, ringed by a band of laurel leaves [2.33]. The backside of each button reads 'EDINBURGH 1822'. These are clearly a set of commemorative 'welcome buttons' of the type being advertised by William Steven & Co. in the days leading up to the King's arrival.

Questions of cultural and historical authenticity were at the forefront of the criticism levelled at this broadly Lowland parade of Highland style. Such contemporary concerns are reflected in the provenance of a formal suit of Highland dress, purchased by National Museums Scotland in 1994 [2.34].[114] It was made for William Blackhall, who lived at Blackfaulds, near the village of Torphichen in West Lothian. Born in 1792, notice of his death in 1863 mentions that he was formerly a comb maker in Edinburgh. Trade directories indicate that he became active in 1812 and, according to Blackhall's will, the family business was still in operation on his death.[115] It has been suggested by Sally Tuckett that his occupation as a comb maker may have influenced his decision to wear a tartan ensemble during the 1822 visit, perhaps in a bid to promote cloth woven by a business associate. Whether that be the case or not, it is probable that his role in supplying a necessary tool in the process of textile production would have allowed him access to purveyors of quality tartan and the expertise required to tailor it appropriately.[116]

Blackhall's suit is a fine example of the revivalist influence on Highland dress construction, blending elements typically found in fashionable menswear of the era with details characteristic of the historic lines of the costume. The coat and waistcoat are made from a version of an eighteenth-century sett, known as Glenorchy, whereas the fringed plaid and narrow box-pleated kilt are made from a version of the Cumming tartan. As aesthetically complementary setts, it is likely that

Fig. 2.34: Kilt suit belonging to William Blackhall of Blackfaulds, West Lothian, *c.*1822

Blackhall's fashionably cut kilt suit is composed of four tailored pieces: a coat, waistcoat, box-pleated kilt, and shoulder plaid. Despite Sir Walter Scott's invitation, relatively few heads of Highland families attended the Royal Visit. As Lowland Scots, such as Blackhall, donned Highland dress and paraded through Edinburgh, commentators questioned the cultural authenticity of the event and complained that a romanticised ideal of Highland history had been imposed upon the whole of Scotland.

Fig. 2.35: Bonnet

By the early 19th century, Highland bonnets had become more structured. While wigs had been favoured during the 18th century, by the close of the Georgian era men often wore their hair cropped or kept it tied back into a ponytail or 'queue'. The slit at the rear of Blackhall's bonnet is designed to accommodate a queue, while also allowing the bonnet to fit snuggly over the crown and forehead of the wearer.

the choice to combine them in the making of a single outfit was a deliberate one. There is no familial reason for Blackhall to have chosen these patterns, meaning that his choices were probably driven by a personal liking for the colours and their arrangement in the grid. Accompanying the ensemble is a sophisticated bonnet, modelled on the broad blue bonnets associated with the rural mode of the costume, which were normally flat and knitted in the round [2.35]. Blackhall's bonnet references this shape and method of manufacture with its flat round top. However, it has been stretched over a wire frame and lined with a linen skull cap to create a more structured iteration of the traditional headgear, the fit loosened or tightened by the use of silk ribbon ties.

These two costumes – in their own ways – embody much of what was considered inappropriate about the 'plaided panorama' of 1822. The visit took place at a time of industrial unrest in urban Scotland and of economic crisis in the Highlands and Islands. The idealised representations of clanship and feudalism pushed to the fore by the organisers of the visit, combined with the material excesses enjoyed by those in attendance, struck an uncomfortable balance between fantasy and reality. The universal application of tartan and the brandishing of claymores on the streets of Edinburgh succeeded in reinforcing a distinct national character for Scotland within Britain, yet this character ran contrary to the lived experience of most of its citizens. In casting the revivalist style of Highland dress as a national icon, its advocates ensured that the cultural relevance of the costume survived beyond the confines of Georgian high society. However, in doing so they also exposed it to the scorn of those who did not recognise themselves in it.

Legacy

National Museums Scotland holds many bound volumes of clan tartan samples, compiled by various collectors and manufacturers over the course of the nineteenth and twentieth centuries. Among these is a small scrapbook containing a discrete collection of twenty 'Highland Tartans', amassed by English antiquarian Sir Samuel Rush Meyrick in 1822.[117] Considered by his contemporaries to be an authority on arms, armour and regional costume, Meyrick's interest in tartan stemmed from its patriotic promotion as an ancient emblem of Highland heraldry. Like other collections of its time, all of Meyrick's specimens have a commercial provenance. The cuttings of fabric glued upon each page are fixed with a neat handwritten label, such as might be seen in a sample book kept behind the counter of a textile merchant for the perusal of customers: 'Small Caledonia' [3.6], 'Colquhoun (silk)', 'No. 158 or Graham in white', 'Large 78th or MacKenzie', 'Abercromby' [2.16]. At the front of the book is a letter written by retailers Millar & Ewing of Glasgow. While no mention is given of the samples themselves, it seems probable that this was the firm that supplied Meyrick with his array of high quality patterns. The focus of the letter is a 'List of the Badges of Distinction used by the Clans of Scotland as sanctioned by the Highland Society of London', seemingly obtained by Miller & Ewing directly from the HSL and subsequently relayed to Meyrick. The list is composed of four columns which, from left to right, give the name of the clan, the plant badge they use, the Gaelic name for the plant, and its proper botanical name. The information contained within the list is presented as inherited fact derived from a trusted source, bound into Meyrick's tartan collection to act as a useful preface for the fabrics [2.36].

Through their various promotional and antiquarian activities, Highland clubs and societies firmly established themselves as the national authorities on what had become – by 1822 – a national costume. Inspired by their own romantic interpretation of Scotland's past, the Highland silhouette they had worked for decades to create had emerged as the recognised sartorial standard. This search for a standard was accompanied by an encroaching sense of rigidity, proscription and mystique. Over time, these features have come to be regarded as defining attributes of modern Highland dress culture.

Notes

1. *The Edinburgh Evening Courant* (14 July 1828), 3.
2. As stated in the rules and regulations of the club, distributed in 1825.
3. *London Courier and Evening Gazette* (31 July 1827), 4.
4. *The Edinburgh Evening Courant* (14 July 1828), 3.
5. NMS H.MCR 2.
6. *The Edinburgh Evening Courant* (14 July 1828), 3.
7. See in particular: McCullough 2011.
8. Nenadic 1999, 220.
9. The material culture of Highland clubs and societies is not well-represented in existing scholarship, with analysis of their cultural legacy largely focusing on the role of these organisations in the investigation of James Macpherson's *Ossian* and associational influence over the standardisation of pipe music. For exceptions see: Watt 2021; Watt and Waine 2019, 34–43.
10. The Dress Act was passed in 1746 as a direct response to the use of Highland dress by soldiers serving in the Jacobite army, and by civilian supporters during the last Jacobite Rising of 1745–46. Enforcement was proposed from 1 August 1747. However, the Act was amended twice – in 1747 and 1748 – effectively pushing back the official date of enforcement until 25 December 1748.
11. *The Kentish Gazette* (19 June 1782), 4.
12. *Caledonian Mercury* (22 June 1782), 2. As discussed in Chapter 1, the ban on Highland dress did not apply to the uniforms of Scottish soldiers serving in the British army, effectively transforming an emblem of rebellion into a symbol of state power. See in particular: Carswell 2012.
13. Hansard 1814, 113–14.
14. *Ibid.*, 114–15.
15. Pentland 2011.
16. Both prints under discussion can be found in the collection of the British Museum: 1868,0808.4866 and 1868,0808.4865.
17. 22 George III, Chap. 63 (1782).
18. Celebrations reportedly took place across the county of Argyllshire in the wake of the repeal, with bonfires lit and toasts drunk to the supporters of the bill. See: *Caledonian Mercury* (27 July 1782), 3.
19. Highland Archive Centre HCA/D238/D/1/16/2 (Archibald Fraser of Lovat to Simon Fraser of Boblainy, 1 July 1782).
20. Greig 2013, 1–3, 6; For the experience of Scots in London, see Nenadic (ed.) 2010.
21. Norman 1997.
22. NLS Dep. 268/23 (Minutes &c, 21 January 1793 – 18 May 1805), 125; NLS Dep. 268/24 (Minute book, 15 March 1802 – 25 March 1808), 84.
23. George IV was an honorary member of the HSL. Although it was hinted at on several occasions, there is no substantial evidence to suggest that he ever attended a meeting. His brothers, meanwhile, each occupied the position of President at various points throughout the early nineteenth century. The Duke of Sussex and the Duke of York and Albany appear to have been the most enthusiastic of the HSL's royal patrons, occupying the presidential role on multiple occasions and frequently attending club events in person.
24. The sale was spread across several days in June and July 1843. Catalogues produced for the sale indicate that the Highland dress collection of the Duke of Sussex was sold on or around 28 June 1843. When it was offered for sale again in 1990, it became apparent that later pieces had been added to the collection by the Glennie family during their period of ownership. See: Christie and Manson 1843, 38; Sotheby's 1990, 12–14.
25. The Duke of Sussex Highland dress collection is currently recorded under the series NMS IL.2015.39 and contains thirty individual pieces of costume and associated weaponry.
26. Royal Collection Trust RCIN 29023–7.
27. Royal Collection Trust RCIN 405420.
28. Dalgleish 2000, 98–99; Dalgleish and Wyld 2016.
29. Corp and Rimer 2020.
30. NLS Dep. 268/1 (William Philip Colyear Robertson to Alexander Fraser, 21 February 1807). Colyear Robertson describes having provided the Duke of Sussex with a 'Gaelic Grammar' and notes that the Duke had already engaged a tutor in Litchfield.
31. NLS Dep. 268/21 (Minute book, 8 February 1783 – 17 December 1793), 13.
32. NLS Dep. 268/22 (Committee book, 4 January 1793 – 17 February 1802), 51. It was also suggested at the meeting that Sinclair commission an engraving of his proposed uniform. However, there is no substantial evidence to suggest that this ever came to fruition.
33. NLS Dep. 268/17 (Accounts and Receipts, 1817–29). See tailoring bill dated 22 February 1819.
34. Highland Archive Centre HCA/D24/1/1/1 (Northern Meeting Minute Book, 11 June 1788 – 10 August 1818), 13.
35. See in particular: NMS A.1993.62 A, currently on display in the 'Jacobite Challenge' area of the *Scotland Transformed* gallery in the Museum of Scotland.
36. Sinclair 1813, 10.
37. NLS Dep. 268/26 (Minute book, 10 December 1814 – 18 May 1816), 34.
38. Sinclair 1813, 6–11.
39. NMS H.TTA 15. A three-piece suit of Prince Charles Edward tartan in the NMS collection has also been identified as a probable example of Highland Society clothing, dating to *c.*1830. However, further research is required to identify whether it can be reliably associated

40. with a particular Highland club. See: NMS A.1994.102 A–C.
40. The jacket was purchased alongside a basket-hilted broadsword, but there does not appear to be any relationship between the two objects other than the identity of the vendor.
41. See original description in NMAS accession register, entry number 1953.1322.
42. I would like to thank Professor Hugh Cheape of Sabhal Mòr Ostaig, University of the Highlands and Islands, for sharing his thoughts on this inscription in 2018.
43. Sinclair 1813, 10.
44. Stewart 1974, 20.
45. NLS Acc. 13156/23 (James Hamilton to David Stewart of Garth, 27 February 1816).
46. NLS Acc. 13156/23 (James Hamilton to David Stewart of Garth, 4 March 1816).
47. NLS Acc. 13156/23 (James Hamilton to David Stewart of Garth, 2 May 1816). Simon MacGillivray was a Treasurer and Secretary of the HSL at the time, alongside Divie Robertson and James Hamilton.
48. Sir Augustus Frederick d'Este (1794–1848) was the only son of Prince Augustus Frederick and Lady Augusta Murray. As the marriage contravened the Royal Marriages Act of 1772, he and his younger sister were considered illegitimate. They subsequently assumed the name d'Este as both parents were descendants of the royal House of Este.
49. NMS H.TTC 44.1.3 ([On behalf of] Sir Augustus Frederick d'Este to Messrs Wilson of Bannockburn, 11 November 1816).
50. NMS H.TTC 44.1.2 (D. Macintosh & Co. to Messrs Wilson of Bannockburn, 16 November 1813).
51. MacDonald 2012, 20.
52. Hoock 2010, 168–69.
53. NMS H.TTC 44.1.4 (George Maitland to Messrs Wilson of Bannockburn, 15 January 1819) and NMS H.TTC 44.1.5 (George Maitland to Messrs Wilson of Bannockburn, 6 February 1819).
54. NMS H.TTC 44.1.7 (Alexander Sinclair to Messrs Wilson of Bannockburn, 16 March 1821).
55. NMS H.TTC 44.1.8 (Donald Coghill to Messrs Wilson of Bannockburn, 26 April 1821).
56. This association continued into the twentieth century, with members of the current royal family attending HSL functions and accepting honorary positions.
57. NLS Dep. 268/26 (Minute book, 10 December 1814–18 May 1816), 86.
58. The presentation of this address to the Prince Regent was reported in *The Sun* (30 May 1816), 1.
59. 56 George III, cap. 20 (1816).
60. Sanger and Kinnaird 1992, 192–93.
61. *Ibid.*, 193.
62. NLS Dep 268/34, 'Credit and debit book, 1784–1815'. See entry for 20 September 1785.
63. *Ibid.* See entries for 29 August 1785 and 20 September 1785.
64. Sanger and Kinnaird 1992, 194.
65. NLS Dep. 268/34, 'Credit and debit book, 1784–1815'. See entry for 1 March 1786.
66. NLS Dep. 268/34, 'Credit and debit book, 1784–1815'. See entries for 15 February 1785, 29 March 1785, 25 June 1785, 12 August 1786, 5 July 1788, [n.d.] April 1789, 27 June 1791, [n.d.] March 1792, 20 February 1797, 7 January 1803. These various entries cover payments for tailoring and cleaning various garments and for the purchase of storage boxes. When Neil MacLean considered quitting the HSL's service in November 1797, the Treasurer noted in the 'Credit and debit book' that the club would not pay him his full due until he surrendered the Highland dress purchased for him.
67. NLS Dep. 268/16 (Accounts and Receipts, 1796–1808). See tailoring bill dated 20 February 1797.
68. *Ibid.* See tailoring bill dated 19 January 1801.
69. NLS Dep. 268/43 (Extracts of the Proceedings of the Society from the 6th February 1819 to the 15th of May 1824), 9.
70. Bell 2011.
71. *Caledonian Mercury* (22 July 1820), 4; *Caledonian Mercury* (4 August 1821), 3; *Caledonian Mercury* (3 August 1822), 4; *Caledonian Mercury* (2 August 1823), 3; *Caledonian Mercury* (31 July 1824), 3.
72. NMS K.2000.56 and NMS M.1930.294. I would like to thank Dr Sarah Laurenson for sharing her thoughts and expertise on the material culture of Scottish jewellery.
73. NLS Dep. 268/2 (Charles Gordon to John Wedderburn, 27 October 1826).
74. The individual cost of all the prizes and, in some cases, from where they were obtained, is fully outlined in: NLS Dep. 268/17 (Accounts and Receipts, 1817–29), see account drawn up for 'Competition of Pipers – 1829'.
75. *Caledonian Mercury* (1 August 1829), 3.
76. *Ibid.*; NLS Dep. 268/17 (Accounts and Receipts, 1817–29), see account drawn up for 'Competition of Pipers – 1829'.
77. NLS Dep. 268/17 (Accounts and Receipts, 1817–29), see account drawn up for 'Competition of Pipers – 1829'.
78. See in particular: NLS Dep. 268/1 (Anthony Coblenz to John Mackenzie, 9 June 1802), requesting guidance on painting a 'correct representation' of Highland dress for a patron in Vienna; NLS Dep. 268/1 (William Philip Colyear Robertson to the HSL, 6 April 1803), requesting on behalf of the Marquis of Douglas whether his clan had a particular tartan; NLS Dep. 268/3 (William Munro to the HSL, 20 March 1829), asking the HSL to pass judgement on a recently purchased portrait of a man in Highland dress believed to date to the early eighteenth century.
79. NLS Dep. 268/26 (Minute book, 10 December 1814–18 May 1816), 104–6.

80. NLS Acc. 13156/23. See also Irvine Robertson 1998, 73–81.
81. NLS Acc. 13156/23 (Donald Macleod to David Stewart of Garth, 24 December 1815); NLS Acc. 13156/23 (Helen Cumming Gordon to David Stewart of Garth, 9 December 1815).
82. NLS Acc. 13156/23 (James Hamilton to David Stewart of Garth, 27 February 1816).
83. NLS Acc. 13156/23 (Alexander Robertson of Struan to David Stewart of Garth, 5 December 1815).
84. NLS Acc. 13156/23 (Duncan Macpherson of Cluny to David Stewart of Garth, 5 December 1815).
85. NLS Acc. 13156/23 (Duncan Macpherson of Cluny to David Stewart of Garth, 26 February 1816).
86. NLS Acc. 13156/23 (Duncan Macpherson of Cluny to David Stewart of Garth, 5 April 1816).
87. NLS Acc. 13156/23 (David Ogilvie to David Stewart of Garth, 26 March 1816).
88. NLS Acc. 13156/23 (David Ogilvie to David Stewart of Garth, 16 April 1816).
89. NLS Acc. 13156/23 (David Ogilvie to David Stewart of Garth, 8 January 1816).
90. NLS Acc. 13156/23 (William Farquharson to David Stewart of Garth, 8 December 1815).
91. NLS Acc. 13156/23 (John MacGregor-Murray to David Stewart of Garth, 2 December 1815).
92. NLS Dep. 268/30 (Minute book, 21 March 1885–22 June 1893), 449. At a meeting held on 2 May 1893, it was revealed that D. W. Stewart had appealed to the HSL to view its tartan collection in preparation for *Old and Rare Scottish Tartans* (1893). To the surprise of the HSL, Stewart claimed to have already seen specimens from the collection in the possession of Dr W. F. Skene, verified with the seal of former HSL secretary John Wedderburn. These specimens are now part of NMS H.TTB 9.1.
93. NLS Dep. 268/2 (Martin Smith Metcalfe to Alexander Macdonald, 3 February 1827).
94. NLS Dep. 268/17 (Accounts and Receipts, 1817–29), see bill from Harper, Pearce & Co. dated 7 November 1827. The account was not settled until 1 March 1829.
95. NLS Dep. 268/30 (Minute book, 21 March 1885–22 June 1893), 97–107.
96. *Ibid.*, 99–100.
97. NLS Acc. 10615/115 (Inventory of property including details of manuscripts, draft copy of inventory, and photograph of some property), 49. The collection is noted as having been stored at The Scottish Hall, Crane Court, Fleet Street, London.
98. Formerly Q.L.1985.81, the collection can now be found under series NMS IL.2018.93. The loan includes a collection of documents relating to the reorganisation of the HSL tartan collection in the early twentieth century, largely addressed to the administrators of the scheme Hugh Pirie Gordon and Ian Cameron (NMS IL.2018.93.8.3).
99. NMS H.TTB 11.
100. NMS X.2018.44, 1–2.
101. Irvine Robertson 1998, 74.
102. Nenadic 1999, 222. See also: McLean 1991; Osborne 2001.
103. *Inverness Courier* (14 June 1821), 3. Significantly, this issue of the paper also carried an article criticising the Celtic Society for enabling its members to celebrate Highland culture, while also operating policies of clearance.
104. NLS Acc. 12898/1 (Minute book, 1820–24), 1.
105. *Ibid.*, 4, 25, 83.
106. *Ibid.*, 102.
107. *Inverness Courier* (14 June 1821), 3; NMS K.2002.977.
108. Although the pamphlet was published anonymously, Scott's authorship was apparent to contemporaries given his guiding hand in visit preparations.
109. *The New Times* (26 July 1822), 1.
110. *Caledonian Mercury* (29 July 1822), 1.
111. *The Morning Herald* (10 August 1822), 3.
112. NLS Acc. 12251/62 (John Duff to Messrs Wilson of Bannockburn, 24 July 1822).
113. NMS A.1987.20.
114. NMS A.1993.208 A–E.
115. *Newcastle Journal* (12 September 1863), 3.
116. Tuckett 2009, 147.
117. NMS H.TTB 8.

Fig. 2.36 (opposite): List of clan badges

This detailed list of emblematic plant badges used by the Highland clans was presented to Sir Samuel Rush Meyrick by Miller & Ewing, cloth merchants of Glasgow. The retailers had acquired the list directly from the Highland Society of London.

List of the Badges of Distinction used by the Clans of Scotland as Sanctioned by the Highland Society of London

Clan	Plant (English)	Plant (Gaelic)	Latin
Buchanan	Birch	Beatha	Betula
Cameron	Oak	Darach	Quercus
Campbell	Myrtle	Roid	Myrica
Chisholm	Alder	Fearna	Betula
Colquhoun	Hazel	Calltain	Corylus
Cumming	Common Sallow	Seilach	Salix
Drummond	Holly	Crcil Fhionn	Ilex
Farquharson	Purple Fox Glove	Meuran Sith	Digitalis
Ferguson	Poplar	Criothan	Populus
Forbes	Broom	Bealaidh	Spartium
Frazer	Yew	An-tiudhar	Taxus
Gordon	Ivy	Lavintin	Hedera
Graham	Laurel	Boidhcraobh	Laurus
Grant	Cranberry Heath	Muileag	Vaccinium Oxycoccus
Gunn	Rosewort	Lus nan laugh	Rhodiola
Lamont	Crab Apple Tree	Abhal Bradhaugh	Pyrus
McAlister	Fine leaved Heath	Dluie Fraoch	Erica Cinerea
McDonald	Bell Heath	Fraoch Derig	Erica Tetralix
McDonnell	Mountain Heath	Fraoch Gorum Briabh	Erica Vulgaris
McDougall	Cypress	Miniehd	Cupressus
McFarlane	Cloud Berry Bush	Lus nan Eighreag	Rubus
McGregor	Pine	Guithas	Pinus
McIntosh	Boxwood	Nighban	Buxus
Mackay	Bulrush	Luachair	Scirpus
Mackenzie	Deer Grass	Garbhaga Feidh	Lycopodium Silago
McKinnon	St John's Wort	Achlasan Challum Chilla	Hypericum
McLachlan	Mountain Ash	Chaorin	Sorbus
McLean	Blackberry Heath or Crowberry	Diarca Fitich	Empetrum
McLeod	Red Whortle Berries	Lus nam Craosleag	Vaccinium vitis Idoa

CHAPTER 3

Designing and trading tartan in Georgian Britain

'I have made out a sort of pattern which I think will do well enough to guide Mr. Wilson ...'

Sir Patrick Craufurd Bruce to Messrs Wilson of Bannockburn (16 November 1811)

Messrs Wilson of Bannockburn archive at National Museums Scotland

Pages 100–101: Pattern design for a bespoke commission (detail)

Watercolour of a tartan sett, submitted to Messrs Wilson of Bannockburn by Sir Patrick Craufurd Bruce in 1811.

(See Fig. 3.18)

THE weaving company, Messrs Wilson of Bannockburn, was founded in Stirlingshire in the late 1750s under William Wilson. The firm first gained a foothold in the tartan industry during the French Revolutionary Wars, securing military contracts to provide cloth to Scottish soldiers serving in the ranks of the British army. They also subcontracted the production of regimental bonnets and hose to garment-makers in their network, thereby acquiring a reputation as a knowledgeable military outfitter. The repeal of the Dress Act in 1782 broadened the commercial marketplace for tartan considerably, and by the end of the eighteenth century Wilsons had succeeded in becoming a major supplier of both civilian and regimental patterns to British consumers. By the early decades of the nineteenth century, the firm had come to be regarded as the national authority on the manufacture of the cloth, as well as the custodian of its material history.

With their eventual liquidation in 1924, Wilsons' immense archive of eighteenth- and nineteenth-century business correspondence, pattern books and textile samples, was dispersed among various collectors. Many of these collectors were prominent tartan scholars, whose interest in the firm stemmed from a desire to better understand its role in the commercialisation of tartan in the Georgian era. While some manuscripts remain in private hands to this day, a substantial amount of material has found its way into the collections of Scottish heritage institutions, most notably those collected and arranged by costume historian John Telfer Dunbar and presented to the National Library of Scotland in the second half of the twentieth century. The collection had formerly been in the possession of Scottish artist and antiquarian William Skeoch Cumming and was bequeathed to Dunbar on his death by Cumming's wife, Belle Sutton, arranged within five tea chests.[1]

The archive of Wilson material held by National Museums Scotland has been growing since the middle decades of the twentieth century and is composed of donations and purchases acquired from numerous sources. Chief among these was a substantial gift of manuscripts and textiles made by Lord David Crichton-Stuart in the years 1952 and 1953, which had been in the collection of his father the 4th Marquess of Bute. Much of this material was originally assembled by William Skeoch Cumming and by the celebrated Scottish sculptor, James Pittendrigh MacGillivray.[2] Alongside correspondence and accounts spanning both the Georgian and Victorian periods, the archive is complemented by an assemblage of nineteenth- and early twentieth-century tartan samples donated by a descendant of the Wilson family, and numerous examples of late eighteenth- and early nineteenth-century costume which incorporate fabrics produced by the firm. Together it is an important resource for the study of early tartan and its many and varied sartorial applications.[3]

By the early decades of the nineteenth century, a diverse global market for tartan had emerged. Wilsons' surviving business records offer invaluable insight into this rapidly evolving process, from the perspectives of both the weavers and their growing customer base [Fig. 3.1]. The collection of documents held by the museum has national and international dimensions, containing orders sent from within Britain and by customers living and working abroad. Stories from the archive illuminate how people in late Georgian society experienced tartan as a tradable commodity, whether they be manufacturers, retailers, or wearers of the cloth. The scope of the archive allows us to look at both the military and civilian sides of Wilsons' business, bearing witness to the myriad ways in which tartan could be applied to the bodies and homes of consumers: from uniform tartans

DESIGNING AND TRADING TARTAN IN GEORGIAN BRITAIN

Fig. 3.1: *High Street, Edinburgh*, by Joseph Mallord William Turner (1775–1851), *c.*1818, watercolour, pen, ink and graphite on paper

Turner's depiction of fabric sellers hawking their wares in the shadow of St Giles' Cathedral captures the lively back and forth between retailers and their customers. As necessary articles, textiles were lucrative commodities in Georgian Britain. Shoppers were well-versed in spotting quality products and often knew what different types of cloth were worth, what they could be used for, and what was in style.

(Yale Center for British Art)

equipped to soldiers serving in Scottish regiments, to fashion tartans woven for women's cloaks, gowns and mantles, to patterns destined for use by enslaved individuals working the plantations of the American South.

The exceptional survival of the business records of Messrs Wilson of Bannockburn has caused the firm to become a focal point in the study of early tartan manufacturing and collecting. The firm, like the cloth it produced, has attained an almost mythic quality in contemporary scholarship; its retention of documents and fabric samples between generations of makers, and the relationships that Wilsons forged with tartan scholars throughout the nineteenth and early twentieth centuries, has led to a privileging of their voice within the annals of tartan history. Though the firm was undoubtedly a prolific maker for much of the late Georgian era, the level of influence it exerted over the general design and function of tartan in this formative period of its popularity has the potential to be overstated by historians. This is especially true when studying the commercialisation of clan tartans in the first quarter of the nineteenth century, a movement that saw specific setts produced or repurposed by tartan manufacturers to construct a sartorial system of Highland heraldry. Wilsons is often positioned as a central player within this story. Most significantly in 1983, Hugh Trevor-Roper portrayed Wilsons as opportunistic 'inventors', taking advantage of a gullible public obsessed by the nascent material landscape of Scottish Romanticism.[4] Trevor-Roper's characterisation, although not wholly inaccurate, is hampered by a lack of understanding of the Georgian textile trade and the place of tartan within it. Notably, he fails to consider the collaborative opportunities that existed between weavers and their clients that enabled creative input from both sides of a transaction. Dress historian Sally Tuckett, in her work on the rise of tartan as a popular commodity within late Georgian society, has emphasised the need for scholars to approach the cloth from the perspective of a materially-minded consumer, thus balancing the draw of the symbolic with the appeal of the aesthetic.[5] While it is certainly valuable to foreground the role played by tartan manufacturers in the contentious reframing of Highland dress culture in the early nineteenth century, it is also important to appreciate how the use and appearance of the cloth has been historically refined by the material needs and preferences of purchasers.

In this chapter, we will look to the surviving documents in the Messrs Wilson of Bannockburn archive at National Museums Scotland and ask, what did the customer want and expect from tartan at the turn of the nineteenth century and how influential were Georgian shoppers and retailers in shaping the appearance, the applications and the mythologies of tartan throughout this period?

The weaver's eye

One of the earliest examples of Wilsons' work held by National Museums Scotland is a length of tartan dated *c*.1790 [3.2]. As well as being one of the oldest commercial tartan samples in the museum, it is also one of the most intricate in terms of colour mixing and density, demonstrating the visual and material richness that could be achieved when a weaver employed a broad spectrum of colours in the execution of a single web. Unlike the later clan and family tartans more recognisable to modern eyes, this tartan does not have a designated name. Instead, it was most commonly referred to as a 'fancy' sett.[6]

Surviving tartans from the late Georgian era are normally a balanced twill-weave worsted fabric, flexible yet highly durable in structure. A tartan pattern – also known as a 'sett' – is created in the loom by joining an identically arranged warp with an identically arranged weft, which utilises at least two solid colours. The meeting of these warp and weft threads creates a particoloured web, producing a pattern that pivots and repeats across the desired length of the fabric to a scale determined by the weaver. This basic method of calculated, repetitive weaving can result in quite complex or simple looking tartans, depending on the number and arrangement of the colours used. As a rule, where the warp and weft threads meet in a tartan web, a solid or a blended colour results. If a weaver were to use only two solid colours – such as red and black, as in the popular 'Rob Roy' sett – the result would not resemble a two-tone chequerboard. Rather, the resulting pattern would be composed of three individual shades: a solid red, a solid black, and a 'blend' of these two colours.[7]

The unnamed 'fancy' tartan in the museum's collection has been worked using eight solid colours, which can be more easily appreciated when examining the rough edge of the fabric, where the cut warp yarns are visible [3.2]. These eight solid colours – dark green, light green, white, purple, blue, red, pink and black – combine in the web to create a crowded pattern composed of thirty-six individual colour shades. It is an example of one of the firm's old superfine tartans, made from very fine wool and extremely durable in structure. This style of hard tartan was commonly used in the making of women's plaids, the density of colour and the sheer quality of the wool making it a highly desirable, luxury commodity. Tartans such as this, designed to simulate a riot of colour enveloping the body of the wearer, went out of fashion among Wilsons' customers at the end of the eighteenth century.

For many, the process of tartan design represents a gateway towards identity formation, even legitimisation. However, in the late eighteenth and early nineteenth centuries, it was fundamentally a commercial exercise. The drive to create was tempered by the need to manufacture a saleable range of practical and attractive goods, which would appeal to as broad a

DESIGNING AND TRADING TARTAN IN GEORGIAN BRITAIN

Fig. 3.2 (overleaf): Tartan fabric, *c*.1790

The visual depth of a finished tartan is determined by the number of colours used when planning the web. This superfine tartan is composed of 8 solid colours, which when woven interact to create 36 individual solid and blended colours. Busy patterns, such as this, were most popular at the end of the 18th century.

FANCY

DRESS MACINTOSH

TTC1 (1)
NA 1132
1953·1296

cross-section of customers as possible. The processes of tartan design and manufacture was therefore quite fluid and reactionary, particularly when it came to patterns marketed towards civilian consumers that tended to reflect the tastes and trends of each passing season. Tartans named after Scottish towns and districts vied for attention alongside commemorative and celebratory sets – such as the 'Waterloo', 'Regent' and 'Walter Scott' – produced in an assortment of textures and scales to suit multiple budgets. Tartans woven for use by the British military, meanwhile, had to conform to strict regimental specifications, leaving little opportunity for deviation or creativity. In a competitive marketplace, gaining repeat custom from merchants and securing military contracts relied on a maker's ability to deliver consistency and quality. Curating and maintaining a dependable system of reference material was therefore an essential business practice for any firm hoping to cultivate a reputation for reliability and variety.

Textile workers across the industry recorded their patterns in different ways, depending on their area of expertise and the complexity of the cloth being produced. For those who worked with ornamental fabrics, such as linen damasks or brocaded silks, a patternmaker would typically be employed to create an exact visual guide for the weaver to follow. Figured patterns were mapped onto point paper, which was ruled with a series of crossed parallel lines that effectively mimicked the grid of intersecting warp and weft threads in the body of the loom.[8] The relative simplicity of tartan weaving rendered such elaborate and costly recording methods unnecessary. However, tartan manufacturers still needed to document their various designs in a way that was easy for weavers in their employ to intuit, consistently reproduce and – if necessary – amend.

Among the working papers in the Wilsons archive at National Museums Scotland is a battered, well-thumbed account book.[9] Its middle pages are filled with a series of pattern tabulations, recording over fifty different tartan designs. As the accounts scattered throughout the entire book range in date from the 1780s to early 1820s, it would be reasonable to assume that these tabulations also date from across that forty-year period. As numbered, district and regimental setts form the majority of those listed, it is likely that most of these patterns were being woven by Wilsons in the final decades of the eighteenth century, before the rising fashion for clan and family tartans came to dominate the output of the firm [3.3].

The pattern tabulations contained within Wilsons' account book provide us with a sense of the firm's creative process as tartan designers and manufacturers, while also representing a baseline standard for identifying and dating their work in surviving swatches and garments. Each pattern listed is the configuration decided on and executed by Wilsons, with each individual design choice informed by the equipment and materials at their disposal and their knowledge of what the market required. At the same time, the patterns listed in these pages should not be regarded as definitive

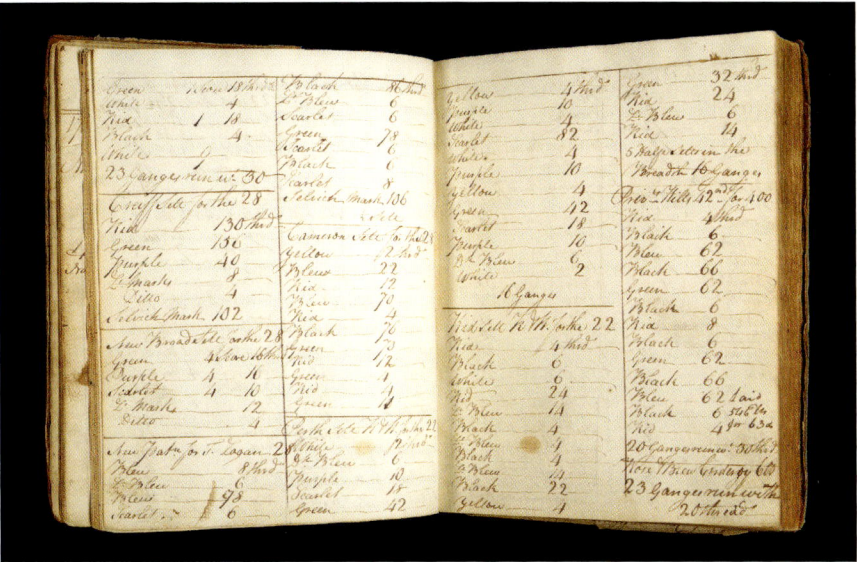

Fig. 3.3: **Pattern tabulations,** *c.*1780–1820

The middle pages of this account book are covered by a series of pattern tabulations. Beneath the name of each given pattern, the arrangement of the colours in the warp and the number of threads per colour has been calculated for the reed size of a specific loom. When reaching the end of the tabulation, the pattern would typically pivot and repeat.

and inflexible. Tartan design was an organic and evolutionary process. If a customer wanted something different, Wilsons was more than capable of supplying it.

Remnants

Most of the letters contained in the Wilsons archive at National Museums Scotland were written by individuals who worked in the textile industry themselves. They were mostly merchants based in towns and cities across Britain – largely in Scotland and England – who acted as the intermediaries between consumers and producers, purchasing tartan to turn to stock in their shops and warehouses, or conveying commissions on behalf of their own clients [3.4].[10] These trade customers were used to handling fabrics on a regular basis, meaning that the sensory language of goods came readily to mind when they put pen to paper.[11] They wished for their wares to be 'fine', 'coarse', 'stout', and 'bright', and trusted Wilsons as an experienced producer to understand what was meant by that. Nevertheless, it was often deemed necessary to send a cutting of fabric that encapsulated the material qualities that they were searching for, to act as a guide.

Circulating remnants of fabric was common practice in the textile and clothing trades during the long eighteenth century.[12] Wilsons' agents were known to carry samples of cloth with them whenever they toured the country on business, using them as representative examples of the types of goods that the firm was capable of supplying to existing and prospective clients. They also routinely sent packets of patterns out by post, if requested to do so by a customer.[13] Samples of Wilsons' work would remain in the establishments of the merchants they visited or corresponded with; while some might be kept loose, others were fixed into the pages of pattern books kept behind counters, which customers would browse when making a fabric selection for an item of clothing. The chosen sample would often be returned to Wilsons in the form of an order, tucked inside the folds of a retailer's letter alongside detailed instructions. For those conducting their business largely by mail, the inclusion of these offcuts introduced a much-needed element of tactility to an otherwise long-distance transaction. Although a written language of goods existed and was heavily utilised by consumers when stating preferences or requesting alterations, it had its shortcomings. By sending along a remnant, customers were thus able to articulate their needs and expectations of the finished product in a way that augmented written directions.

There are over two hundred textile fragments attached to letters in the Wilsons archive at National Museums Scotland. The majority of these are worsted tartans of varying qualities, ranging in date from the 1790s to 1840s. Most, though not all, of these tartans are the product of Wilsons' looms. Alongside these tartans sits a smattering of other fabrics, largely made by Wilsons' subcontractors and competitors: white, black and green serge, lilac camblet, scarlet and striped garter tapes, plaid silk ribbons and chequered hose cloth, to name a few.[14] This diverse range of textiles is an indication of Wilsons' place within a broad network of complementary manufacturers, who seldom worked in complete independence from one another. When seeking to form a business relationship between firms, these scraps functioned as exemplars of a maker's unique identity and skill.

For Wilsons, providing customers and fellow makers with small offcuts of their work made good business sense. The circulation of samples was a fairly cheap and direct method of self-promotion. It also allowed them to manage expectations from the outset of a transaction, as both sides would be working from the same physical reference. For Wilsons' customers, receiving a packet of samples – either in person or by post – provided them with a tactile understanding of the range and quality of fabrics on offer at any given time. The addition of a pricelist also helped them to directly weigh the monetary value placed on a product by its maker against the actual material present in their hands, an important consideration when

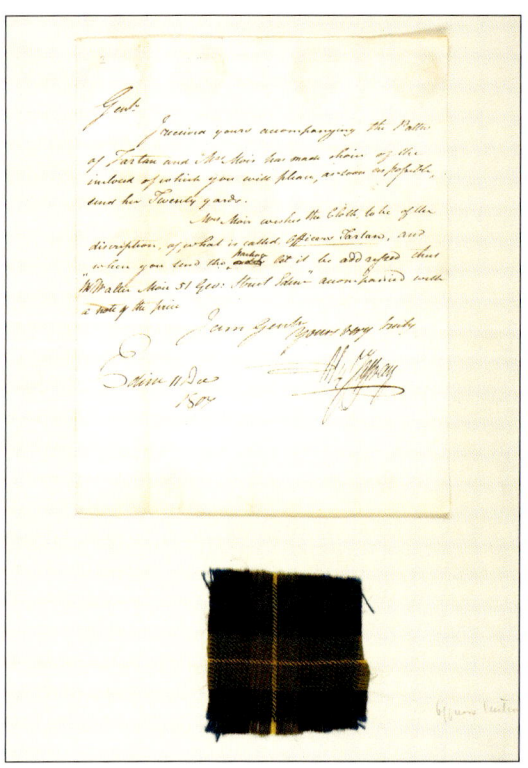

Fig. 3.4: Ordering by proxy

This letter was written on behalf of Mrs Moir by Alexander Jaffray. It is an order for 20 yards of Gordon regimental tartan, intended for Walter Moir. It was common for Georgian shoppers to order goods by proxy, which meant nominating a trusted individual to mediate the transaction and negotiate matters of cost and quality. This was usually a family member, friend or a business acquaintance. Walter Moir was an accountant who lived and worked in George Street, Edinburgh. He and Jaffray organised property auctions in the city.

ordering textiles by mail.[15] They could judge whether the price specified was a fair one by assessing the quality of the tartan before them. Were the colours right? Was the structure of the weave consistent? Did the handle of the cloth answer the needs of the intended garment? By possessing fabric samples in advance of placing their order, the customer was given a solid basis on which to dictate terms and secure the best possible deal. Subsequent haggling could cover a number of issues, from simple questions of cost to more complex demands that impacted the look and feel of the fabric itself.

When selling tartan abroad, fabric samples were even more important for communicating the reality of goods purchased by proxy. As well as the difficulties posed by the long-distance nature of correspondence shopping, transatlantic transactions were hampered by the length of time it would take for deliveries to reach their destination, and the additional costs of conveyance and taxation were often greater than purchasing a domestic product.[16] Making sure one got what one paid for and that it would suit the purchaser's needs was therefore of paramount concern. In lieu of living with one's disappointment, resolving any mistake was a protracted and expensive affair. In tandem with such practical considerations, the presence of a material sample could be used to gauge whether the textile would complement the tastes of a particular region. What might please a customer in Edinburgh or London, for instance, might not meet the satisfaction of customers in New York, Halifax or Rio de Janeiro.[17]

A way of tackling such obstacles was for merchants based abroad to place their orders well in advance and to try to anticipate – or indeed shape – what the local population might favour from one season to the next based on the samples already in their possession. In December 1824, David Hadden sent word from New York that green tartans 'with Scarlet stripes to enliven the appearance' had been favoured by his customers that year. Red-based patterns had done poorly by comparison, as the large amount of cochineal required to execute them effectively made them prohibitively expensive. In preparation for the arrival of the next shipment in summer 1825, Hadden requested that the firm send on more quality green-based tartans and enclosed three samples of those that had sold best in recent months: the 'Colquhoun', the 'Glenorchy' and the 'Prince Charles Edward' [3.5].[18]

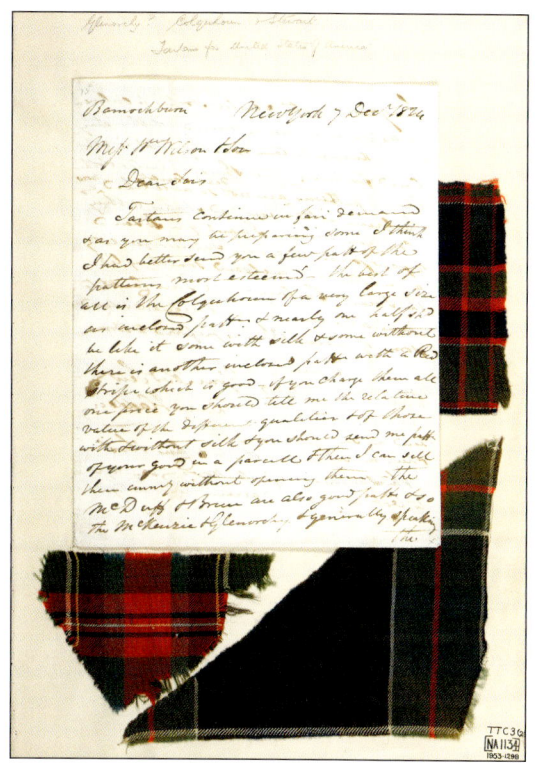

Fig. 3.5: Selling tartan abroad

Tartan became increasingly fashionable outside of Scotland during the early 19th century. In this letter from David Hadden of New York, the merchant noted that red and green tartans were in high demand among his customers and sent a selection of offcuts to Messrs Wilson of Bannockburn as examples of the specific setts he wanted to re-order.

Fig. 3.6: Cutting of Small Caledonia tartan, *c.*1822

A cutting of tartan labelled 'Small Caledonia', sent to the English antiquarian Sir Samuel Rush Meyrick by cloth merchants Miller & Ewing of Glasgow in 1822. Someone has overwritten the label with the name 'Macpherson' at a later date, reflecting the changing identity of the pattern over time.

One of the main reasons for passing offcuts of tartan between weavers and their clients was to provide both sides of the transaction with a definitive pattern guide. Early tartan was a notoriously variable product, particularly during the final decades of the eighteenth century when naming conventions were continually evolving to suit the needs of the moment. A tartan might be identified in various ways: a manufacturer's numbering system, the intended function of the cloth, or its material traits such as the predominant colour, the scale of the design, or the weight of the fabric. A tartan may also be known by conflicting monikers, depending on the purchaser: 'Caledonia', 'Kidd', 'MacPherson' [3.6].[19] The rigid, codified system of named tartans we recognise today came into existence only gradually, as the affiliations built up between specific patterns and specific families, clans, districts and military regiments were strengthened by years of repeat custom and habitual wear. The inclusion of a sample would therefore minimise the risk of a customer receiving a different sett to the one they had requested.

In a letter dated 21 February 1821, Miller & Ewing of Glasgow sent Wilsons a piece of what they called 'Stewart' tartan, requesting that the firm provide them with four identical pieces as quickly as possible – 'at all events it must <u>equal in quality to the pattern</u> and the whole four pieces must be <u>exactly the same shades.</u>'[20] The sample attached to their order is an example of one of the many variations of the popular 'Royal Stewart' that began to circulate in earnest during the first quarter of the nineteenth century [3.7]. The piece submitted by Miller & Ewing is a variation known as the 'Prince Charles Edward', the major difference being the reduction of the red ground in favour of bringing the azure to greater prominence. The naming of the pattern reflects the growing fascination with Jacobite history and culture in late Georgian society and the romanticisation of Bonnie Prince Charlie in popular art and literature of the era.

By sending a swatch with their order, a customer could also effectively redesign an existing pattern to suit their needs without them ever having to meet the manufacturer face to face. Requests for alterations were not unusual, especially when it came to the selection of alternative shades and the adjustment of overall colour schemes. In an order for four tartan shawls made in 1832, Edinburgh-based retailers Romanes & Paterson asked Wilsons to modify the agreed upon pattern to include the colours of two yarn samples, noting alongside the specimens glued to the writing paper: 'the Blue must be darker than this' and 'this is the Green we like' [3.8].[21] Such a request, while relatively straightforward to fulfil, highlights the

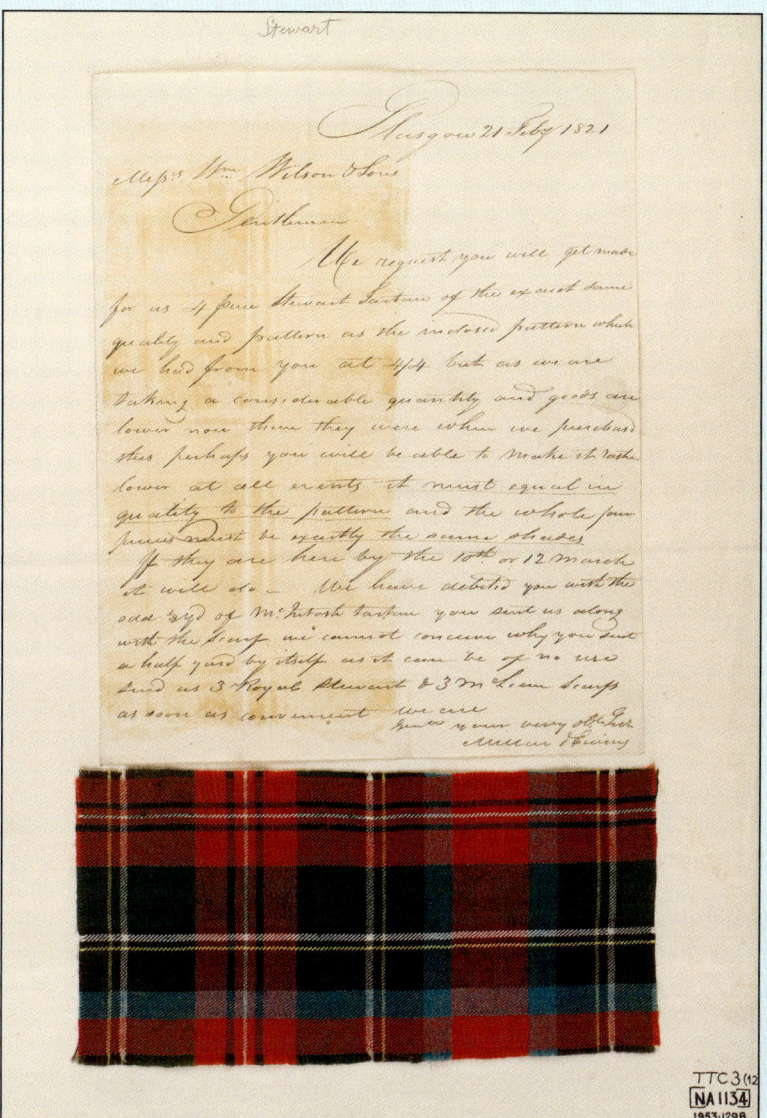

Fig. 3.7: Tartan to match

To avoid confusion and facilitate quick service, customers would provide Messrs Wilson of Bannockburn with remnants of fabric to pattern match. In this letter from Miller & Ewing of Glasgow in 1821, the firm provided a cutting of Prince Charles Edward with the demand that the finished product be identical to it in every way.

Figs 3.8: Yarn samples

As well as sending swatches of tartan, retailers also sent samples of yarn for colour matching. In this letter from Romanes & Paterson in 1832, the company sent snippets of blue and green yarn for the weavers to reference when fulfilling its order for tartan shawls.

power dynamic that existed between trade customers – those people ultimately responsible for promoting and selling the fabric to consumers – and the producers of the cloth. Altering the blue and green hues in the tartan may seem slight, but it represented a fundamental change to the aesthetic character of the product.

This type of customer intervention could be quite radical in nature, resulting in the creation of a new pattern that bore only a passing resemblance to the original sent. In a letter dated 14 March 1800, Alexander McIntyre of Fort William enclosed a small cutting of red, purplish pink, and black tartan with an order for cloak cloth. Although happy with the scale of the given pattern, he was less pleased with the colourway and requested that Wilsons change it completely. He asked the weavers to keep the solid black that acted as the ground-colour, but directed them to introduce 'Green in place of the Cudbear Red [a purplish pink, derived from lichens]', 'blue in place of the Scarlet Red, and Light blue in place of the Black break in the Red'.[22] For McIntyre, the sending of a swatch was essential in articulating his needs. Without it, it is unlikely that Wilsons would have been able to follow his written directions accurately and produce a tartan that was both the exact scale required and the desired colourway.

By the close of the Georgian era, the range of tartans manufactured by firms like Messrs Wilson of Bannockburn had become more heavily standardised. There was an expectation of regularity and availability, particularly around popular patterns, such as clan setts. Customers could now order a tartan by name and be fairly confident they would receive the correct one in return, without needing to resort to sending a material reference. Still, if a named pattern was complex, had variations, or was somewhat obscure, providing a sample for Wilsons to work from remained a useful tool for ensuring a degree of accuracy.

When Romanes & Paterson wrote to Wilsons in September 1828, they included a small fragment of what they called 'Drummond of Strathallan', a sett that has considerable stylistic overlaps with the 'Ogilvie'. Both tartans are characterised by a densely packed, colourful web that would require great skill and patience to execute. As a well-established firm with decades of experience on which to draw, the retailer hoped that Wilsons would be able to advise them on where to source the correct pattern:

> *We are sorry to trouble you regarding such a little matter, but as we cannot procure the* [attached] *in this city & are very anxious to oblige the Lady we apply to your house as the most likely in Scotland to have it. It is for fourteen yds of Drummond of Strathallan Superfine tartan (we inclose a pattern to prevent mistakes) & if you have it not on hand & are willing to make perhaps 30 yds we would be glad to take that quantity.* […] *please to return us the pattern* […] *unless you can make it as we must give it back to the Lady.*[23]

As the fragment remains with the letter in the archive, it appears likely that Wilsons were able to oblige Romanes & Paterson on this occasion. Having the sample to hand would have helped them to determine quickly whether what they had in stock would answer the commission – not only in terms of the desired pattern, but also the specified quality of the weave – or if a new length should be put in the loom.

The popular perception of early clan tartans as a fixed array of unchanging products is belied by evidence from the archive. Though patterns were indeed becoming more rigidly defined by the close of the Georgian period, a customer could still insist on subtle refinements to suit their own tastes and expectations of what a clan tartan should be. Charles Blair Junior, a merchant from Dunkeld, had very particular ideas about the execution of the 'Atholl' sett, which he regularly purchased from Wilsons for the local gentry [3.9]. In an order for four fringed shawls, placed in June 1827, he praised the quality of the offcut in his possession, but suggested how it might be further improved:

> […] *make the shades of <u>Green</u>, <u>Black</u> and <u>Blue</u> in the shawls <u>the very same</u> as in the pattern sent, and let the Scarlet be of the very best. Will not the Scarlet appear better in the shawl if the thread is <u>somewhat</u> heavier than the other yarns? <u>I want a noble article</u>, as I expect to sell of them to the nobles of the land. […] I have seen Dark Tartans such as this Atholl made more dull than they ought to be by rights from having the red yarn put in very small. Now let me*

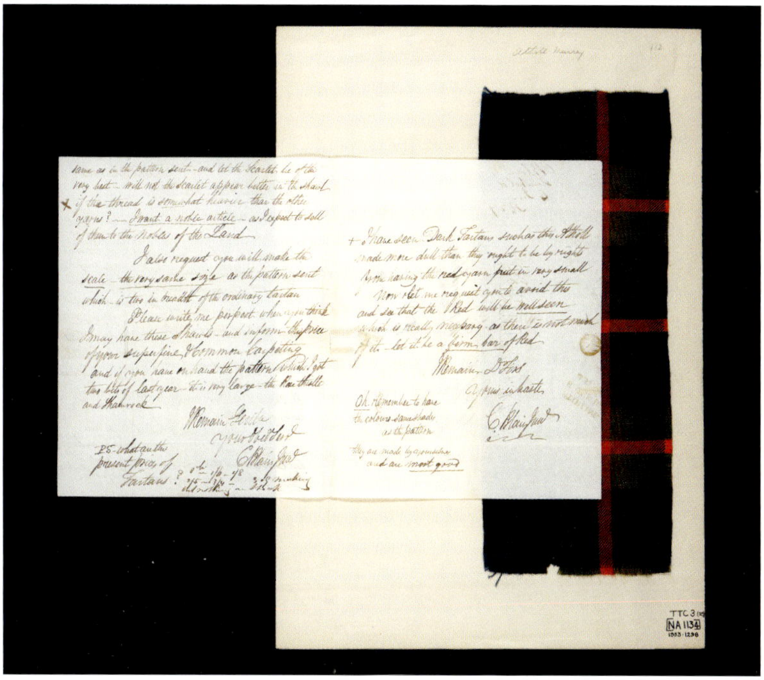

DESIGNING AND TRADING TARTAN IN GEORGIAN BRITAIN

Fig. 3.9: Altering a clan sett to taste

Charles Blair Junior was a successful and well-respected merchant in Dunkeld, Perthshire. He operated a drapery business for over 30 years, specialising in tartan cloth, tartan outerwear, and outfits of Highland dress. Blair demanded only the very best from his suppliers and was not afraid to ask for changes to existing setts. In this letter, he requested that the red in the Murray of Atholl be made larger and brighter than usual.

115

request you to avoid this and see that the Red will be <u>well seen</u> which is really necessary, as there is not much of it. Let it be a <u>firm bar</u> of Red. […] <u>Oh</u>. Remember to have the colours same shades as the pattern, they are made by yourselves and are <u>most good</u>.[24]

Of course, just as a textile sample could be used to measure a high level of quality and consistency in a customer's order, it could also be used to enforce low standards of dress in the intended recipient of the cloth. On 5 June 1817, Wilsons received a letter from Wilson, Stow & Co. of Glasgow, confirming receipt of a packet of tartan samples from the firm. They informed Wilsons that although they had dutifully forwarded the packet on to their client, they thought the selection of patterns sent had been ill-judged given the intended use case of the fabric. As the tartan was destined to clothe the enslaved population of Charleston, South Carolina, the company deemed Wilsons' selection unsuitable for the purpose – too fine and too expensive. They counselled Wilsons that if they wanted to make a deal, they needed to reconsider their asking price and decrease the quality of the cloth accordingly: 'The house will take a Bale of them about 3 feet square but they want to see patterns considerably lower priced[,] say your very lowest prices you have […] send out to us patterns of your very lowest priced Tartans particularly <u>Dark Tartans</u>[.] [The] house is very safe & good[,] you must go low with them' [3.10].[25]

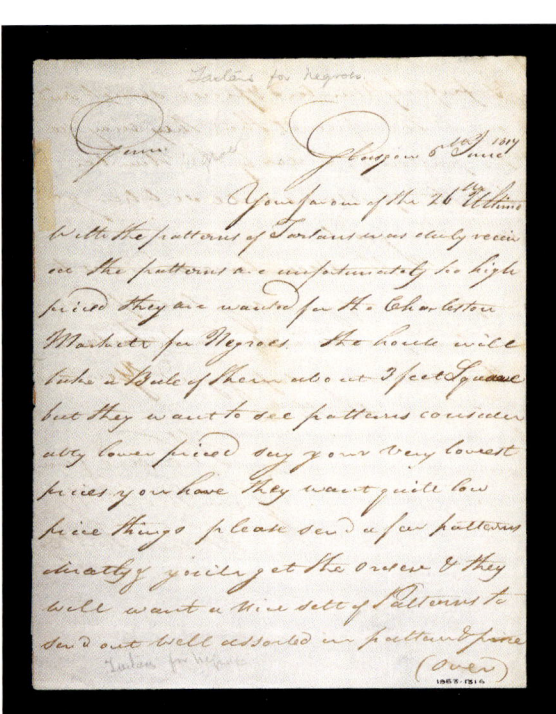

Fig. 3.10: Tartan for South Carolina

Wilson, Stow & Co. were cloth merchants based in Glasgow. Like many such companies based near ports, they had an international clientele. The letter received by Messrs Wilson of Bannockburn in 1817 references an order for 'dark tartans' destined for 'the Charleston Market for Negroes'. Though not explicitly stated, the tartan was probably intended for field slaves. Inexpensive woollen plaids were among the small body of textiles deemed appropriate for use in slave clothing in the 18th and 19th centuries, with plantation owners importing bales of cheap cloth seasonally from Britain.

Diagrams and keys

When discussing issues of quality and personal preference in tartan design, Wilsons' customers did not always limit themselves to descriptive instructions or to the tactile advantages of tartan samples: some chose to express their requirements visually through carefully drawn diagrams and keys. These surviving drawings, though rare, give a sense of how the Georgian consumer understood the physical construction of tartan and their own place within the journey of its fabrication. Through the acts of drawing and annotation, a customer could exert a level of creative agency in the process of tartan design from the very outset of a commission. These drawings articulate a range of aesthetic qualities over which consumers might wish to exercise their control as paying customers: colour choice, colour brightness and texture, pattern arrangement and scale. Although the power over such decisions ultimately rested with the maker and was informed by what resources they had available to complete an order, by providing Wilsons with a clear visual template of their needs and expectations customers were able to closely influence how a finished tartan might look upon its delivery.

This form of concerted visual direction also proved useful when a customer wanted to request alterations to a pattern that they had already received and were dissatisfied with. In February 1838, Messrs Walker of London wrote to Wilsons to inform them that a piece of Chisholm tartan that they had received had not been approved of by their client. Although the pattern itself had been correct, the scale of it was deemed unsuitable for use in a plaid: 'We must therefore request you will put forward another exactly to the size of the pattern on the other side same quality as before.' On the back of the letter, the merchant had meticulously mapped the Chisholm to the scale desired by their customer. Should the firm not already have a piece to hand that would suit the purpose, they now possessed a precise diagram from which to weave a new length [3.11].[26]

A diagram could also serve a useful function if the client was unable, for whatever reason, to send a physical specimen of the thing they wanted. An order submitted by Robertson & Wigham of Glasgow in June 1811 contained two sett diagrams in lieu of fabric. 'Being in want of a small quantity of Tartan; and understanding from John McIntire that you have generally a supply of that article on hand – The purport of this is to request you will have the kindness to send us [per] 1st Carrier the

DESIGNING AND TRADING TARTAN IN GEORGIAN BRITAIN

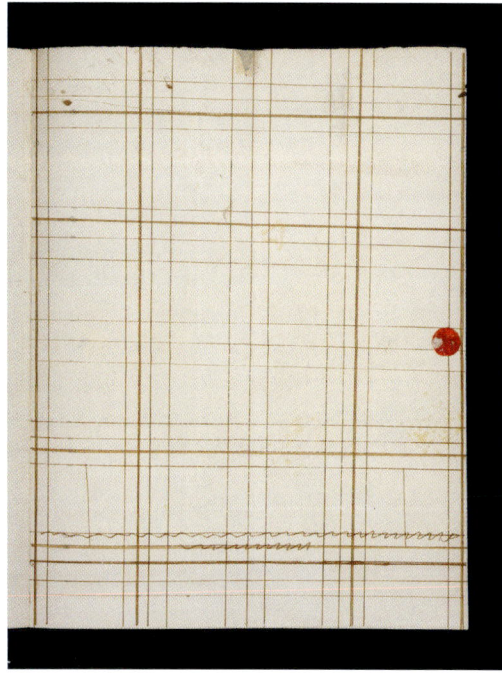

Figs 3.11: Customer drawing of the Chisholm sett

Having received a length of Chisholm tartan deemed unsuitable for use in a plaid in 1838, Messrs Walker of London submitted this scale drawing dictated by a customer.

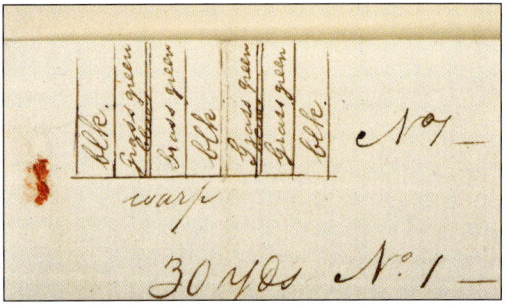

Figs 3.12 and 3.13 (left and below): Diagrams in lieu of fabric

In June 1811, Robertson & Wigham of Glasgow submitted these two sett diagrams instead of sending fabric samples. These were not meant as references for weaving, but guides to help Messrs Wilson of Bannockburn identify whether they had the desired patterns immediately to hand.

lengths as mentioned on the annex'd – if good qualities, bright colours and rather fine.' The order was sent 'in the expectation the Goods are on hand', meaning that the two diagrams were not meant to act as instructions for the weaver to follow. However, the way that the tartans were recorded indicates that they were drawn using a piece of cloth as a reference, possibly brought in and shown to Robertson & Wigham by one of their clients. The patterns, labelled 'No. 1' and 'No. 2' and running along the edges of the page, replicate the arrangement of the coloured warp threads as they would appear along the ragged edge of a piece of fabric [3.12, 3.13].[27]

Most of the diagrams in the collection demonstrate that their authors grasped the most basic aspect of tartan design – that the arrangement of the warp threads mirror that of the weft. As such, most customers who submitted drawings to Wilsons adopted a similar approach to that of Robertson & Wigham, choosing to reproduce the warp in isolation rather than replicate the web in its entirety. We can imagine how simple it would have been for a weaver to employ these hand-drawn guides as reference tools when dressing the loom. Using the paper as a measure, they could space the coloured threads out in the way specified by the client.

A. McCallum & Son, proprietors of a textile warehouse in Glasgow that dealt largely in silk, lace and muslin, wrote to Wilsons in 1824 with a request for a piece of 42nd Officer's tartan, a piece of McDuff and '1 [piece] Superfine Campbell to pattern described'. Orientating the paper to landscape, the merchant has outlined the desired setting of the Campbell of Argyll and provided a key, summarising how the diagram should be interpreted by the maker. The pattern is presented to scale, in two halves, reading from point A to point B, and from point B to point C. When the two halves are joined, the full width of the cloth is given from selvedge to selvedge: 'N. B. From A to B is the one half & from B to C is the other half; giving the whole width of the Tartan. B. B. is the Centre of the Tartan – the Yellow and White stripes are alternate, the Divisions give the Width of each colour.' The drawing has also been used to indicate the expected material quality of the finished tartan, with directions to execute the alternating yellow and white stripes in silk written alongside each instance of these colours in the scale diagram [3.14].[28]

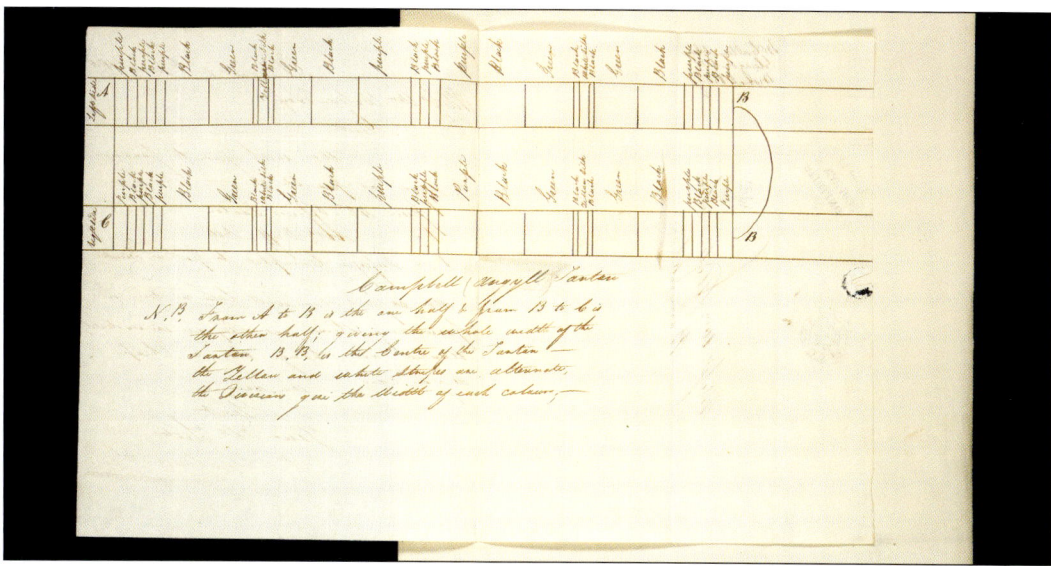

Fig. 3.14: **Customer drawing of the Campbell of Argyll sett**

Pattern scale and correct colours were important considerations for customers, leading some to submit diagrams that clearly outlined their needs and expectations of the finished product. In this letter, A. McCallum of Glasgow included a painstakingly annotated diagram of the Campbell of Argyll tartan. His scale, colour and fibre preferences are clearly marked.

Achieving the correct pattern to a scale determined by the client is a common concern across the collection of customer drawings. However, the use of diagrams to articulate colour preferences is also evident. While some customers employed coloured inks or paints to embellish their diagrams, others relied on simple annotations to indicate what they wanted. Writing to Wilsons from Forres in September 1829, merchant William Purse placed an order for seven yards of the MacLeod tartan. Although a small quantity, Purse assured the firm that if it was delivered promptly and to the given specifications, then a much larger order would undoubtedly follow. The drawing annexed to the order is strict on matters of scale – 'Black exactly this Breadth', 'Yellow 16 threads' – as well as on matters of colour. The red stripe in the sett, being very narrow, needed to catch the eye and hold its own in the sea of interlocking yellow and black. Instead of asking for a plain solid red, as he had for the other colours in the sett, Purse highlighted his desire for boldness by noting and underlining 'Rich Crimson 12 threads' against the slim line [3.15].[29]

Diagrams were an essential tool for those customers who wanted Wilsons to weave designs of their own imagining. Most of Wilsons' customers were content to select or, if necessary, amend an existing pattern to suit their individual needs. However, Wilsons would occasionally receive special commissions for new setts if an event, individual, or institution called for the delivery of something personal and unique. For instance, the raising of a volunteer yeomanry cavalry unit in England in 1794 occasioned a request for 450 yards of bespoke tartan. The fabric was to clothe fifty yeomen, and in terms of texture and weight should conform to 'the Common tartan used by the Highland [Regiments]' and needed to be

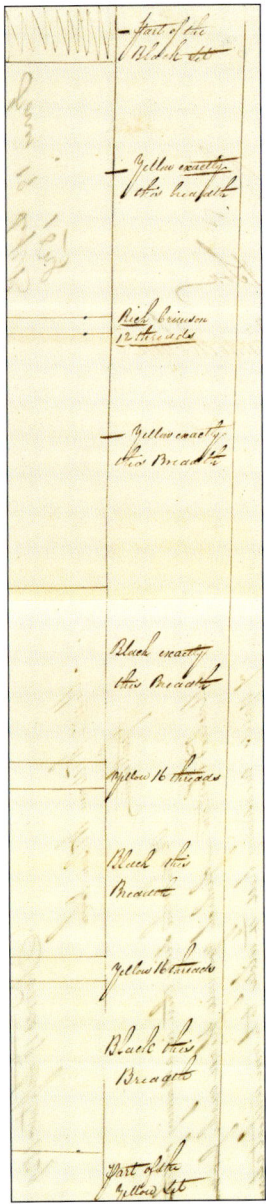

wide enough so that when two lengths were seamed together, the resulting cloak would be sufficiently voluminous to cover both man and horse. The colours were to be 'Dark Blue & Scarlet', reflecting the standard colours used in yeomanry uniform, 'the largest squares to be Blue & the Scarlet to come in by way of Relief'. On the back of the letter, the customer made a light pencil drawing of a grid, labelled vaguely at intervals with 'Blue' and 'Scarlet', with the postscript: 'The above is a rough draught of what is wanted – but I have little doubt, but you will devise some thing that may [be] thought neater of Blue & Scarlet – it is only intended to give you an Idea of what they mean that the above sketch was sent.'[30]

Writing in 1835, James Logan forwarded a design on behalf of the Prince Edward Island Caledonian Society. The newly instituted club wanted to create a tartan of its own for its membership to wear at meetings. Logan's design is accompanied by a colour key for the weavers to follow when making up the tartan, using Wilsons' existing stock of regimental and clan tartans as a common reference point: 'The Green is to be the bright colour of the 92nd – the Blue such as in the plaid of the 79th and the white to be as bright as that in the Clanranald's or Glengarry's'. As the membership of the Prince Edward Island club was not as prosperous as that of its sister

Fig. 3.15 (left): Customer drawing of the Macleod sett

This diagram was submitted to Messrs Wilson of Bannockburn by William Purse of Forres in September 1829, indicating the desired scale and depth of colour for the MacLeod sett. Wanting the red in the weave to stand out against the yellow and black, he specified a 'Rich Crimson'.

Fig. 3.16 (right): Pattern design by James Logan

James Logan was a Scottish antiquarian and historian. His excellent working knowledge of tartan enabled him to design one of his own in 1835, intended for the Prince Edward Island Caledonian Society.

societies in Britain, Logan requested that all silk be omitted from the weave and that the cloth be of a similar quality to that manufactured for Scottish infantry to wear as part of their uniforms. The design is laid out carefully to scale, annotated, and coloured in inks. It was evidently amended prior to being sent off, however, as the central light stripe has been changed from yellow to white [3.16]. To save confusion, Logan has labelled the change clearly, explaining in the colour key that the last time he ordered a yellow stripe from Wilsons it had 'gone off', meaning that the dye had faded or become fugitive.[31]

The most ambitious and visually complex design to be found in the collection of customer drawings held by National Museums Scotland, comes from the pen of Sir Patrick Craufurd Bruce.[32] It accompanied a commission for livery tartan, presumably meant to be worn by Bruce's attendants at one of his many properties in London, Buckinghamshire and the Scottish Highlands. The drawing, and the series of correspondence that surrounds it, represents one of the rare instances in which we can trace the progress of a bespoke commission through several stages of negotiation and thereby gain a sense of how a customer's drawing was incorporated into Wilsons' working practices.

The commission first came to hand in November 1811, when Bruce sent Wilsons a hastily drawn pattern tabulation under cover of his brother William [3.17]. Appended was a note:

> *I have made out a sort of pattern which I think will do well enough to guide Mr. Wilson; Lett him consider what is stated; if he requires further information, he may refer to me – But if he thinks it will make a pretty Tartan, lett him make, in the first instance, as small a quantity as he conveniently can, and as soon as possible, and send it up here for me to Judge and if determined on; when I shall give him the additional orders of what I shall require – Signed P Craufurd Bruce.*[33]

After presumably receiving assurances from Wilsons that the pattern sent could be executed to his specifications, Bruce was aggrieved six months later when he received a roll of tartan that was completely inadequate to the task. In response to this disappointment, he decided to go to great lengths to have the mistake rectified:

> *The Roll of Tartan came safe to hand but is not of the Pattern I wished, – the Ground is Scarlet,*

DESIGNING AND TRADING TARTAN IN GEORGIAN BRITAIN

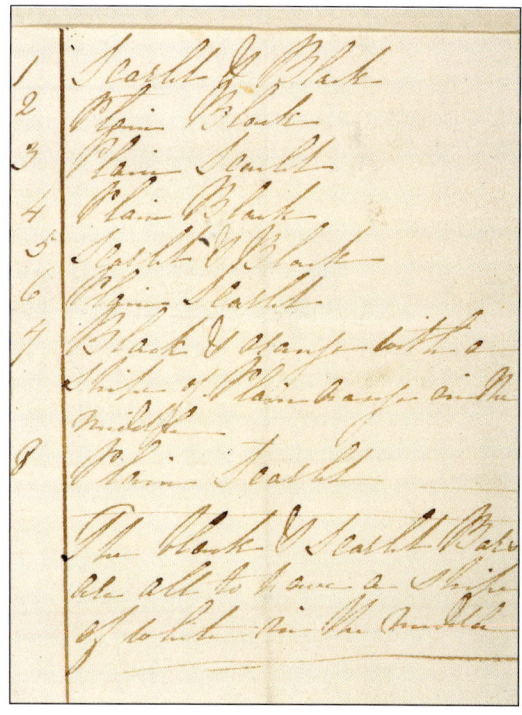

Fig. 3.17: Pattern tabulation for a bespoke commission

Sir Patrick Craufurd Bruce sent this pattern tabulation to Messrs Wilson of Bannockburn in November 1811, shortly after purchasing the Highland estate of Glenelg and becoming a member of the Highland Society of London. The tabulation only specifies the arrangement of Bruce's chosen colours, leaving the firm with a lot of creative freedom in how to interpret his design.

I wished it to be Orange, because the Bruce Livery is that colour with Scarlet Cuffs and Colar and Waistcoat; I have therefore had another Pattern made in which I have endeavoured to introduce all the different colours that are requisite, and it strikes me the assemblage will make a handsome showy Pattern; – I now enclose the Drawing, which is intended to describe the same Sett or sized Pattern as that you have already wove, and in order to ascertain as much as possible the giving a correct idea of the several Colours, particularly where the warp and woof are to be of different colours, I have caused to be wrote on the Margin the respective colours, – with this attention therefore I trust you will be able thoroughly to comprehend and to make out the pattern exactly, in which case I should wish to have the Piece wove for me, but untill I see and approve of the Pattern I should only like to have as small a quantity as you can conveniently manufacture; afterwards if I find it to be what I wish and intend I shall then give you a Further Order; if you could in the course of a Month send me a small quantity just sufficient for two or three Jackets and Waistcoats it would be satisfactory, but it must positively reach here by the Twentieth May.[34]

It is unclear whether Bruce executed the elaborate drawing himself or whether he employed the talents of an acquaintance [3.18]. Whatever the case, it was a fruitless effort. A further letter, dated 23 June 1812, stated that Wilsons' second attempt had come to hand but, yet again, had proved a disappointment. In his terse reply to the weavers, Bruce stated emphatically that 'the Pattern I do not at all like or approve of, and I do not think the Colours are by any means good, particularly the Orange is very bad'. One last time, he attempted to state his needs. He had a new pattern made and, for good measure, included swatches of fabric cut from his servant's livery for Wilsons to use as a guide.[35] Unfortunately, we do not know whether Bruce ever got the pattern executed to his satisfaction. The archive holds no further missives related to the transaction and, as far as can be ascertained from the surviving records of the Bruces, no payment related to the commissioning of the tartan was ever made to Wilsons.[36]

Sir Patrick Craufurd Bruce was born at Stenhouse, Stirlingshire, in January 1748, the fifth son of Mary Agnew and Sir Michael Bruce, 6th Baronet of Stenhouse. He began his working life in Bombay as a writer to the East India Company, eventually progressing to the role of merchant banker with interests in London and abroad. His main residence was at Taplow Lodge in Buckinghamshire, but he also maintained a home in the city. By 1811 he had made two substantial property purchases: a townhouse in Upper Grosvenor Street, London, and the Highland estate of Glenelg in Inverness-shire. He acquired the latter from John Norman MacLeod, 24th Chief of Clan MacLeod, at a cost of £100,000 (with a further £25,000 invested in improvements in subsequent years). Bruce's significant investment in Highland property coincided with a bid to become a fully-fledged member of the Highland Society of London. In their list of members,

Fig. 3.18: Pattern design for a bespoke commission

After receiving what he deemed an inadequate weaving of his design in April 1812, Bruce sent Messrs Wilson of Bannockburn this elaborate watercolour as a more detailed explanation of what he wanted. His main complaint was that the orange in the previous weaving had not matched that of his servant's livery, for which the tartan was intended.

Fig. 3.19: *John Crichton-Stuart, 2nd Marquess of Bute*, by Sir Henry Raeburn (1756–1823), c.1821, oil on canvas

Painted in 1821, Raeburn's portrait of the 2nd Marquess of Bute is among the best representations of a caped tartan cloak worn in the Georgian style. With its crimson lining and great length, the Royal Stewart cloak is a bold and showy accompaniment to Bute's fitted suit of dark broadcloth, stark white cravat and stiff leather walking boots. His tartan outerwear is a fashionable yet practical piece of elite male clothing.

(The Bute Collection at Mount Stuart)

published in Sir John Sinclair's *Account of the Highland Society of London* (1813), Bruce is noted as having joined the club on 1 June 1811. He styled himself as being 'of Glenelg' as opposed to his familial home at Stenhouse or main residence at Taplow, despite the relative newness of that acquired identity.[37] Shortly after his membership was accepted and he began attending meetings, Bruce sent his commission to Messrs Wilson of Bannockburn. As a younger son whose lands in Scotland were purchased as opposed to inherited, it is possible that his hopes of creating a unique tartan – and his anxiety about getting it right – was fuelled by a desire on Bruce's part to display his social and cultural credentials in sartorial form, thereby raising his pedigree in the eyes of his peers.

Tartan as fashion fabric

The Wilsons archive at National Museums Scotland offers invaluable insight into the level of control that customers were able to exert over tartan design and the refinement of its manufacture. Perusal of the firm's correspondence also indicates the types of garments its tartan was used to create. Georgian tartan was evidently an adaptable commodity. Beyond the realms of Highland dress tailoring, the cloth found its way into a variety of everyday and occasional garments.

During the early 1800s, tartan was in vogue as cloaking fabric. The cloth was a popular option for outdoor wear as the tight twill structure of the weave and natural water-repellent qualities of the wool provided excellent protection from the elements [3.19]. Surviving tartan cloaks of the era often betray their practical function, the bright particoloured fabrics soiled by mud and accumulated damp. A man's caped cloak of Royal Stewart tartan, acquired by the museum in 1993, was so well worn upon its accession into the collection that curator Naomi Tarrant noted in the catalogue that it was 'the kind of item which eventually was relegated to the hall for anyone to use if they needed to go outside in bad weather'. With its interlined collar, deeply pleated neck and red twill lining, it would certainly have been warm and serviceable. The fact that the hem is badly stained and has been turned up at a later date indicates that it had a long and useful life, well past the point of stylishness [3.20, 3.21].[38]

Tartan cloaks went in and out of fashion with the turning of the seasons. Retailers timed advert-

isements of their availability to coincide with the colder months, when customers were looking for suitably sturdy attire. In December 1802, the firm James & Walters of London announced it had made 'an invaluable improvement upon Scotch plaids and cloaks' by devising a new waterproofing method, designed to make plaid cloaks, pelisses and boat cloaks 'defy all weather, as rain cannot possibly penetrate them'.[39] Walker's Warehouse in Covent Garden, meanwhile, boasted that if its customers were pushed for time in the run up to the winter season, they could choose from an array of ready-made cloaks of equal quality to those made to order.[40] Such ready-made pieces were not only available to shoppers in Britain. The export of gentlemen's tartan cloaks and great coats is well-documented in the pages of colonial papers, such as the *Calcutta Gazette*, which regularly carried advertisements for goods lately arrived on the vessels of the East India Company: 'Tartan Plaid Great Coats, with sleeves, lined with green baize.'[41]

The Wilsons archive contains numerous requests for cloaking material made during this period. Appended to an order for 30 yards of Macduff

Figs 3.20 and 3.21 (detail): Royal Stewart tartan cloak, lined with red twill

The dynastic and military associations of the Royal Stewart combined to make it a highly desirable fashion fabric in the early 19th century. Of all the tartan cloaks known to survive in private and museum collections around the world, the Royal Stewart is among the most commonly observed patterns.

sent on 7 December 1824, Robert Fotheringham of Kincardine requested the firm send him a packet of 'some Good samples of Tartan for Gowns & Cloaks'.[42] As well as supplying yardage, there is also evidence that Wilsons had their cloth tailored into ready-made cloaks for direct sale to dealers in Scotland and for export abroad.[43] In November 1814, Hector Macome wore a tartan cloak made for him by Wilsons when visiting a haberdashery in Paisley owned by his niece, Mrs McWalter. He wrote to inform the firm that several of McWalter's customers had enquired after the cloak and were keen to make a purchase. One gentlemen, standing at 6 feet 2½ inches, would require quite a large cloak to fit him comfortably and Macome hoped that Wilsons would be able to oblige.[44]

Acting on behalf of a friend, John Sommers of Mid Calder wrote to Wilsons in February 1818 regarding a commission of 'a few dozen of Tartan Cloaks with sleeves for the Brazil market'. Sommers wanted to know how much tartan typically cost per yard, how many yards went into a cloak, and how much it would cost to have them made up. He had an idea of what patterns might suit his friend's needs, but asked the firm to send him a packet of patterns with their prices attached, from which he could make a selection: 'The tartans must all be of the brightest colours such as the Grant, Stewart & Douglas. The greater the quantity of red & yellow so much the better.'[45] Later correspondence, dated 9 March 1818, indicates that while Sommers was happy to proceed with the transaction, he wanted the style and quality of the garments to meet his exacting standards. The distance they would have to travel and the costs involved in their conveyance meant that they had to be attractive and saleable, and Sommers insisted that before the cloaks were shipped he would need to inspect them. The sett and weight of the cloth had to reflect local tastes and the demands of the hotter climate. If they were not sufficiently 'handsome', Sommers warned, he would not bother sending them:

> *In regard to the Plaid it occurs to me that the sleeves might be an inch & half or even two inches shorter & that a single cape is quite sufficient, & the neck or collar need not be so broad & does not require to be turned down, if it were only about half the breadth. The cloth thus saved would enable you to make the cloak perhaps an inch longer. The upper cape is not enough cut out & does not hang flat on the shoulders. Indeed, I think one cape quite sufficient & as the cloaks are not intended for warmth they should be made as light & simple as possible. If the appearance of a double cape be necessary, which I should think is not the case, it might be made a false one. The cape if possible should not be pieced, or should if necessary be done so as to suit the Tartan. I need not say that you will of course make them of different sizes. […] The Tartan cannot be too showey & splendid, & the greater the proportion of bright colours such as red & yellow with a little light blue & green so much the better. The Brazillians are not fond of dark colours.*[46]

Sommers' exacting description corresponds to an existing cloak within the museum collection [3.22].[47] Accessioned in 1942, it once belonged to the great-grandmother of the donor, thus placing its date of manufacture comfortably within the first quarter of the nineteenth century. The cut of the cloak is both practical and elegant. An interior drawstring allows the garment to be cinched at the upper back, creating a tapered silhouette that would have followed the line of the high-waisted gown worn beneath. The armholes are covered by tabs of matching tartan fabric which, if desired, can be buttoned at the wrist to form a tight-fitting sleeve. The dark silk ribbon used to close the cloak at the neck complements the warm tones of the worsted tartan, while the matching of the sett along the seams gives the illusion of wearing the pattern all of a piece. As well as being among the earliest tartan cloaks held by National Museums Scotland, this garment is also notable for being the earliest known example of the Buchanan tartan [3.23]. The use of the pattern in the cloak significantly pre-dates its christening as a clan sett, meaning that whoever commissioned the garment would have known and ordered it under another moniker. Rather than

Fig. 3.22 (left): Buchanan tartan cloak, *c.*1800–10

This caped cloak trimmed with green silk ribbon is tailored from one of the earliest known examples of the Buchanan tartan. At the time the cloak was made, this busy asymmetric pattern was not known as a clan tartan and would likely have been sold under a different name.

Fig. 3.23 (right): Sample of Buchanan tartan

This cutting of the Buchanan is contained within a folio of 58 clan tartans, compiled during the first half of the 19th century. The descriptive card and silk binding sewn to each sample suggests that the collection once belonged to a tailor, merchant or weaver. Such books were commonly kept in shops and workrooms, as a reference for customers and manufacturers.

choosing it for its clan affiliations, the customer would have picked it because they liked the way the fabric looked and because it suited their needs as a purchaser.

Manufacturing authenticity

Elizabeth Gaskell's *Wives and Daughters, An Every-Day Story*, follows the fortunes of Molly Gibson, a shy young woman living in a provincial town in England during the 1830s. At the prospect of visiting the house of a venerable country squire and having nothing suitable to wear for the occasion, Molly is persuaded by her widowed Scottish father to purchase a new gown from a local milliner, Miss Rose. The exchange is weighted with personal and familial significance. Engaging the services of a milliner for the first time was an important milestone for young women of a certain class. Being permitted to choose the fabric for a new outfit represented a move towards greater autonomy in the day-to-day running of their lives, when a girl was given more direct control over how she presented herself to the world. Unfortunately, Molly's inexperience in sartorial matters – coupled with a lack of maternal supervision and insight – leads her to make a rather questionable choice.

> *Miss Rose persuaded her to order a gay-coloured, flimsy plaid silk, which she assured her was quite the latest fashion in London, and which Molly thought would please her father's Scotch blood. But when he saw the scrap which she had brought home as a pattern, he cried out that the plaid belonged to no clan in existence, and that Molly ought to have known this by instinct. It was too late to change it, however, for Miss Rose had promised to cut the dress out as soon as Molly had left her shop.*[48]

Aggrieved that the milliner would sell her something that was 'not a true clan tartan', Molly comes to resent 'the terrible, over-smart plaid gown' that makes her feel so strange and unbecoming in the company of others. Throughout her time at Hamley Hall, Molly dreads the moments when social etiquette compels her to don the dress. Her low opinion of the silk is shared by her hosts who, though kind, privately pity her for her lack of taste and sophistication. When the squire's son Roger meets Molly over dinner, he considers her 'badly-dressed and rather awkward', but does not embarrass her by voicing the opinion aloud. Mrs Hamley, meanwhile, gently steers Molly away from wearing the 'horrid plaid silk' when she is invited to tea with her future stepmother at the Towers. Wanting Molly to make a favourable impression among the local aristocracy, the older woman tactfully suggests that a plain white muslin, while somewhat old fashioned, would suit her better.[49]

For Molly, her first commercial experience of tartan is tainted by notions of its inauthenticity. To be told by her father that the fabric she chose specifically to please him lacks a distinctive clan identity – combined with his disappointment in her inability to recognise this, given her Scottish ancestry – makes her feel inadequate, even foolish. She had placed her faith in the worldly Miss Rose, whose lack of knowledge on the subject of clan tartans had caused her to lead the novice shopper astray.

The arrival of the 1830s marked an interesting transitional moment in the commercial history of tartan. For decades the market had been flooded with new patterns jostling for position within a continually evolving canon. The tartan trade had reached a tipping point of standardisation and a rigidly defined array of clan patterns emerged as the prevailing articles. Certain rules and expectations shaped their manufacture and sartorial applications, effectively guiding how they were retailed to consumers. To specialise in the sale of clan tartans, vendors learned to trade upon the appealing aesthetics of the cloth, while also promoting the culture of Scottish Romanticism that surrounded and demarcated its fashionability. Scholarly interest in the origins of clan tartans soon dovetailed with the ambitions of manufacturers and retailers, who wanted to cement the historical credentials of their wares in the popular imaginations of customers.

As clan tartans had grown in popularity during the early 1800s, those who retailed them began to employ artful language in how they described them to consumers. Ladies fashion magazines, such as *Ackermann's Repository of Arts*, underscored the 'ancient character' of the cloth, even as it was absorbed into the making of the latest styles [3.24].[50] Others incorporated words such as 'real' and 'authentic' in newspaper advertisements, investing their wares with a sense of rarity and value that befitted their emerging status as cultural curiosities. Exactly what made a clan tartan 'real' and 'authentic', however, was a fluid concept.

In the eyes of some buyers, foregrounding the cloth's geographical – as well as ancestral – provenance was key. From 1810 to 1813, R. Menzies & Co. of Carmarthen in Wales frequently stocked Highland tartans for use in ladies' mantles and pelisses, as well as gentlemen's morning gowns. The firm characterised its tartans as specialty items, offering them for wholesale and retail without reserve as 'the great distance betwixt them and their

Fig. 3.24: *Evening Dress*

Published in the October 1822 edition of the fashionable periodical *Ackermann's Repository of Arts*, this plate details an evening dress of Mackenzie silk tartan. The accompanying description contains an allusion to the supposed antiquity of clan tartans, claiming that, 'The families of the ancient Scotch nobility were distinguished by their different plaids'.

HIGHLAND STYLE

Manufacturing Friends' in Scotland meant that they were difficult fabrics to reliably keep in stock. While it may have been possible to source tartan from elsewhere in Britain by this point – such as from the textile hubs of Norwich and Manchester – R. Menzies & Co. clearly felt that there was no benefit in stocking tartan unless it came directly from a Scottish maker. This may account for an advertisement they posted in *The Cambrian* in February 1815, which boasted of their acquisition of 'a few pieces of real Highland tartan' after a year of silence on the topic.[51] For others in the trade, the origin of a tartan was seemingly less important than the quality of its production. George Fox of Covent Garden, for example, advertised himself as 'the only Ladies' Woollen Draper in London who Manufactures and Retails real Highland Tartan Plaids of all the Clans' during the winter season of 1819. His claim implies that he considered his manufactures just as 'real' as anything a Scottish weaver could supply, as he had the skill to replicate an established set of patterns to a recognisably high standard.[52]

The first scholarly publication specifically to address the merging of the historical and the commercial properties of tartan was James Logan's *The Scottish Gaël; or Celtic Manners as Preserved among the Highlanders*.[53] Appearing in two volumes in 1831, it was based on Logan's observations of Highland life and surviving antiquities, collected on a walking tour he had undertaken over the course of 1826. The descriptive plates and appendices Logan prepared were toted by the publishers as unique selling points of the work, with particular emphasis given to the utility of the 'accurately coloured Engravings of the Costumes of the various Highland Clans; with correct Specimens and Descriptions of their respective Badges, Tartans, &c'.[54] Notably, the second volume included an appendix of more than fifty clan tartans designated by Logan as historically 'authentic' specimens, accompanied by instructions on how the various thread counts should be read and interpreted. This list was aimed at manufacturers and consumers alike, who Logan deemed in equal need of enlightenment on the subject.[55]

There is recognition in Logan's text that national events, chiefly the Royal Visit of 1822, had given rise not only to an influx of new tartan patterns, but also to widespread public interest in the supposed antiquity of the cloth and its historical associations with the culture of the Scottish Highlands. Though he regarded this as a broadly positive development, he had his reservations about the direction the industry had taken in recent years. 'This creditable feeling unfortunately led to a result different from what might have been expected: fanciful varieties of tartan and badges were passed off as genuine, and the attempt to set the public right on these matters is likely to meet the objections of many.'[56] In other words, in publishing his list of 'authenticated' tartans, Logan expected both to upset and to improve the tartan industry by imposing order upon chaos. He noted:

Opposite: Frontispiece to subscriber questionnaire

After the favourable reception of *The Scottish Gaël* (1831), James Logan began to elicit subscriptions for a new work on the history of the clans. He circulated a questionnaire among the Scottish elite, hoping to gather authentic information on clan lore, heraldry, and surviving material culture. This copy of the questionnaire was sent by Logan to Messrs Wilson of Bannockburn in November 1831, covering a request for example swatches of all known clan and family tartans produced by the firm.

The utility of these lists is apparent. Any one desirous of possessing the tartan of his clan, may, by inspecting the table, inform himself of the exact pattern, and with this knowledge he cannot be deceived in making a purchase. The advantage of these accurate descriptions to the manufacturer and the dealer is obvious. They will, by this guide, be able to provide the true sett of any clan tartan.[57]

DESIGNING AND TRADING TARTAN IN GEORGIAN BRITAIN

Notes

1. Dunbar 1981, 19; Dunbar presented this material to the National Library of Scotland (NLS) in 1952, which may be consulted using the identifier MSS.6660–7000. NLS holds further material related to the firm, acquired from various sources.
2. Until recently, the Wilson material donated to the National Museum of Antiquities of Scotland by Lord David Crichton-Stuart was only partially recorded. Following a period of reassessment and record enhancement funded by the William Grant Foundation, the 1952 and 1953 donations are now fully searchable on the museum catalogue as part of the NMS H.TTC series.
3. For previous studies that have consulted aspects of this National Museums Scotland (NMS) material, see in particular: Mills and Carswell 1998; Tuckett 2016.
4. Trevor-Roper 1983, 30.
5. Tuckett 2016. See also Dyer and Wigston Smith (eds) 2020.
6. NMS H.TTC 1.1.
7. On tartan design, see in particular: Stewart 1972; Sutton and Carr 1984; Scarlett 1990.
8. Duncan 1807, 105–7.
9. SAS Mss No.610. This account book is part of the Society of Antiquaries of Scotland Numbered Manuscript Collection, which can be accessed through the Research Library at National Museums Scotland. It was donated by Lord David Crichton-Stuart in 1952–53, alongside transcriptions of Messrs Wilson of Bannockburn's 1819 Key Pattern Books, made by James Pittendrigh MacGillivray in the early twentieth century. See also: MacDonald 2012.
10. NMS H.TTC 3.8.
11. Cox 2015; Dyer 2016.
12. It is very common to find fabric offcuts appended to the correspondence of purchasers, retailers and manufacturers. Fabric sample books are also numerous in archives and museum collections. See in particular: Miller 2014.
13. There are numerous examples of this type of request scattered throughout the archive, from both new and returning customers. As goods changed seasonally, customers would request the most up-to-date selection of patterns available.
14. NMS H.TTC 4.29; NMS HTTC 4.8; NMS H.TTC 4.5; NMS H.TTC 4.27; NMS H.TTC 4.13; H.TTC 4.24; NMS H.TTC 4.9.
15. Walsh 2006, 167–72.
16. Textiles were among the most highly prized commodities during the long eighteenth century, with places such as North America heavily dependent on imports from British merchants due to a lack of domestic manufacturing and a general preference for European style. Political tension and military conflicts across the British Atlantic region caused the taxation of imported goods to fluctuate throughout this period. See in particular: Montgomery and Eaton 2007; Haulman 2011.
17. The majority of orders in the Messrs Wilson of Bannockburn archive relating to the firm's participation in foreign markets can be found in the NMS H.TTC 44.3 series.
18. NMS H.TTC 3.23.
19. NMS H.TTB 8. See registration notes for 'Kidd', Scottish Register of Tartans; Trevor-Roper 1983, 30; Scarlett 1990, 75–76, 137–39; MacDonald 2012, 25–26, 35.
20. NMS H.TTC 3.12.
21. NMS H.TTC 4.48.
22. NMS H.TTC 4.11.
23. NMS H.TTC 3.31.
24. NMS H.TTC 3.29.
25. NMS H.TTC 44.3.13. On the history of textiles worn by slaves in North America, see in particular: Baumgarten 2002, 133–39; Ramsey 2019. Language surrounding textiles was quite fluid in the Georgian period. It is important to note that when a textile was described as 'tartan' or 'plaid' in the late eighteenth and early nineteenth centuries, the author did not necessarily mean a patterned fabric. The term could also refer to a cloth of a solid colour. That the letter NMS H.TTC 44.3.13 refers specifically to 'Dark patterns', however, implies that in this instance patterned fabrics are being discussed.
26. NMS H.TTC 3.14.
27. NMS H.TTC 4.15.
28. NMS H.TTC 3.17.
29. NMS H.TTC 3.32.
30. NMS H.TTC 4.4.
31. NMS H.TTC 43.7.
32. For all letters and drawings pertaining to this transaction, see: NMS H.TTC 4.17, NMS H.TTC 4.18, NMS H.TTC 4.19 and NMS H.TTC 4.20.
33. NMS H.TTC 4.17.
34. NMS H.TTC 4.19.
35. NMS H.TTC 4.20.
36. The Bruce family archive is held by the Weston Library (Bodleian Libraries Repository), Oxford.
37. Sinclair 1813, 61.
38. NMS A.1993.209.
39. *The Daily Advertiser and Oracle* (4 December 1802), 1.
40. *The Morning Post* (7 February 1803), 2.
41. *Calcutta Gazette* (12 September 1811), 2.
42. NMS H.TTC 3.21.
43. Tuckett 2016, 194–95.
44. NMS H.TTC 44.3.7.
45. NMS H.TTC 44.3.10.
46. NMS H.TTC 44.3.11.
47. NMS A.1942.40. For a comparison Buchanan sample, dating from *c.*1830, see piece bound into folio NMS H.TTB 11.
48. Gaskell 1866, vol. I, 56–57; Waine 2019, 8.

49. *Ibid.*, 59, 83–84, 124.
50. NMS H.RHI 91.94.
51. *The Cambrian* (11 February 1815), 3. R. Menzies and Co. consistently advertised their stocks of Highland tartan between 1810 and 1813.
52. *The Morning Post* (20 December 1819), 1. It is worth noting that Fox applied the same strategy to the marketing of 'real' Welsh flannels, made by him in 1814. See: *London Courier and Evening Gazette* (28 October 1814), 1.
53. Logan 1831, 2 vols; Cheape 2006, 76.
54. *Inverness Courier* (19 January 1831), 1.
55. Logan 1831, vol. II, 401–8. The technical accuracy of Logan's tables has been questioned by historians since their publication in the early nineteenth century, in particular by those with a practical knowledge of weaving, such as Scarlett and MacDonald.
56. Logan 1831, vol. I, 238.
57. *Ibid.*, 238–39.

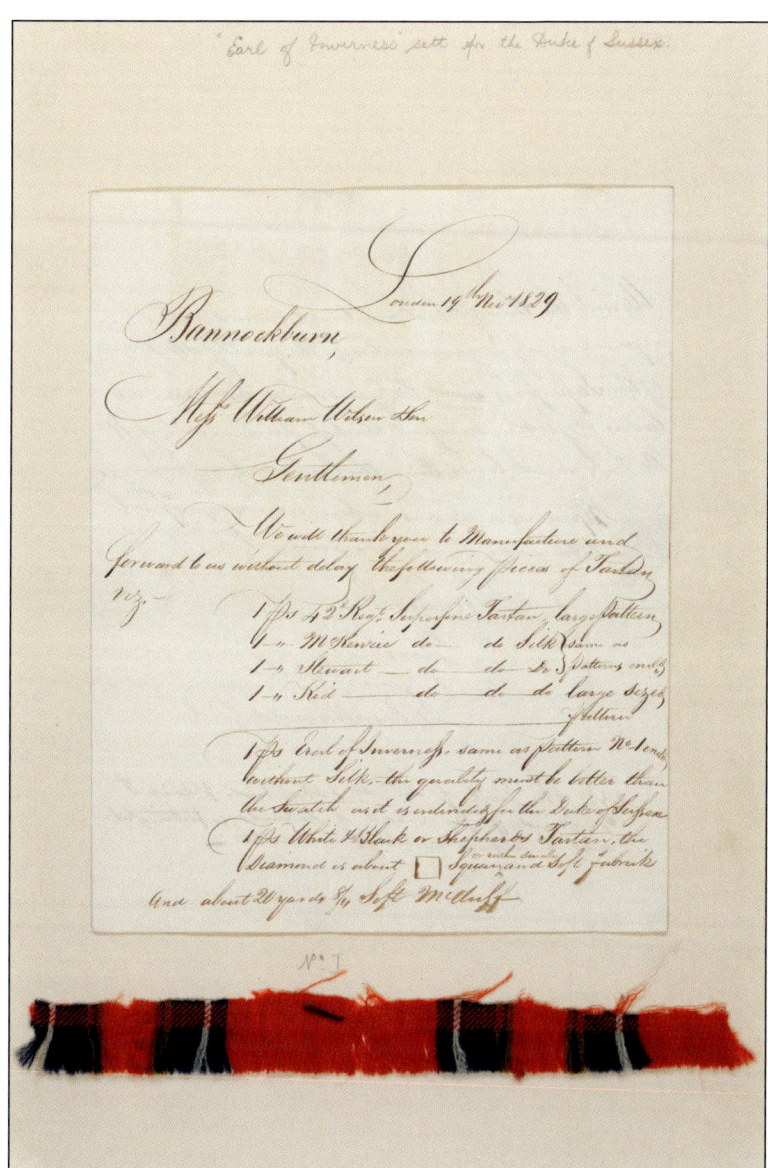

An order for Prince Augustus Frederick, 1829

This order from Harvey & Co. of London was received by Messrs Wilson of Bannockburn on 19 November 1829. Alongside various regimental and clan setts, the firm also asked for a quantity of Earl of Inverness tartan 'intended for the Duke of Sussex'. The firm stipulated that the quality must exceed that of the swatch sent, as the commission had to meet the needs of their royal customer.

CHAPTER 4

Highland style in Georgian society

'At present everything Highland is the rage both in London and on the Continent, and as we are apt to borrow our fashions from the south, it is gratifying to see that there is something like a reciprocity. Most cordially, therefore, do we say – success to the philabeg!'

Inverness Courier (16 December 1835)

Pages 134–35: Back of little boy's kilt dress, c.1815–20

(See Fig 4.47)

IN 1812, Sir Henry Raeburn exhibited a portrait of Colonel Alastair Ranaldson MacDonell of Glengarry at the Royal Academy in London. Standing proudly in the archaic setting of an old baronial hall, Glengarry is depicted as the quintessential Highland chief, arrayed in the latest iteration of revival style [Fig. 4.1]. On the walls behind him hang an assortment of ancestral Highland weapons, including a studded targe and a pair of crossed basket-hilted broadswords. A new-fangled *sgian dubh* is just visible tucked into the side of his diced hose [4.2], while a modern broad bonnet sits atop his head.[1] The felted wool has been stretched over a wire frame to give the headgear its rigid dimensions, its harsh lines contrasting sharply against the antique folds of his belted plaid. The sett of the kilted cloth corresponds to that used in his finely tailored short coat; four years after Raeburn's portrait was displayed to the public, Glengarry submitted a specimen of this same pattern to the Highland Society of London for inclusion in their clan tartan collection, authenticated with his seal. In comparing this portrait with that created for him by Angelica Kauffman during his Grand Tour of Europe in 1799–1800 [2.28], it is plain that Glengarry had retained many pieces of his Highland costume over the intervening years. However, the silhouette he presented to Raeburn had subtly altered to reflect prevailing fashions in British menswear. The composition of his dress is a blending of ancient and novel, of inherited, acquired and innovative objects.

In this, our final chapter, we turn to the details of construction and styling that typified formal Highland dress costume of the late eighteenth and early nineteenth centuries. Although these garments represented a distinct point of view

HIGHLAND STYLE IN GEORGIAN SOCIETY

Fig. 4.1 (left): *Colonel Alastair Ranaldson MacDonell of Glengarry (1771–1828)*, **by Sir Henry Raeburn (1756–1823), 1812, oil on canvas**

Raeburn's portrait of the 15th Chief of Glengarry encapsulates the revivalist style of formal Highland dress favoured by the Scottish gentry during the early 19th century. Glengarry's interpretation of the costume had evolved since he sat for Angelica Kauffman in Rome a decade before. However, there were some elements that remained constant. His elaborate dirk, fork and skinning knife with their gold mounted ivory handles appear in both portraits.

(National Galleries of Scotland)

within Georgian society, it is important to remember that they were not isolated from the broader landscape of fashionable consumption in Britain, or indeed the rest of Europe. Despite its characterisation as ancient by those who sought to preserve and promote its use throughout the long eighteenth century, there was much about the Georgian style of Highland dress that was materially modern. It was a reactive and highly adaptable mode of ceremonial costume, that steadily altered to reflect the changing times and cultural preoccupations of its wearers. It was this malleability that ensured its longevity as a living tradition and strengthened its position within the pantheon of Scotland's national iconography.

Fig. 4.2 (opposite): *Sgian dubh*

A *sgian dubh* is a small knife with a leather sheath, usually worn tucked into a hose top. It was a late addition to the Highland dress silhouette, with little evidence for its inclusion in the formal costume prior to the Georgian period. This example has a carved cow horn handle mounted with brass, and likely dates from the early 19th century.

HIGHLAND STYLE

Refining the Highland silhouette

The early nineteenth century witnessed an evolution in elite male tailoring. Inspired by the aesthetics of ancient sculpture and archaeological discovery in Italy and Greece, British tailors began to cut, piece and manipulate cloth in ways that played with the statuesque qualities of the human form. In fashionable menswear, inventive shaping techniques were employed to give the illusion of fuller chests, broader shoulders, toned thighs and slim waists. The resulting silhouette sought to celebrate a classical ideal of the masculine shape.

Coat skirts were shortened and cut away from the hips, inviting the observer to intuitively scrutinise the relative proportions of the upper and lower body. Tailors honed cutting and finishing methods to take greater advantage of the flexibility of natural fibres – such as wool – thereby enabling artfully moulded profiles to appear effortless in motion. As discussed by dress historian Anne Hollander, '[w]ith the help of nearly imperceptible padding, curved seams, discreet darts and steam pressing, the rough coat of dull cloth was gradually refined into an exquisitely balanced garment that fitted smoothly without wrinkles and buttoned without strain to clothe what appeared to be the torso of a Greek athlete'.[2] These changes to the male silhouette were reinforced in the pages of professional tailoring manuals and further refined by the invention of the measuring tape. Now a standard piece of equipment, its introduction enabled tailors to take swift and accurate measurements of their clients for the first time.[3]

It was during this period of sartorial innovation and experimentation that a more formulaic approach to the fashioning of men's Highland dress costume started to appear. Those who specialised in crafting suits of Highland dress adopted the techniques born of the popular fascination with the neoclassical, producing form-fitting garments that lent a sculpted appearance to the clothed body. At the same time, they sought to reference the ancient origins of this once regional, martial costume by employing fabrics and notions that materialised a romantic ideal of historic clanship: family tartans, emblematic buttons and badges, and military stylings such as bullion ribbon and braiding [4.3].[4] Certain features of cut, construction and embellishment became standard practice within a relatively short period of time, laying the foundations for the costume we recognise today.

The intricate matching and manipulation of tartan cloth emerged as a defining feature of early nineteenth-century Highland costume; when examining extant garments in the stores of National Museums Scotland, it is particularly noticeable in the seaming of coats and the pleating of kilts. Whereas the prevailing neoclassical style in men's dress favoured a strictly monochromatic palette – the crisp white linens and sober broadcloths evoking the smooth tones and textures of worked stone – the makers of Highland dress costume invested heavily in the vibrant intermixing of

Fig. 4.3 (opposite): Kilt suit belonging to Andrew Clark, c.1815

This formal suit of Highland dress is tailored from MacLean hard tartan, comprising a coat, waistcoat and kilt. Each piece has been cut and constructed to emphasise the athletic qualities of the human form, in deference to the prevailing neoclassical mode of elite male fashions. Clark's suit also incorporates romantic, patriotic and militaristic elements characteristic of Georgian Highland dress culture. In addition to the presence of a bold clan tartan, the green velvet collar of the coat is ornamented with silver thistle insignias. The horizontal button placement and epaulettes of gold bullion ribbon, meanwhile, echo the style of regimental uniforms worn in the Napoleonic era.

shades and the manipulation of surface patterns upon the body. In contrast to the solid blues, greens, blacks, browns and buffs that dominated elite male fashion in the late Georgian era, the particoloured tartans used in the manufacture of coats, kilts and plaids enveloped the wearer in the colours of a wild, natural world.

The balanced grid of tartan setts complemented the new sculptural quality favoured in elite male dress, moulding to the shape of the body like scaffolding encasing and supporting the outlines of a building. When working with tartan, a tailor could combine the curved seams of a coat with the variegated grid of the tartan to achieve striking kaleidoscopic patterns that mapped imperceptibly onto the contours of back, chest and arms. This approach to the material allowed makers to interpret the same standard pattern in a variety of ways. A popular sett, such as the Royal Stewart, could be treated quite differently even within the wardrobe of a single individual.

In 1954, the Scottish United Services Museum acquired an extensive collection of clothing from an estate sale at Springwood Park, Kelso. This large assembly of dress and accessories once belonged to members of the Scott Douglas family, with the majority of pieces dating from the nineteenth century. The estate sale included several garments from the wardrobe of Sir John James Scott Douglas, 3rd Baronet (1792–1836), including two coats of Royal Stewart tartan worn by him as a young man.[5]

The two coats appear remarkably similar on first glance; each utilises the same tartan pattern, both have silk velvet cuffs and collars, decorated with a patriotic thistle insignia alternately worked in silver and gold metal thread. Closer inspection, however, reveals that the materials and tailoring exhibited in each coat vary markedly in terms of quality. The tartan used in the coat with the blue silk velvet cuffs and collar is a serviceable worsted [4.4], while the tartan used in the coat with the green finishing is a finer combination of worsted and silk [4.5]. The introduction of the silk into the weave would have made the cloth harder to work with when constructing the garment, given the different tensions and textures of the fibres in the web. The precision of the seaming and lack of buckling across the surface of the coat can be taken as a sign that whoever made the garment possessed the knowledge and intuition required to execute the commission to a high standard. If we also take into consideration the fine horizontal braiding, gold metal thread work, and the rows of cut glass buttons that frame the front closure, cuffs and tails, it is apparent that the second coat was intended for an event of some significance.

Scott Douglas was fastidious when it came to marking his costume with identifying stamps and inked signatures. This orderly habit enables us to trace when certain garments in the Springwood Park collection were worn with a reasonable degree of accuracy, constructing a life from the clothes left behind. The coat with the blue collar and cuffs contains the signature 'Captain Douglas', written into the linen lining of the sleeve [4.6].

HIGHLAND STYLE IN GEORGIAN SOCIETY

Fig. 4.4 (opposite): Tartan coat, c.1819

This short coat of Royal Stewart hard tartan belonged to Sir John James Scott Douglas. It is made of worsted tartan with blue velvet facings, decorated with silver thistle motifs about the cuffs and collar. Single-breasted with a straight cut-away at the hips, the coat is fastened by a row of domed white metal buttons of a type commonly seen in military clothing.

Fig. 4.5 (opposite): Tartan coat, c.1822

Also belonging to Sir John James Scott Douglas, this second coat is made of a fine worsted and silk Royal Stewart tartan with green velvet facings. It is decorated with gold thistle motifs at the cuffs and collar, with two rows of cut-glass buttons backed with foil. These frame the centre front of the coat, the sleeve closures and coat tails. The curved cut-away of the coat over the hips is suggestive of elite court styles of the era.

Figs 4.8 and 4.9 (opposite): Tailoring with tartan

Each maker has interpreted the Royal Stewart sett in their own distinctive way, cutting and piecing the pattern to suit the required style, cost and function of the commission.

Figs 4.6 and 4.7: Inked signatures

Marking clothing with a personal identifier was extremely common in the Georgian period. Both coats contain the signature of Sir John James Scott Douglas. The variance of his name indicates that the two coats were made and worn during different phases of his life, as a professional soldier and as a husband.

After serving as Lieutenant in the 15th Light Dragoons, the wearer purchased a captaincy in the 22nd Light Dragoons in 1819, at the age of 27. The regiment was disbanded in 1820, meaning that the coat can be linked quite definitively with this short period of his professional army career; it may even have been made by an army clothier. The coat with the green collar and cuffs, enlivened by a series of cut-glass buttons, contains the signature 'J J Scott Douglas' [4.7], relating to the next chapter of its wearer's life, when his financial and personal circumstances had drastically changed. Shortly after succeeding his father as 3rd Baronet of Springwood Park in 1821, John married his cousin Hannah-Charlotte Scott on 15 August 1822. In anticipation of their marriage, he took the name Scott by royal licence and legally became known as Sir John James Scott Douglas. This means that the second, more elaborate of the two coats can only have been worn by him as a married man of means.

Bringing the two coats together and comparing them side by side allows us to appreciate how two different makers of varying ability approached the grid of the Royal Stewart, cutting and manipulating the cloth to suit their own inclinations and skill levels. As in the Royal Stewart coat associated with the activities of the Highland Society of London, discussed in Chapter 2 [2.15], we can see how the back of each of Scott Douglas' tartan coats has been pieced to give the impression of colliding, interlocking shapes [4.8, 4.9].

It might be supposed that this exacting method of construction would lead to excessive wastage. However, an economical tailor could always find ways to turn the surplus fabric to their advantage. The pile of scraps that resulted from carefully cutting and piecing the carapace of a tartan coat were frequently repurposed in areas hidden to the eye, such as the lining. A fine example of this repurposing technique can be observed in a kilt suit of MacGregor tartan, dating to around 1820.[6] When mounted upon a figure, the level of sophisticated pattern manipulation across the entirety of the outfit becomes apparent [4.10, 4.11]. In comparison to the Royal Stewart used in Scott Douglas' coats, the MacGregor appears a much simpler sett: a red ground, crossed by relatively small quantities of green, white and black. However, the minimalistic nature of the pattern would have made the pursuit of balance and symmetry all the harder to achieve for the maker. It was easier to conceal mistakes when working with a small or busy sett, as the density of the colours distracted from issues caused by improper cutting and pattern placement, such as the buckling of fabric at the seams or a lack of harmony in the manipulation of the grid. The exterior of the coat

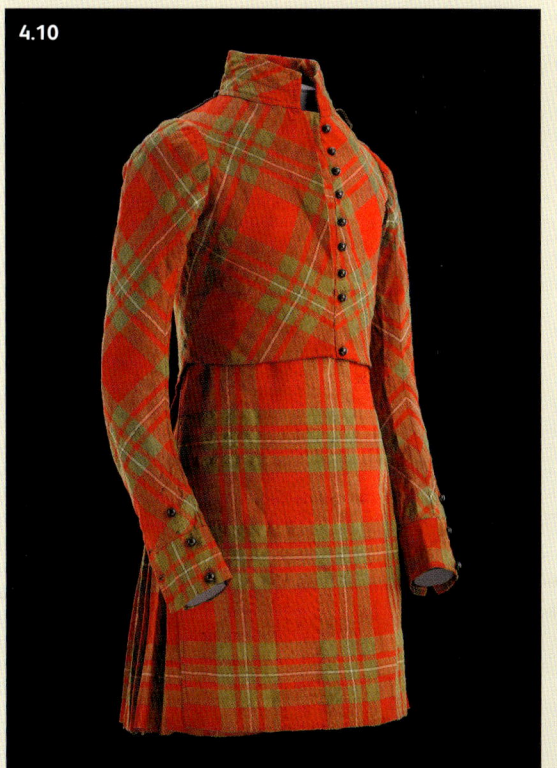

Figs 4.10 and 4.11: Kilt suit, *c*.1820

This coat and kilt of MacGregor hard tartan have been tailored with great skill and attention to detail. The MacGregor sett is well-matched across the entirety of the coat, from the curved back seams to the convergence of the pattern at the front closure. The straight cut-away of the coat at the hips and the tapered construction of the kilt combine to create the illusion of a slim waist, offset by a muscular upper body.

Fig. 4.12: Piecing

The internal construction of this MacGregor hard tartan coat is an object lesson in economical tailoring. It is half-lined with blue hessian, with the remaining areas pieced together using differently shaped tartan off-cuts salvaged from the making of the kilt suit.

demonstrates a high level of skill and attention to detail on the part of the tailor in their use of the MacGregor, most notably in the construction of the coat tails where the outline of two pockets are almost indistinguishable due to the expert quality of the pattern matching. The interior of the coat, meanwhile, is a carefully considered patchwork of leftovers [4.12].

The ability to tailor both competently and creatively with tartan was a recognised talent in the trade. In 1808, a story was reproduced in several British newspapers praising the skills of an old tailor in the service of Macdonald of Clanranald, who had become blind due to the length and technical precision of his labours. His inability to see had not stopped him from working the tartan, however. He was seemingly so attuned to the task of making suits of Highland dress for his master that he could intuitively distinguish the different stripes of colour in a tartan web by relying on his sense of touch alone. While this may seem improbable, if one considers that the lighter stripes in finer quality hard tartans of this period were often woven in silk then the tailor's ability to navigate the pattern using only the sensitive pads of his fingers is not beyond the realms of possibility. In admiring the tailor's remarkable proficiency, the article reminded its readers: 'It is well known how difficult it is to make a Tartan dress, because every stripe and colour (of which there are many) must fit each other with mathematical exactness: hence it is that very few tailors who enjoy their sight, are capable of executing this task.'[7]

Aside from the evolving intricacies of pattern manipulation, the most drastic of the material changes to occur within the construction of Highland dress costume during this period was the introduction of what Scottish antiquarian James Logan termed 'the modern belted plaid […] made up by the tailor to imitate the ancient form'.[8]

Of all the elements that have contributed towards the making of the archetypal Highland dress silhouette since the eighteenth century, one of the most constant has been the plaid. Today it is commonly fringed, sewn to shape, and worn pinned at the shoulder. However, earlier iterations looked and functioned much like a mantle or cloak. Such plaids are numerous in museum collections, though few are associated with full costumes. A notable exception can be found in a suit of Highland dress that once belonged to English Jacobite and Tory MP, Sir John Hynde Cotton [4.13].[9] Thought to have been acquired by Cotton on a visit to Scotland in 1744, the suit consists of a single breasted tartan coat embellished with green silk braid and tassels. The construction and cultural context of the Cotton suit was the subject of a meticulous study by former curator Helen Bennett in 1980, in which she noted that the plaid was composed of two lengths of tartan cloth joined selvedge to selvedge by a central seam, forming a rectangular garment measuring approximately 160 cm wide by 493 cm in length.[10] The prodigious size and shape of the plaid was well suited to providing the wearer with additional protection in inclement weather, either wrapped close about the body, pulled up over the head, or hand-pleated and belted about the waist to form a loosely kilted skirt.

Numerous prints from the Georgian period demonstrate an enduring popular interest in the apparent versatility of the plaid, based largely on descriptions published by travellers passing through the Highland region and observing its use first hand. Artists concentrated on communicating the form and function of the plaid, with many depictions representing how the garment could be physically re-shaped by the wearer to suit the needs of the moment. The impression was one of liberation and ease, suited to the demanding nature of the Highland terrain.

An engraving by George Philipp Rugends, published in Augsburg by Johann Christian Leopold in the early decades of the eighteenth century, shows the plaid wearer in three iterations. The central figure has the plaid pulled up to cover his shoulders, revealing the belt which keeps the fabric securely gathered about his middle. The figures to the left and the right provide side profiles of the plaid with its folds allowed to hang [4.14].[11] These same poses were later referenced in the work of Johann Sebastian Müller, whose engravings of Highland men in regional dress were published by John Bowles of the Black Horse in Cornhill, London. Müller has captioned his prints with descriptions of how the plaid can be worn in varying states, depending on the taste and requirements of the wearer [4.15]. A further print by Müller, also published by John Bowles, attempts to underscore the historical credentials of the costume in deference to the tenor of contemporary debates, which aligned its appearance with the Roman occupation of Scotland.[12] Beneath representations of a piper, soldier and a drummer, the print is captioned: 'The beautiful Dress used by the Highlanders is in great part the Ancient Roman Habit; for Tacitus tells us that the celebrated Roman Consul Agricola to soften this fierce and warlike People by his good address prevail'd upon them not only to learn the Roman language, but to accept the Habit and build Houses and Publick Buildings of all sorts.'[13] While such prints give a useful indication of how Highland dress and its history were popularly viewed within Georgian society, it is debatable whether they reflect the material realities of the costume as it became more formalised.

Although the belted form of the plaid remained an integral aspect of Highland costume, it became less ubiquitous with the introduction of tailored alternatives. By the middle decades of the eighteenth century, the

Fig. 4.13: Highland suit belonging to English Jacobite and Tory MP, Sir John Hynde Cotton, c.1744

Comprising a tartan coat, plaid and trews, Cotton's suit is among the earliest and most complete examples of Highland dress to survive in public hands. There are five different tartans used in the construction of the suit, with the trews showing significant signs of alteration. Quality tartan costume which pre-dates the last Jacobite Rising of 1745–46 is exceedingly rare, due to the Highland dress ban that followed in its wake. The good condition of the suit indicates that it was a prized family heirloom, which attained the status of a Jacobite relic with the passage of generations.

Fig. 4.14 (above): Print

George Philipp Rugends is thought to have created this engraving of plaid wearers around 1743. Its appearance may have been prompted by the popular fascination with Highland soldiers occasioned by the mutiny of the Black Watch (42nd) Regiment in May 1743. A spate of prints and ceramics featuring Highlanders emerged around this time, focusing largely on those mutineers executed on Tower Hill in London.

Fig. 4.15 (below): Print

This print by Johann Sebastian Müller recycles the central figure that appears in Rugends' depiction of plaid wearers in three attitudes. This instance of repetition raises the question of whether Müller really drew his plaid wearers from life, as his caption claims. Müller's description of the plaid is couched in practical terms, focusing attention on how the garment can be worn over the shoulders 'in rainy weather'.

HIGHLAND STYLE IN
GEORGIAN SOCIETY

plaid and kilted skirt had separated to become two distinct garments. This stratification of style is evidenced in a portrait of Alasdair Ruadh Mac-Donell, 13th Chief of Glengarry, and his attendant, in the collection of the Museum of the Isles [4.16]. The chief is depicted standing to the fore of a grand chamber, resplendent in full Highland regalia. One hand rests atop a studded leather targe lain across a table, while the other cradles his hip. The subtle quarter-turn of his body concentrates the eye on the voluminous folds of tartan cloth girded about his waist, the end of which is visibly gathered across his back and secured at his shoulder in traditional fashion. Behind the chief stands his attendant, proffering a beribboned bonnet and fowling piece. As is to be expected, the manservant is dressed simply and practically, his plain cloth coat and corresponding waistcoat missing the opulent gold lace embroidery of his master's garments. Notably, the servant's kilt lacks the characteristic bulk of a belted plaid. Instead, it hangs straight down from the hips and hugs closer to the outside line of the man's leg. The comparatively narrow shape of the servant's kilt has been achieved by manipulating and stitching the material into place, rather than gathering and strapping it around the body to please the whim of the wearer, as would be done with the *feileadh mòr*. This economically tailored incarnation of

Fig. 4.16: *Alasdair Ruadh MacDonell, 13th Chief of Glengarry* (c.1725–61), unknown artist, mid-18th century, oil on canvas

MacDonell was a commander of the Royal Écossais, a regiment of the French army mostly composed of Scottish Jacobites. On his way to provide military support for Prince Charles Edward Stuart in 1745, he was captured by British government forces and imprisoned in the Tower of London. Although outwardly a staunch Jacobite, on his release in 1747 he allegedly became a secret government agent. Operating under the codename 'Pickle', MacDonell is said to have passed information about the exiled Stuarts and their supporters directly to the Crown.

(Armadale Castle, Gardens and Museum of the Isles)

HIGHLAND STYLE

Figs 4.17 and 4.18 (opposite): Kilt suit, *c*.1790–1800

This is the earliest kilt suit held by National Museums Scotland. It is composed of a sewn kilt and corresponding coat, both tailored from the same tartan pattern. Variations of this sett, which originated in the 1790s, include the 'Kidd', 'Caledonia' and 'Macpherson'. The suit would likely have been worn with diced hose and brogues, a white linen shirt, neckcloth, and a long silk waistcoat with a high collar.

Fig 4.19 (opposite): Sewn kilt, *c*.1790–1800

Lain flat, it is easier to appreciate the irregular construction of this early tailored kilt. Unlike later examples in the museum's collection, the grid of the tartan sett has not been artfully manipulated when forming the sewn pleats. Note the two sets of silk ribbon ties, which would fasten the kilt closed at the hip and above the knee to create the characteristic conical shape.

the garment became known as a *fèileadh beag* – meaning little or small kilt. It can be regarded as the forerunner of the contemporary kilt, still habitually worn as part of formal Highland dress today. As an early refinement in the history of Highland dress, the innovation and popular adoption of the sewn kilt was an indication of more radical changes to come.

A rare example of this new tailored approach to kilt-making and wearing was acquired by National Museums Scotland in 1988 and forms part of a Highland dress costume thought to date to *c*.1790–1800 [4.17].[14] When it first entered the collection, curators ascribed a date of *c*.1820. However, there are numerous material details about the outfit which suggest a revised periodisation is required. The exaggerated height of the turned down, pointed collar, the snugly-fitting sleeves, scallop-edged pockets and the curved cut away of the coat are all strongly reminiscent of 1790s fashion, when elite male clothing began to make the transition towards a more form-fitting, athletic style of suit.[15] There is also the question of identifying the tartan from which the outfit is made; a busy pattern, composed of red, green, black, yellow and azure, it belongs to a group of variations which originated in the 1790s. The first reference to it can be found in an order placed by Mr Kidd with Messrs Wilson of Bannockburn for tartan destined to clothe slaves on his West Indian plantation. Variations of the sett would be produced by the firm for decades to come, as numbered patterns, under the customer name 'Kidd', under the patriotic name 'Caledonia', and under the clan name 'Macpherson' [3.6].[16]

The way that the tartan has been employed to construct both the coat and the kilt does not reflect the characteristic precision and creativity that had become standard practice in Highland dress tailoring by 1820, as discussed above. This is especially noticeable when examining the dressed figure from behind, which evidences a lack of balance and symmetry in how the tartan has been cut, pieced and pleated [4.18]. The collar and the sleeves of the coat demonstrate a distinct disinterest in pattern matching, echoing the style and composition of other tartan outfits known to have been made and worn in the second half of the eighteenth century, such as Sir John Hynde Cotton's irregularly pieced trews.[17]

The first tailored kilts were typically constructed from a single length of hard worsted tartan, with sewn pleats at the rear and two plain sides that folded around the lower half of the body, one resting atop the other [4.19]. As is still the case today, the kilt was not hemmed but relied instead upon the selvedge of the cloth to create a tidy appearance at the knee. Any raw edges, such as where the tartan length had been cut from the loom, were turned and stitched to prevent fraying. The addition of a soft cotton waistband, as can be seen in this example, helped to reinforce the shape created by the layered folds, while also accommodating the weight of the fabric as it hung from the body. To maintain the conical profile of the kilt, the wearer would have tucked the folded layers high up beneath a long, fastened waist-

4.17

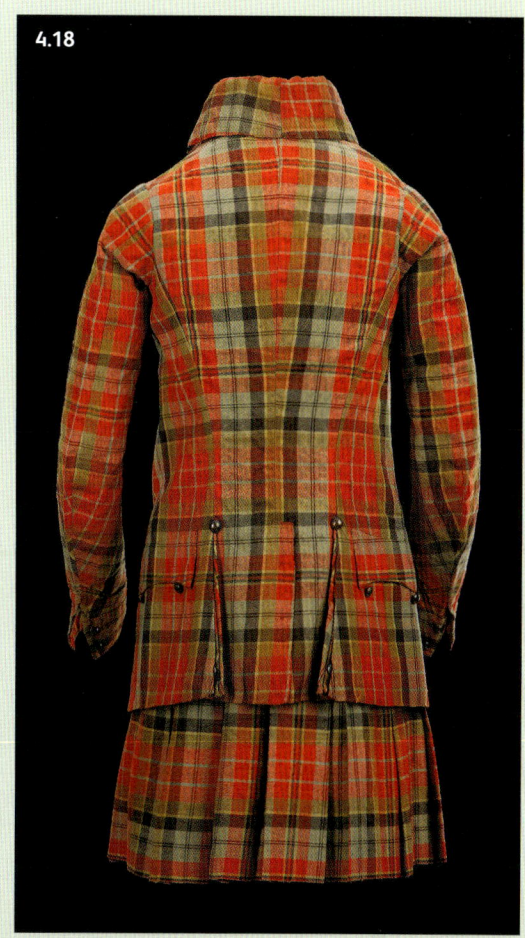

4.18

4.19

coat. Two sets of silk ribbon ties, positioned at the hip and thigh, prevented the kilt from slipping down or becoming undone. Other examples of early sewn kilts incorporate buttons at the waistline to give additional stability. However, there is no evidence to suggest that this particular kilt ever carried an internal fastening. A further indication that this kilt hails from the earlier side of the Highland dress revival is the style of pleating at the rear. As can be more easily appreciated when laying the garment flat, it is evident that there is no rhyme nor reason to how the tartan has been gathered and stitched. The size of the pleats are not equal, and the tartan pattern has not been pleated to sett or to stripe, as became common practice in the early decades of the nineteenth century.[18]

Sewing the kilt into a predetermined shape made it easier for tailors to replicate and refine it, while also bringing the garment further in line with the existing conventions of British menswear. As pleating styles gradually grew more regimented, the internal construction of the little kilt began to echo the practical benefits exhibited in modern breeches and pantaloons. Convenient fob pockets were sewn into carefully shaped waistbands and sets of buttons were positioned at the front and rear to accommodate the use of braces [4.20]. Although ribbon ties were retained as fastenings, their function – much like the silk rosettes sewn at regular increments to the front fold of the garment – was largely decorative [4.21]. These stylistic and practical adjustments arguably ensured the survival of the kilt within the ever-evolving world of fashionable dress.

By fixing the pleats in place with the application of needle and thread, the versatile and voluminous nature of the traditional *feileadh mòr* was lost. However, makers soon developed a tailored alternative to act as a complement to the sewn kilt, should the wearer desire it as an option. Designed to be worn in seamless conjunction with the *fèileadh beag*, the tailored plaid was shaped and sewn to replicate the cascade of fabric from shoulder to waist that had so distinguished the traditional belted plaid of the eighteenth century. James Logan's description of this sartorial novelty in *The Scottish Gaël* (1831) notes that this fresh interpretation of the belted plaid was 'more convenient, as well as better adapted to the altered state of society'. In his account of how to don the 'modern belted plaid', he explained the relationship between the two halves:

> *where, formerly, the lower and upper parts of the garb were attached, they are now separated, the lower part* [the little kilt] *having the folds fixed by sewing, and being often worn without the other appendages. The plaid is fastened round the body and pended from the shoulder, being, in like manner, made up by the tailor to imitate the ancient form. The loose end is represented by a small triangular piece of cloth suspended from the right side, where the end of the breacan* [plaid] *was tucked under the belt.*[19]

Figs 4.20 and 4.21 (opposite, above and below): Constructing a sewn kilt

Examining this kilt of Mackintosh hard tartan both inside (above) and out (below), we can see how the basic shape of the kilt has been formed around a structured waistband, of the type commonly observed in men's breeches and pantaloons of the era. Note the incorporation of a white cotton fob pocket, convenient for carrying a watch. This hybridised approach to kilt making combined antiquated style with progressive tailoring methods, seeking to strike an aesthetically pleasing balance between old and new modes of fashionable dress.

National Museums Scotland has several examples of the Georgian tailored plaid within its stores. While it is often the case that accessory garments are collected without the beneficial context of a full outfit, the museum is lucky to possess three tailored plaids with their corresponding costumes, all dating from the first quarter of the nineteenth century.[20] In comparing the individual construction of each piece, it is plain that tailored plaids of this period did not necessarily conform to a standard shape, size or mode of embellishment. Despite Logan's exacting description, all three iterations are materially quite different. Each one has been carefully made with a vision of how the sewn gathers and folds should interact with the rest of the costume. Creating the illusion of a full belted plaid was evidently a bespoke process, befitting the experimental nature of British tailoring during this period [4.22–4.30].

Figs 4.22 (this page) and 4.23 (opposite): Kilt suit with a tailored plaid, *c*.1820

Purchased in 1961, this suit entered the collection of the National Museum of Antiquities of Scotland with no biographical information regarding its former owner. It is a fine example of the revivalist style of Highland dress. All three elements of the suit – coat, kilt and tailored plaid – are made from Mackintosh hard tartan. Each piece has been carefully cut and constructed to allow for pattern matching between overlapping garments. Note how the triangular tab of the tailored plaid interacts with the front apron of the kilt.

Figs 4.24 (this page) and 4.25 (opposite): Kilt suit with a tailored plaid, belonging to Malcolm McCallum, *c*.1822

Malcolm McCallum was one of twenty pipers from Glenlyon who travelled to Edinburgh in August 1822 to perform before George IV, in celebration of the monarch's landing at Leith. The coat and kilt are of Drummond tartan, while the tailored plaid has been constructed using the Robertson sett. Both clans have traditional ties to Perthshire, as well as histories of affiliation with the Jacobite cause. Originally purchased by the Royal Scottish Museum in 1915, the suit was transferred to the National Museum of Antiquaries of Scotland in 1977 to reflect its status as a textile object representative of 'national' culture.

Figs 4.26 and 4.27: Creating the illusion

The Mackintosh plaid (above) and the Robertson plaid (below) have been tailored and styled in vastly different ways. However, they each achieve the same visual effect when tied about the waist and pinned up onto the shoulder. Both garments provide a convincing illusion of an 18th-century belted plaid girded about the hips and bulging at the back, yet they have been cut and constructed according to the individual taste and ability of the maker.

Figs 4.28 and 4.29: Kilt suit with a tailored plaid, *c*.1820–30

This suit of Murray of Atholl tartan was purchased by National Museums Scotland from a sale at Fingask Castle, Perthshire, in 1993. The outfit probably belonged to Sir Patrick Murray Threipland, 5th Baronet (1800–82). Threipland was made a Captain of the Royal Perthshire Militia in 1825, which may account for the overt military styling of the tartan coat with its double-breasted front and profusion of domed white metal buttons. As with the previous two outfits, note how the tails of the coat have been tucked up inside the folds of the tailored plaid to create more volume.

Fig. 4.30: The option of a full plaid

Tailored plaids were not made to provide warmth, but to mimic the appearance of a full plaid without the prohibitive weight of gathered yardage. The suit of Murray of Atholl tartan has been made with both a light tailored plaid and a full fringed plaid, allowing the wearer flexibility when dressing.

HIGHLAND STYLE

Transforming the arisaid

On 20 December 1832, Sarah Justina Davidson of Tulloch married Ewen Macpherson of Cluny, 14th Chief of Clan Macpherson, at St George's, Hanover Square, in Mayfair. It was a small ceremony, followed by a celebratory breakfast attended by close friends and family members. The party was hosted at the house of the bride's brother, Henry, who lived just a short distance from the parish church in Berkeley Square. Afterwards, as reported by a journalist for the *Morning Post*, the couple embarked on their wedding journey to the fashionable resort town of Leamington Spa.[21] The following June, husband and wife took up residence at Cluny Castle in Badenoch, where they were welcomed by a deputation of kinsmen and tenantry in Highland dress, accompanied by pipers playing 'The Macpherson's Gathering'.[22] At the time of their arrival, Sarah was six months pregnant with their first child, Duncan, who would be born on 9 October 1833. The announcement of the birth referred to Sarah as wife of the Chief of Clan Chattan, a not so subtle nod towards the long-contested nature of that title between the Macphersons and Mackintoshes, an ancient dispute inherited by her new husband on the death of his father in 1817.[23]

National Museums Scotland possesses two gowns from this early period of Sarah's married life, donated by a family member to the Royal Scottish Museum in 1934.[24] The first is a high-waisted gown of white watered silk with puff sleeves, worn by Sarah on her wedding day in London. In contrast to this elegantly simple silhouette, the second gown is a riotous interplay of colour and exaggerated shaping. Believed to have formed part of her *trousseau* – the collection of clothing and moveable goods traditionally brought into the marriage by a wife – the gown is made from a vivid silk tartan, trimmed with a profusion of lace and finely worked embroidery [4.31]. A detachable belt has been introduced beneath the bust to give the appearance of a high, nipped-in waist, a trick of proportion further accentuated by the broad neckline of the bodice and capaciousness of the sleeves. The hem of the garment is padded, the additional weight enabling the skirt to keep its distinctive bell profile when the wearer walked or danced. The construction and style of this second gown is characteristic of the influence of historical romanticism on women's fashions during the 1820s–30s, but with a distinctly Scottish twist.[25]

Overwhelmingly regarded as a movement driven by the consumer habits of men, it is important to recognise that women also played a role in the advancement of Highland style within Georgian and early Victorian society. The silk thread embroidery that adorns both the skirt and the belt of Sarah's gown is a reference to red whortleberry, a clan plant badge with significance to both the Davidsons and the Macphersons as members of the Clan Chattan association.[26] The tartan sett used in the gown may also be regarded as a form of familial heraldry. By the 1830s, this pattern was

Fig. 4.31 (opposite): Silk tartan trousseau, 1832

Sarah Justina Davidson was born in 1812, the youngest daughter of Caroline Elizabeth Difell and Henry Davidson, 3rd Laird of Tulloch. When she married Ewen Macpherson of Cluny in 1832, this silk tartan gown formed part of her wedding trousseau.

being produced by Messrs Wilson of Bannockburn under the name 'MacPherson, Dress'.[27] Although it is unclear whether the silk used in Sarah's trousseau was the product of Wilsons' looms or those of London or France, the reasons for its inclusion in the gown are more transparent. In commissioning the dress – coded with the iconography of her clan – Sarah was celebrating her acquired identity as a Macpherson and emphasising her new social position as wife of the Chief. Garments such as this offer a glimpse into how upper-class Highland women engaged directly with the revival of Highland dress culture in the first half of the nineteenth century, imbuing the seeming frivolities of fashion with their own personal sensibilities.

There are many reasons why historical textiles and dress represent a specialised field within the museum world, and why certain things tend to survive where others do not. The fine or unusual clothing of the upperclasses has a better chance of enduring the passage of time than the everyday dress of the poor. Prior to their entry into a collection, aristocratic dress would typically have been cared for by a servant, whose job included periodically mending, storing, cleaning and occasionally refashioning the expensive wardrobes of their employers. The survival and excellent condition of Sarah's *trousseau* suggests that it was well looked after, from its first use in 1832 to its donation to the Royal Scottish Museum in 1934. Wedding clothes are considered among the most precious of family heirlooms and are often carefully preserved by their owners, passed down between generations.[28] The fact that the luxurious textiles used to make the tartan gown were never harvested to fashion something new, testifies to the emotional place it occupied within Sarah's home and thoughts.

Whereas the revivalist style of Highland dress costume is visually, materially and textually well-defined for the male wearer, the picture is harder to draw for women of the era. Rarities, like Sarah's tartan *trousseau*, suggest that women also sought to combine modern lines with antique ideals in the hopes of creating a historically resonant costume. In a similar fashion to male wearers, women would look to iconic articles plucked from traditional Highland dress cultures of the past as inspiration for the dress of the present.

The dress of eighteenth-century Highland women has not received as much scholarly attention as that of Highland men. However, if a particular garment can be said to have characterised women's dress in the region, then the arisaid would emerge as a likely candidate [4.32]. Much like the belted plaid favoured in male Highland dress, arisaids were an extremely versatile piece of clothing. It was reserved for smart or occasional wear, such as attendance at church or for social visits. Typically composed of two lengths of heavy plaiding material joined by a central seam, the wearer could comfortably enclose themselves within its ample folds and even draw it up over the head for additional warmth and privacy. When not employed as outerwear, such pieces could also act as a form of household plenishing, the large amount of fabric used to construct them easily doubling as a blanket or a bed cover. Anita Quye and Hugh Cheape have observed that this secondary function likely ensured the preservation of such garments once they had fallen out of common use, their material quality and utility guaranteeing their absorption into the workings of the domestic space.²⁹ That many surviving arisaids are marked with the initials of erstwhile owners is an indication of their intrinsic value, both as serviceable objects and as family heirlooms [4.33a,b].

By the closing decades of the eighteenth century, the arisaid had become less favoured by Highland gentlewomen. However, its lingering

Figs 4.32 and 4.33a,b: Arisaid

A late 18th-century barred plaid or arisaid, from Melrose, Gamrie, Banffshire. Surviving arisaids are seldom brightly coloured, often combining a plain white or cream ground with alternating bars of red, yellow and blue. This example is marked with the stitched initials of its former owner, 'I B'.

Fig. 4.34: *Woman Sketching in a Landscape*, by Barthélemy Vieillevoye (1798–1855), c.1830, oil on canvas

Belgian artist Vieillevoye is noted for his accurate depictions of fashionable hairstyles and clothing. The prominence of the Royal Stewart plaid in his painting of a young woman indicates the growing popularity of such tartan mantles in European womenswear during the early 19th century. Regarded as practical and stylish accessories, fringed plaids were favoured for outdoor leisure pursuits, such as recreational walking, painting and sketching. The identity of the sitter is unknown. However, the landscape around her is thought to be a rural location near the city of Liège, where Vieillevoye lived and worked from 1834 until his death in 1855.

(Acquired by The Clark Art Institute, 1982.60)

sartorial influence can be observed in the rising popularity of fine worsted plaids, silk tartan scarves and fringed tartan mantles in the fashionable dress of middling and upper-class women, both within Scotland itself and the world beyond [4.34].[30]

Fashion follows soldiers

Patriotic styles were a recurrent theme within European dress culture throughout the eighteenth and nineteenth centuries, especially during periods of open hostility between nations.[31] By the terms of the Dress Act of 1746, Scottish soldiers serving in the British army had been given explicit permission to retain aspects of Highland dress as part of their regimental uniforms. This would prove to be a significant exemption, as it ensured the martial qualities of the costume could only be employed *en masse* when worn by those contracted to serve in the interests of the state. Military service during the second half of the eighteenth century has often been cited as a major contributing factor in the rehabilitation of Highlanders in the public imagination following the last Jacobite Rising. Over the second half of the eighteenth century, the military interpretation of Highland costume became intimately tied to the processes of British commercialism and imperial expansion [4.35]. With the glorification of Scottish soldiers in British popular culture, civilian costume reacted accordingly. In times of conflict, the individuals who wore that distinctive garb became celebrated icons of a nation at war, and their uniforms a pattern card for milliners to follow.[32]

Writing to tartan manufacturers Messrs Wilson of Bannockburn in April 1810, Dornoch merchant William Munro asked the firm to send him two pieces of 42nd regimental tartan, as worn by the soldiers of the Black Watch. He asked that the cloth be 'very good' quality, 'fit for Gentlemens dresses'. In addition to the 42nd pattern, Munro asked Wilsons to send him an array of tartan samples that might appeal to his regular customers. Although he had been in business for upwards of seven years, Munro had never 'done anything in the Tartan Line' and was anxious for guidance on what would suit:

> … as our local militia are to be dressed in the Highland Garb and of course a number of our high and low Classes will follow the same example, I would wish to keep a few [patterns] for that purpose and as I am unacquaint[ed] with your prices and the patterns that might answer best I therefore wish if you would take the trouble to send in the parcel swatches of all your Tartans […] with their prices fixed to each and at same time Numbered so that I can order an assembly.[33]

Exchanges such as these were reflected in the fabrication of pseudo-military garments, with explicitly regimental materials repurposed into the dress of non-combatants as a form of patriotic display. An example of this approach can be seen in a coat and kilt of Cameron of Erracht tartan, once belonging to artist William Skeoch Cumming and donated to the Scottish Naval and Military Museum in 1930. Both garments are thought to date to the first quarter of the nineteenth century [4.36]. The Cameron of Erracht sett was first used by the 79th Regiment of Foot (Cameron Highlanders), a regiment raised by Sir Alan Cameron of Erracht in 1793. However, the cut of these two garments and the light colourway of the tartan itself suggest that these are a civilian interpretation on military style.[34]

Fig. 4.35: *Officer of a Grenadier Company in a Highland Regiment*, unknown artist, unknown date, oil on canvas

By the end of the 18th century, around sixty Highland regiments had been raised by the Crown. The equipage of these Highland soldiers referenced the traditional martial culture of clan society, encompassing dress and weaponry. Painted around 1778, this portrait exemplifies the style of military Highland dress uniform worn during the late 18th century. The kilt and plaid of Black Watch tartan worn by the sitter appears alongside a sporran, basket-hilted broadsword and the characteristic red coat of British infantry. The yellow facings and silver detailing of the coat denote regimental affiliation and rank.

It was not only civilian menswear that echoed the qualities of regimental dress. Following the Battle of Waterloo in 1815, the city of Paris was occupied by allied forces and the distinguishing silhouette of the Highland regiments quickly emerged as an object of fascination among the French citizenry. Their costume was deemed both exotic and risqué by spectators, particularly the kilt which exposed the naked legs – and, if the ensuing deluge of satirical prints was to be believed, the naked posterior – of military men to the curious gaze of local women [4.37].[35]

This clash of cultures in the public space came to express itself in the execution of voguish clothing.[36] That summer, the *Gazette de France* informed its readers that the ladies of Paris had developed 'a sudden taste' for Highland uniform and the pages of fashionable periodicals were fast becoming populated by plates, detailing 'complete suits of female dresses *a l'Ecossaise*'. Among these was a head-to-toe ensemble, reportedly worn to the opera in August. It consisted of a red spencer and a short petticoat of tartan taffeta, accessorised by a pair of red and white diced hose and 'a black hat adorned with red feathers, and tied under the chin with a tartan ribband'.[37] While the spencer and petticoat were blatant homages to the scarlet regimental coatee and kilt, the distinctive headgear was the most obvious sartorial reference to the

Fig. 4.36: Jacket and kilt, *c.*1820

Originally a regimental sett worn by the 79th Cameron Highlanders, the Cameron of Erracht tartan transitioned into civilian use during the early 19th century. Perusal of the Messrs Wilson of Bannockburn business archive at National Museums Scotland reveals numerous instances of regimental setts being purchased for everyday civilian wear, especially during or in the wake of war.

Fig. 4.37: *Les Écossais à Paris ou La Curiosité des Femmes*

This satirical print was one of many published in Paris during the allied occupation of France following the Battle of Waterloo. Artists were drawn to the unusual appearance of the Highland soldier and often dwelled on the comedic potential of the kilt.

equipage of the occupying forces, echoing the tall, plumed bonnets worn by Highland soldiers when on duty.

The fashionable emulation of Scottish military headgear can also be observed in the pages of British periodicals of the period. If we compare an early nineteenth-century forage cap with a fashion plate published in *Ackermann's Repository of Arts* in 1817 [4.38], it is obvious that the intricate latticework of black and blue ribbons that trim the model's 'Glengary cap' are inspired by the characteristic diced band of a Scottish soldier's bonnet [4.39]. This particular creation was credited to London milliner 'Miss McDonald of 29, Great Russel-street, Bedford-square', and is typical of women's fashion *à la militaire*.[38]

With the advent of the French Revolutionary and Napoleonic Wars, many upper-class women in Britain began to employ fashionable dress as a medium to express their support for relations involved in the fighting.[39] Jane Maxwell, Duchess of Gordon, is often credited as the first woman to introduce silk tartan into the wardrobes of London high society during this period, in an effort to champion the military ambitions of her husband, the Duke of Gordon, and her son, the Marquis of Huntly. The Duchess's valet, Matthias d'Amour, recorded in his memoirs that his mistress had appeared at the Queen's Drawing Room in 1792, arrayed in an abundance of silk tartan woven for her in Spitalfields. The stunt was widely reported, earning her the moniker of the 'Tartan Belle' [4.40]. According to d'Amour, the demand for silk tartan was soon so high in the capital that lengths of unfinished plaid were cut straight from the loom to fulfil the mounting orders. 'At last the tartan influenza reached even Paris,' he recalled, 'and the Duchess had the gratification of knowing that she was the leader of fashion for London and the French metropolis.'[40] Her daughter Charlotte, Duchess of Richmond, engaged in similar spectacles at the height of the Napoleonic Wars. In May 1808, she accompanied her husband as he reviewed the Argyllshire Highlanders at Phoenix Park in Dublin, dressed in a Highland bonnet and tartan plaid in deference to the soldiers before her. It was reported by the *Morning Chronicle*, 'never did her Grace look more truly elegant than she did in the national dress of her country'.[41]

Although such demonstrations of sartorial patriotism were often heartfelt, they could also reflect the transitory nature of wartime fame. When Admiral Adam Duncan led the British navy to victory at the Battle of Camperdown in October 1797, ladies who attended a celebratory subscription ball in Windsor adopted tartan turbans in recognition of his birthplace. They adorned them with white satin ribbons, decorated with an anchor and the motto 'Admiral Duncan, and the Navy' in gold letters.[42] Less than a year later, the *Hampshire Chronicle* informed its readers that Duncan's celebrity had been eclipsed by that of Admiral Horatio Nelson, following the defeat of the French at the Battle of Aboukir Bay: 'Our Ladies will dress themselves *a l'Egytienne*. We shall have the *Mummy Shroud*

Fig. 4.38 (above): *The Glengary Habit,* 1817

This plate was published in *Ackermann's Repository of Arts* in September 1817. The title is a direct reference to the diced glengarry, a form of military headgear that first appeared in the early 19th century. Her spencer is also reminiscent of regimental attire, with its frogged detailing and shoulder wings.

Fig. 4.39 (above, right): Forage cap

The diced band of this knitted and felted undress bonnet is characteristic of those worn by Highland regiments during the Napoleonic Wars. The foundational red and white check could also incorporate green, blue or yellow, depending on the regiment for which it was made. Edged with black silk ribbon, traces of feathers found during conservation suggest it once had a plume, secured by a ribbon cockade.

Fig. 4.40 (above): *A Tartan Belle of 1792,* by Isaac Cruikshank (1764–1811), 1792, hand-coloured etching on paper

Jane Maxwell, Duchess of Gordon, was a leading figure in fashionable metropolitan society. She was a political hostess, agricultural reformer and a military recruiter for the 92nd Regiment of Foot (Gordon Highlanders). This satirical print by Isaac Cruikshank was published in London in 1792, immediately following the appearance of the Duchess in tartan at the Queen's Drawing Room.

(Courtesy of The Lewis Walpole Library, Yale University)

instead of the Tartan plaid, and the head *a la Crocodile* instead of the *Cockernony.*'[43]

Employing tartan as a symbol of support for Scots serving in the armed forces extended beyond the occasional dress of ordinary citizens and the aristocracy. It also appeared in ensembles adopted by members of the British royal family, no matter their age. In early November 1802, Colonel John MacLeod of Colbecks waited on the Prince of Wales at Carlton House. During his visit, he presented his wife and daughter to Princess Charlotte, the Royal Patroness of the Loyal MacLeod Fencibles. MacLeod had commanded the regiment from 1799 until it was disbanded in June 1802. As a compliment to their military guest, the six-year-old child was 'dressed for the occasion in the *Macleod tartan*'.[44] It was not unusual for children to be incorporated into such public displays of support for Scotland's naval and military men, with Highland dress styling frequently used to transform them into little emblems of the nation.

While young boys could not join the military effort as soldiers, they could certainly be dressed in imitation of them by their parents or guardians. Although elements of fantasy and play were undoubtedly at work in the commissioning of such costumes, it is also possible that adults chose to dress their children in this manner in anticipation of their future military careers.[45] This was certainly the case at the Caledonian Asylum in London, a charitable institution established by the Highland Society of London to care for Scottish children orphaned during the Napoleonic Wars. The administrators viewed the adoption of Highland dress by children at the asylum as essential not only to the development of their national spirit, but of their martial characters. It was also regarded as a viable strategy for securing regular and enthusiastic subscribers to their cause.

In a report prepared on the asylum's progress in 1807, the administrators recommended that in addition to receiving a steady education in all the usual accomplishments, 'the Boys might be taught Sword play, and Military Exercises; and the whole should be clothed uniformly in Tartan Jackets, Trouse, or Philabeg, and the Bonnet. The Girls also should be clothed in Tartan'.[46] When fundraising for the Caledonian Asylum in 1810, committee members proposed that 'two boys & two girls, children of Soldiers who had distinguished themselves in the Battle of Alexandria might be sought for & introduced in the Highland Garb, as Emblems of the Institution, to distribute the asylum cards to the Gentlemen assembled'.[47] In 1816, committee member James Hamilton wrote of his intention to continue the practice once the doors of the asylum were open to general admission, writing: 'When the children are placed in the Asylum, I intend to stand out for their being clothed in Tartan. It will keep up the national feeling, and in fact unless some national distinction in dress is preserved, they would pass for the Objects of any common parochial Charity.'[48]

Most children's Highland dress costumes held in museum collections today date from the 1840s or later, when Victorian interpretations on the garb entered the mainstream of British fashion and Scotch suits, and tartan frocks became commonplace articles in popular children's wear.[49] National Museums Scotland is fortunate to possess a rare, early example of Highland style clothing for children, which significantly pre-dates this trend: a little boy's kilt dress of Prince Charles Edward tartan, thought to have been made and worn *c*.1820. Judging by its proportions, it would have fit an infant, no older than three or four. Purchased from a private vendor in 1994, the original wearer of the costume is unknown.[50] However, despite a lack of biographical information about its erstwhile owner, by assessing the object and conducting contextual research we can catch a glimpse of how the physical needs of small children and the cultural preoccupations of adults converged within the Georgian revival of Highland dress [4.41].

Fig. 4.41: Kilt dress, *c.*1815–20

Infant boys were kept in skirts until they were old enough to make the transition to trousers. The cut and construction of this Georgian kilt dress incorporates many of the features found in the revivalist style of adult Highland dress costume, but with an eye towards the practical concerns of child-rearing in the early 19th century.

From at least the sixteenth century, the form and function of children's clothing tended to reflect the status of children in society as 'little adults'. Boys and girls were typically dressed in miniature raiment, the image of their fathers and mothers.[51] In surviving portraiture of the era, the standard silhouette of boy's Highland dress depicted on canvas tends to adhere to that worn by their elders. A useful example of this can be found in the famous double portrait of the Macdonald boys, painted by William Mosman in the mid-eighteenth century [4.42].

James Macdonald, the senior of the pair, leans his weight into the barrel of a handsome fowling piece, while his younger brother Alexander stands holding a golf club, preparing to swing at a black leather ball at his feet. These luxurious props relate to the sporting pursuits of the Scottish gentry during the eighteenth century, symbolising pastimes outside the purview of most ordinary folk: both hunting and golfing required the use of sophisticated and expensive equipment, as well as unfettered access to large areas of land. The Macdonald boys' Highland clothing is equally lavish and further denotes their high rank in society as the sons of Macdonald of Sleat. Both wear tartan coats and waistcoats, trimmed with gold braid and velvet: dark green for James and red for Alexander. The base colour of the tartan – a lustrous scarlet, achieved by the use of imported cochineal – is a clear indication of their wealth. Each carries a tan leather sporran at their waist, the purse decorated with knotted tassels and closed by way of a brass cantle. The netherwear differs between older and younger, but neither garment falls outside the definition of formal Highland dress during this period. James wears the tailored little kilt and Alexander the trews. Two blue bonnets with red headbands can also be observed, one cast to the ground and the other hooked onto the bow of a tree. When worn, such bonnets fit snugly over the crown of the head, secured at the nape by black ribbon ties. Scots bonnets like this were typically knitted in the round and felted, making for a warm and relatively waterproof head covering, well-suited to outdoor activities. They were also worn by men serving in Scottish regiments, illustrating the ebb and flow of sartorial influence between soldiers and civilians, even at this relatively early date.

Images of lower-class children sporting Highland costume, while rarer by comparison, evidence a similar interpretation on this theme of adult dress in miniature. The boy depicted in a sketch of camp followers in 1742, for example, wears the blue bonnet, the diced hose, and a plaid of green military tartan kilted at the waist. Given his small stature, the folds of the plaid fall well below his knees, while his scarlet coat marks him out as the son of a soldier, on whom his outfit would have been closely modelled [4.43].[52]

By the second half of the eighteenth century, new ideas about the meaning of childhood and the practicalities of child-rearing had begun to circulate in Europe. Influenced by publications such as Rousseau's *Emile* (1762),

Fig. 4.42 (below, left): *Sir James Macdonald (1741–66) and Sir Alexander Macdonald (1744/45–95)*, by William Mosman (*c*.1700–71), about 1749, oil on canvas

James and Alexander were the sons of Sir Alexander Macdonald of Sleat, a Highland chieftain with estates on the Isle of Skye. The Macdonalds of Sleat supported the Jacobites in the 1715 Rising, but in 1745 raised a militia in support of the British government. Despite the restrictions on wearing Highland dress imposed in the wake of the last Jacobite Rising of 1745–46, the boys were painted by Mosman in 1749 wearing formal Highland costumes. The work illustrates the selective nature of enforcement surrounding the ban, as well as the adult mode of Highland dress imposed upon children in the mid-18th century.

(National Galleries of Scotland)

Fig. 4.43 (above): *Scottish woman with child and dog*

This is one of a collection of twelve hand-coloured engravings of Scottish troops and camp followers, thought to have been made in 1742 during the War of Austrian Succession.

(*Prints, Drawings and Watercolours from the Anne S. K. Brown Military Collection.* Brown Digital Repository. Brown University Library)

Fig. 4.44: *Sir Evan John Murray-MacGregor, 2nd Baronet (1785–1841)*, by Sir Henry Raeburn (1756–1823), *c.*1797–99, oil on canvas

The tartan skeleton suit worn by Murray-MacGregor exemplifies the changing attitude towards Highland dress for children by the close of the 18th century. Young boys were no longer expected to dress as miniature adults, with new types of clothing tailored specifically to meet the needs of growing bodies. Although physically different in many ways, the revivalist style of Highland dress for children continued to reference the martial character of the garb.

(History and Art Collection / Alamy Stock Photo)

there were those who came to question what constituted appropriate attire for the growing child. The 1770s witnessed the advent of children's wear – a category of dress stylistically and functionally distinct from the dress of adults and tailored to meet the physical needs of the young. There was a stronger desire for simplicity and comfort, loose-fitting garments and lightweight materials.[53] Perhaps unsurprisingly, the revival of Highland dress culture was not immune from this pivotal shift in attitude. While it superficially retained the slightly stiff, embellished characteristics common to ceremonial dress, surviving visual culture appears to indicate experimentation in the fit and feel of the Highland dress outfits worn by children during this period. Sir Henry Raeburn's depiction of Major-General Sir Evan John Murray-MacGregor, 2nd Baronet (1785–1841), is a prime example of this [4.44]. Thought to have been painted at some point between 1797 and 1799, the portrait was produced when Murray-MacGregor was in early adolescence.

Opposed to the belted plaid, philabeg or trews characteristically worn as part of adult Highland dress at the turn of the nineteenth century, Raeburn's portrait of the young Murray-MacGregor shows his subject dressed in a tartan skeleton suit, paired with archetypical Highland dress accessories. The skeleton suit first appeared in the 1770s and was a form of transitional dress that bridged the stages of skirted infancy and breeched boyhood.[54] The skeleton suit usually consisted of two pieces: a pair of straight, ankle-length trousers and a short-fitted jacket, buttoned together at the child's waist. This arrangement gave the child a neat and tidy appearance yet allowed for a roomy seat, which wouldn't restrict the movement of the child's hips and legs while running or jumping in play. As in Raeburn's portrait, these suits were often worn over a wide-collared linen shirt edged with muslin, accompanied by plain stockings and flat black shoes.

Uniquely, the skeleton suit worn by Murray-MacGregor is faced with hard tartan – a complete departure from the simple, serviceable fabrics often observed in surviving skeleton suits of the period, the most common being nankeen or plain cotton. The use of tartan as the upper fabric transforms the skeleton suit worn by Murray-MacGregor into something altogether more formal, symbolic of the wearer's familial and national self. He also wears an ornate ostrich feather bonnet, with a white, red and green diced band, decorated with a black silk ribbon cockade. This is a significant addition to the child's ensemble, further cementing its ceremonial nature and elevating it from an example of tartan fashion into a hybridised form of Highland dress costume. The bonnet depicted in the portrait is a direct reference to the distinctive headwear worn by soldiers serving in Scottish regiments at the time [4.39]. Its inclusion here signifies the growing influence of military Highland dress uniforms on civilian styles in the Georgian era, as well as the expectation of military service placed on the shoulders of some sons. Murray-MacGregor would himself purchase a commission as an Ensign in the 81st Regiment of Foot in December 1801, at the age of 16.[55]

There is no definitive way of knowing whether the tartan skeleton suit worn by Murray-MacGregor in Raeburn's portrait was a real or an imagined garment. As is often the case with clothing worn by the very young, no tangible evidence of it has survived and only a painterly impression of the dress remains. Material rarities, such as the little boy's kilt dress in the collection of National Museums Scotland, allow us the unique opportunity to test assumptions gleaned from such representative visual sources against the physical evidence embodied by a contemporary garment. Like the tartan skeleton suit, the surviving kilt dress may be regarded as a piece of transitional costume, suited to the practical realities of infancy yet retaining a whimsical, quasi-ceremonial function [4.41].

The garment is composed of two distinct pieces – a bodice and a kilted skirt – which have been sewn together just above the natural waistline to create the full costume. The kilted skirt has been made using a single piece of fabric, divided into three distinct sections: a tightly pleated portion at the centre back, an interior fold, and an exterior fold. Wrapped over each other and tied using two sets of interior and exterior ribbons, the skirt falls into the characteristic shape of a tailored short kilt, with the pleats to the rear and a flat, straight line created at the front [4.45]. As well as the distinctive profile created by the internal construction of the kilt dress, which closely mirrors that of kilts made for grown men, details of external embellishment lend further weight to the assumption that whoever made the garment was consciously echoing the style of Highland dress worn by adults. The silk ribbon rosettes sewn to the edge of the apron, for instance, closely conform to a standard method of decoration frequently observed in surviving kilts of this period [4.23].

The horizontal *à la Hussar* braiding and domed metal buttons that embellish the bodice at front and back are typical military stylings which, at the height of the Napoleonic era, had come to strongly influence the fashionable dress of civilian men and women [4.46, 4.47]. The tartan used to construct the dress, meanwhile, is a small setting of the 'Prince Charles Edward'. The sett would undoubtedly have been chosen to complement the smaller dimensions required of children's clothing, yet its prominent place within the commercial culture of sentimental Jacobitism should not be overlooked.

Fig. 4.45 (above): Ribbon fastening

The little boy's kilt dress is fastened internally and externally using silk ribbon ties. These ties, as well as the cockades sewn to the front of the kilt dress, have been dyed to complement the red-based tartan from which the garment is made. These stylistic features echo the construction of kilts worn by adult men, manufactured during the same period.

Figs 4.46 and 4.47 (above and below): Buttons and braids

Responding to the high visibility of soldiers in Georgian society, fashions *à la militaire* combined elements of European military uniform with civilian clothing. Domed buttons and elaborate braiding were typical features of this trend, appearing across men's, women's and children's wear.

In terms of the outfit's physical comfort and practicality, a modern observer may assume that the kilt dress is the worst possible thing for a small child to wear. If one focuses only on surface detail, the dress looks quite stiff and restrictive. However, on handling the object, such an assumption is hard to uphold. At first glance the sleeves appear as if they would cut into the flesh of the shoulder. In fact, each sleeve can be loosened and lengthened very easily by the simple act of unlooping a button and unfurling the fabric. This would have allowed for greater flexibility of movement on the part of the child and aided the adult in slipping the dress up and down the boy's arms when changing. While the hard worsted tartan may look heavy and cumbersome, the fabric is actually quite lightweight and relatively smooth to the touch. The tight structure of the twill-weave cloth also makes for a durable and largely waterproof surface. Furthermore, the bodice – the element of the garment which would have sat closest to the body – is lined with brown linen. This would have prevented the wool from chafing against the child's delicate skin and helped to absorb sweat. When worn with a set of cotton or linen undergarments, this added layer of protection would have provided additional warmth to the child's core, while the unlined, lightweight tartan skirt would allow the child's legs ample room to move.

The material rarity of the kilt dress suggests the fashion was not widely adopted within Georgian society. However, there are numerous examples of its kind within the visual record of the period; many versions of the dress appear in fashion plates, prints and portraiture, spanning the 1810s and '20s. These representative sources give a fair indication of how the extant garment in the collection of National Museums Scotland was intended to be worn, by whom, and to what purpose.

A plate from *Ackermann's Repository of Arts* (September 1825) shows a proud mother leading her son forward by the hand [4.48]. The child's body is turned towards the viewer, showing every element of his costume to the best advantage, and imparting a sense of the garment's movement. His kilt dress is made from a green, potentially a military tartan; and like the surviving example at National Museums Scotland the front of the dress is embellished with what appear to be functional, domed metal buttons and decorative braiding on the sleeves and the bodice. The child's costume is accessorised with a shoulder plaid, a sporran, a pair of diced hose and a plumed bonnet. An edge

Fig. 4.48: *Morning Dress*, 1825

Periodicals offered guidance on the fashions favoured by upper-class women, drawing on styles observed in London and Paris. Occasionally these publications reference modish clothing intended for children. This plate, printed in *Ackermann's Repository of Arts* in September 1825, depicts a small boy in a kilt dress walking alongside a woman wearing white muslin.

(Los Angeles Public Library Digital Collection / Ackermann's Repository)

Fig. 4.49: *John Dingwall Younger of Brucklay*, by Charles Turner (1774–1857) after James Holmes (1777–1860), 1819, mezzotint, stipple, and engraving on paper

The kilt dress worn by John Duff Dingwall is accessorised with miniature Highland dress accoutrements, echoing adult military uniform. The original portrait miniature by John Holmes was made in 1818, with Charles Turner's print appearing the following year.

(© The Trustees of the British Museum)

Fig. 4.50: *Augusta, Duchess of Cambridge* (1797–1889), *with Prince George* (1819–1904) *and Princess Augusta of Cambridge* (1822–1916), by Melchior Gommar Tieleman (1784–1864), 1823, oil on canvas

In this group portrait the infant royal is depicted wearing a kilt dress. It is made from Prince Charles Edward tartan. The pattern was named to take advantage of the growing popular interest in Jacobite history at the turn of the 19th century, and was among the most popular setts manufactured by the tartan weaving firm, Messrs Wilson of Bannockburn.

(Royal Collection Trust / Her Majesty Queen Elizabeth II 2022)

of white cotton can be observed protruding from the neckline of the bodice, betraying the presence of a cotton undergarment beneath the dress.[56]

Although the fashion plate shows a fictitious child, drawn to demonstrate the costume to makers and consumers, other sources illustrate how and when kilt dresses were worn by known individuals. The first is an engraving in the collection of The British Museum, published in London in December 1819 by the printer Charles Turner. Based on an original painting by the artist James Holmes, it depicts John Duff Dingwall of Brucklay Castle, Aberdeenshire, as an infant [4.49].[57] Born in 1815, Dingwall would have been around four years old when the portrait was made. As in the fashion plate, his tartan costume is accented by the addition of archetypal Highland dress accessories reminiscent of soldier's attire, such as a feathered bonnet and diced hose. An ornamental sporran is buttoned onto the front of the dress, at waist height, while the boy's fringed plaid is wrapped about him and secured at the shoulder by a ribbon tie. Beneath the portrait is the boy's biographical information, surmounted by a heraldic crest and motto. Combined with his distinctive mode of dress, the inscription underscores the wish of Dingwall's guardians to present him to the world as a patriotic Scot.

A further iteration of the kilt dress can be found in a group portrait of the Duchess of Cambridge and her two young children, Prince George and Princess Augusta. The children's father, Prince Adolphus, is also present, in the form of a bejewelled portrait miniature held aloft by his four-year-old son. The group portrait is attributed to Melchior Gommar Tieleman and is dated 1823, when the family was living in Hanover. The duchess wears a luxuriant red gown and matching turban, paired with what appears to be an Indian shawl. Perhaps meant as a complement to what dress historian Hilary Davidson has described as his mother's 'exoticised ensemble', Prince George is portrayed in the guise of a little Scottish soldier.[58] His richly-braided kilt dress – tailored from Prince Charles Edward tartan – is accessorised with diced hose and red ribbon garters. At his feet is a silk tartan bonnet, trimmed with a diced band, feather plume and black silk ribbon cockade [4.50]. If the use of the kilt dress in the engraving of John Duff Dingwall can be interpreted as a method of familial and national self-fashioning imposed on the young by the old, its appearance within this depiction of the Duchess of Cambridge and her children imparts a rather different message. The presence of the Indian shawl and the Scottish kilt within the visual presentation of members of the British royal family speaks to the cross-cultural bricolage that elite fashion had become by the early decades of the nineteenth century; this is indicative of the growing reliance of luxury consumption on the material gains born of colonial expansion in the Georgian era. This state of affairs is neatly articulated by a passage printed in *The Lady's Monthly Museum*, published in 1812:

> … *now that the couturières have availed themselves of the Grecian costume, the true standard of taste; now that they have had recourse to the artist and the antiquary, who have not disdained to render their assistance, what elegance has appeared! Unconfined even to the statues of antiquity, the genius of dress roves in endless variety; she steals her hues from the rainbow, and the whole habitable world is ransacked for bodily adornment. The wool of Cachimere, the turban of the east, and the plaid of the north, lend their assistance, while the Turk, the Pole, and the Indian, lay their treasures at the feet of the fair.*[59]

Fancy dress

Fig. 4.51 (above, left): Silk tartan banyan

First worn in the mid- to late 18th century, this silk tartan banyan likely had a second life in the 19th century as a piece of fancy dress costume.

Fig. 4.52 (right): Alterations

Originally loose and flowing, the back of this silk tartan banyan has been refashioned to create the structured tails of a frockcoat.

One of the more unusual garments in the fashion and textile collection at National Museums Scotland is a silk tartan banyan, dating to the middle decades of the eighteenth century [4.51].[60] Banyans were commodious housecoats for men, inspired by the Japanese kimono. They first entered European fashion in the late seventeenth century, as a result of cross-cultural exchange born of increased global trade. Loose and long, these comfortable gowns were worn by gentlemen during their leisure time at home and were typically made from soft, patterned fabrics of the highest quality. To own one was a declaration of a man's wealth and social status, suited to a life free of physical toil.[61] Once belonging to the Hays of Yester in East Lothian, at some point during the nineteenth century this particular banyan was reworked to more closely resemble the formal cut of a gentleman's frockcoat. To achieve this metamorphosis, the excess fabric that distinguished the relaxed nature of the banyan was drawn back and away from the hips and formed into rigid coat tails. The change has been poorly made, with one side hanging differently to the other; this is evidence of inexpert hands, trying to direct old fabric into a fresh configuration [4.52]. The purpose of such an intrusive, hasty change is most readily explained by the nineteenth-century vogue of turning hand-me-down clothing into pieces of fancy dress costume, for use in home theatricals and masquerades.

It is fairly common for garments in museum collections to show signs of alteration. In the same way that areas of mending and staining give an impression of the body – or bodies – that once filled a piece of clothing, evidence of remaking is evidence of use. Distinct from the functional necessities of darning, patching and the re-stitching of loose seams, alterations represent the start of a new chapter in the life of a garment. In the case of the silk tartan banyan, it meant its transformation from a male luxury good associated with the informalities of the aristocratic domestic space, into a highly structured piece of occasional costume that enabled its wearer to assume a different identity.

Georgian fancy dress culture was characterised by the meeting of old and new; recycled garments and treasured family heirlooms frequently appeared alongside elaborate costumes, designed and executed by specialist outfitters in Britain's cosmopolitan centres. The genteel masques and fancy balls of the late eighteenth and early nineteenth centuries provided a world beyond the confines of the stage within which wearers could explore the imaginative potential of historical recreation, entertaining an idealised vision of the past as a reaction against the industrialised present. As a living tradition with a rich material legacy on which to draw, Highland dress fits neatly into this landscape of re-use, re-interpretation and conspicuous consumption.

Fancy variations on Highland dress were first introduced in the seventeenth century in the form of theatrical costume, such as that worn by comic actor and playwright John Lacy in the character of Sauney the Scott [4.53]. However, it was not until the late eighteenth century that the fancy style of Highland dress captured public attention as a fashionable pursuit outside the playhouse, most notably when the sons of George III appeared at elite masquerades in the patriotic guises of Highland soldiers in the 1780s and 1790s.[62] Such demonstrations of royal favour led to the swift rise of fancy balls as an avenue of charitable fundraising among the aristocracy, especially in Britain's urban centres. Encouraging one's peers to engage with laudable social causes was tempered by the spirited conviviality of dress-up.[63] The staging of such events by Highland clubs and societies during the early decades of the nineteenth century brought Highland dress more firmly within the sphere of fancy dress culture.

HIGHLAND STYLE IN GEORGIAN SOCIETY

Fig. 4.53: *John Lacy* (d.1681), by John Michael Wright (1617–94), *c.*1668–70, oil on canvas

Lacy was a star performer at the Theatre Royal in London during the 1660s. This unusual triple portrait, painted by John Michael Wright for Charles II, depicts Lacy occupying three of his most popular roles: Sauny the Scott, Monsieur Device and Parson Scruple. In the guise of Sauny, Lacy has adopted tartan trews as a sign of Highland gentility, with a voluminous plaid, a broad blue bonnet, and a large dirk and pistol.

(Royal Collection Trust / Her Majesty Queen Elizabeth II 2022)

On 30 January 1835, the Celtic Society hosted their first fancy ball at the Edinburgh assembly rooms on George Street. Advertising the event in the *Caledonian Mercury*, the club announced that all surplus proceeds from ticket sales would be 'devoted towards Educational Purposes in the Highlands, and encouragement of the Highland Schools, to which the funds and exertions of the Society are principally directed'.[64] In the aftermath of the event, commentators congratulated the organisers for rendering 'the amusements of fashion subservient to the great moral end of national improvement'.[65]

At a meeting of the Celtic Society held on 4 February 1835, it was revealed that the inaugural fancy ball had attracted 906 guests – 417 ladies and 489 gentlemen – with tickets selling at half a guinea and one guinea respectively. Despite the substantial level of patronage and goodwill that the event had generated among the Edinburgh *bon ton*, not everyone present was pleased with the direction the ball had taken. The chairman of the meeting, Macdonald of Staffa, announced that he had been disappointed to see several members of the Celtic Society 'wearing their Bonnets during the whole Evening – and it was his opinion that however proper or customary this might be in a meeting of the Chiefs with their clans in their own country[,] he did not think it was either etiquette or proper to do so in the company of Ladies[,] more especially in the company of our Southern friends'. While he did not wish to chastise or dampen the enthusiasm of his compatriots, he felt that the members of the Celtic Society should formally resolve 'that hence forward it shall not be considered as Etiquette for any member to wear his Bonnet in a room[,] especially in the Company of Ladies'. The motion was duly seconded.[66]

Staffa's preoccupation with formal Highland dress etiquette may seem overzealous, especially in the convivial setting of a fancy ball where guests were given *carte blanche* to exhibit their fantastical creations. However, his comments to the Celtic Society were made in the full knowledge that every detail of the event – from the identity of the guests and the minutiae of their dress, to the decoration of the rooms and the names of their suppliers – had been painstakingly reported in the pages of the popular press. In the wake of any elite social function, it was common practice for newspapers to publish a fulsome account to satisfy the curiosity of the general public, whose access to such events was strictly observational. If the event was deemed particularly significant or interesting, these accounts might be reprinted across numerous titles and circulated around the country.

On the day of the Celtic Society meeting, *The Scotsman* devoted an entire column to the costumes worn by attendees at the inaugural Celtic Fancy Ball, providing succinct accounts of each guest and their mode of dress. A plethora of ceremonial and fancy costumes were noted – not just Highland dress, but character costumes, professional attire, military uniform and the habits of other clubs, such as the Royal Company of Archers, the Six Foot Club, and the Caledonian Hunt. Meant to be informative and entertaining in nature, some entries carried judgements on the calibre and historical authenticity of the costumes worn. The costume of a clan chief, worn by Scottish author and politician Sir Thomas Dick Lauder, was deemed 'remarkably correct' by *The Scotsman*, while the suit of Highland dress worn by John Mackintosh was considered only 'very correct'. Staffa himself had been given one of the longest entries in the paper's list, with every aspect of his clothing and accoutrements specified in full:

> *Mr Macdonald of Staffa – In the complete Highland garb of his family tartan, bearing on his left shoulder an ancient Macdonald silver shield of great antiquity, with the accompanying implements of the Cross, of broad sword, dirk, pistols, purse, silver buckles and bonnet mounted with eagle quills as a Highland Chieftain, with a silver thistle surrounded by the mountain and bell heath.*[67]

Given that the Celtic Society of Edinburgh had spent over a decade building a reputation as the preservers and promoters of Highland dress culture in the city, it is not surprising that Staffa would want to ensure that members maintained rigid attention to detail in the face of such scrutiny.

At the same meeting, Staffa announced that the Duke of Gordon, then President of the Celtic Society, had suggested it was time for the organisation to commission a distinguishing emblem for members to wear at gatherings and at public events. It was decided a small committee should be formed to decide on the design and that members should submit specimens for their consideration. He then produced 'a very antient Button that had been put into his hands by Mr Alexander Macdonald', and exhibited it to those around him as an example of what was considered fitting.[68] The moment represents just one of many in the history of the Highland dress revival, when an artefact was brought forth as inspiration for the fashioning of contemporary style.

The fancy balls hosted by the Celtic Society soon became a hotly anticipated fixture of the Edinburgh social calendar, echoing the success of the Highland Society of London piping competitions of years before. Like other events of its ilk, the Celtic Fancy Ball was timed to coincide with the social season, when the Scottish capital was flush with fashionables in search of diversion. Guests attended wearing antique styles of national costume or dressed as historical figures, inspired by authentic illustrations from medieval manuscripts and the romanticised depictions of pastoral life found within the pages of European costume books. Others looked to the fictive pasts of historical novels and narrative poems, most notably to Sir Walter Scott's Jacobite chronicle *Waverley; or, 'Tis Sixty Years Since* (1814) and chivalric romance *Ivanhoe* (1819).[69]

A lithograph titled *Bal Celtique*, based on a painting by Charles Achille d'Hardivillier, depicts the reception area of the Edinburgh assembly rooms

HIGHLAND STYLE

Fig. 4.54: *Bal Celtique*, by Charles Achille d'Hardivillier (1795–1835), *c.*1836, lithograph

During the first half of the 19th century, romantic tastes increasingly found expression in Gothic art, architecture and literature inspired by medieval history. A new branch of fantasy Highland wear began to appear at society balls and pageants during this period, linking Highland culture to a chivalric interpretation of the medieval past.

(City of Edinburgh Council – Libraries / www.capitalcollections.org.uk)

on the night of the second Celtic Fancy Ball in 1836 [4.54]. The scene provides us with a record of the style of costume commonly adopted by ladies and gentlemen at such events. The popular enthusiasm for medieval historicism on display within the d'Hardivillier print is echoed in the cut and construction of two fancy Highland costumes from the collection at National Museums Scotland. The first is a dark blue silk velvet coat with silk ribbon trim, once belonging to Ranald George Macdonald of Clanranald. Intended to be worn with a matching blue velvet glengarry bonnet, decorated with gold bullion, eagle feather plume, and a red and white silk ribbon cockade, the coat's slashed sleeves and deep gauntlet cuffs are reminiscent of a late medieval doublet [4.55].[70] The second ensemble is a two-piece suit once owned by John Campbell, 2nd Marquess of Breadalbane, dated to *c.*1835–45 [4.56].[71] Both the kilt and jacket of Breadalbane's suit are immaculately tailored examples of fantasy Highland wear, made from a fine weaving of Black Watch silk tartan. In a similar manner to the slashed sleeve detail of the Clanranald coat, the cuffs, waist tabs and shoulder wings of the Breadalbane jacket have been given a rolling scallop edge, trimmed with black piping, as a nod to sixteenth- and seventeenth-century modes of aristocratic male dress. The ornamental sporran that accompanies the outfit is characteristic of the type of accessory commonly worn in fancy dress settings: the gold bullion ribbon and coiled wire tassels that sit against the soft pelt of the purse have been chosen to complement the lustrous shine of the silk used in the corresponding garments [4.57]. Together, these luxurious tones and textures would have combined upon the body to transform the wearer into a compelling spectacle, able to hold their own in a ballroom of similarly sparkling historical *tableaux*.

Fig. 4.55 (left): Doublet belonging to Ranald George Macdonald of Clanranald, *c*.1830–40

The Clanranald collection of Jacobite and family relics, donated to the National Museum of Antiquities of Scotland in 1944, contains a wide variety of Highland dress pieces. The style and quality of this medieval-inspired doublet indicates that Macdonald of Clanranald participated in the vogue for Highland fancy dress in the early decades of the 19th century.

Fig. 4.56 (left, below): Highland dress costume belonging to John Campbell, 2nd Marquess of Breadalbane, *c*.1835–45

This flamboyant kilt suit of Black Watch silk tartan is a rare example of Highland fantasy wear, of the type commonly seen at fancy dress balls and aristocratic fundraisers during the first half of the 19th century. Breadalbane was a notable patron of masquerade culture throughout this period, both as an attendee and host.

Fig. 4.57 (below): Fancy dress sporran, *c*.1835–45

The accessories worn as part of fancy dress were seldom practical. Made from a combination of soft brown fur, chamois leather, gold bullion ribbon and coiled wire, the primary function of this glittering sporran was to catch the eye.

Fig. 4.58: *Viscount Glenlyon as the Knight of the Gael, Followed by the Men of Athol*, by Charles Achille d'Hardivillier (1795–1835), c.1839, lithograph

On 30 August 1839, the Earl of Eglinton hosted a re-enactment of a medieval tournament at his castle in Ayrshire. The tournament was inspired by the chivalric ideals of the Gothic Revival, which drew on tales of honour and bravery from the middle ages. The knights who competed at the Eglinton Tournament, such as Viscount Glenlyon, were mostly drawn from the Scottish aristocracy. Competitors wore family heirlooms and antique or replica armour, decorated with heraldic crests.

When the Breadalbane suit was acquired by National Museums Scotland in 2018, it was thought that the costume may have been a special commission made to welcome Queen Victoria to Taymouth Castle during her first tour of the Highlands in September 1842. The royal visit was famously marked by displays of romanticised clan culture, which included a deputation of pipers, an honour guard, and a ball in the grand gothic hall. The monarch was impressed by the carefully choreographed spectacle put on by Breadalbane and the Perthshire gentry, writing in her journal that 'it seemed as if a great chieftain in olden feudal times was receiving his sovereign'.[72] While the occasion certainly warranted the creation of an immaculate costume, it should be noted Breadalbane was a prominent patron of historical fancy dress culture throughout the middle decades of the nineteenth century. He attended the famous re-enactment of a medieval tournament hosted by the Earl of Eglinton in August 1839 [4.58], was among the named patrons of the Celtic Fancy Ball in January 1841, and was invited by Queen Victoria and Prince Albert to their Plantagenet Ball at Buckingham Palace in May 1842, hosted in aid of the floundering silk-weavers of Spitalfields.[73] The style and quality of the outfit indicates that it could have been worn at any one of these events.

A host of specialist urban retailers stepped forward to meet the demand created by the annual Celtic Fancy Ball. These included the Edinburgh branch of Meyer and Mortimer, which frequently provided banners of clan tartan to decorate the walls and staircases of the assembly rooms, and the Albion Cloth Company, a gentlemen's outfitter based on George Street that produced many of the fancy dresses and military uniforms worn by those in attendance.[74] In addition to the costumes themselves, the Albion Cloth Company also retailed quality Highland dress accessories. Examples of these survive in the jewellery collections of National Museums Scotland, including a silver ring brooch thought to have been made in Edinburgh by silversmith Richard Jack in 1838 [4.59]. The design of the brooch echoes the form and functionality of older pieces then swelling the collections of antiquarians, notably in the style of engraving and the swivelling pin.[75] A notice placed by the Albion Cloth Company in *The Scotsman* in 1838, states that the shop was well stocked with accoutrements suited to 'the Garb of the Celtic Clans, from the plainest style to the most sumptuous'.[76]

Alongside the provision of new pieces, both organisers and guests sought to imbue the Celtic Fancy Ball with a sense of authenticity and grandeur by sourcing genuine historical artefacts to dress the venue and augment their costumes. This included the borrowing of weaponry from the Society of Antiquaries of Scotland, to transform the urban opulence of the assembly room into 'an ancient Highland baronial hall'. In 1836 it was reported:

Fig. 4.59: Silver ring brooch, c.1838

By the middle decades of the 19th century, the plaid brooch had become an integral aspect of male Highland dress culture. Earlier, such pieces had been favoured largely by women. Plaid brooches retained their basic form and function with the passage of time, though some were more highly decorative than others.

The walls were decorated with the arms and accoutrements of past ages, all tastefully grouped, and including, of course, the Highland pistol, dirk, claymore, and Lochaber axe, besides the skins of the wild animals of our mountains, which were interspersed amidst the arms as trophies of the chase. […] The toute ensemble of this design had really a most striking effect, and was well calculated to awaken the associations of the feudal ages and to conjure up the images of the mailed warriors of old, whose brawny limbs could wield those ponderous implements that would baffle the energies of our modern chivalry. We understand that the assortment of armour contained several relics of great historical interest, in particular several pieces which had served to mow down the gallant Highlanders on the field of Culloden, also the gun that shot the last bloodhound that traced the sons of Macgregor. Many of these were very handsomely leant for the occasion by the Antiquarian Society.[77]

Mention of the arrangement appears in the correspondence of the Society of Antiquaries of Scotland for the year 1841; in a brief note, Mr George Potts was granted permission to borrow two swords and shields from the museum 'as usual', the wording implying that the relationship between the museum and the organisers of the Celtic Fancy Ball was of long standing.[78]

Fancy dress culture provided a rich afterlife for Highland dress arte-

Fig. 4.60 (left): Refashioned Highland dress sword belonging to Sir Evan John Murray-MacGregor, c.1822

The fine sterling silver basket-hilt was added to this ancestral weapon in 1822. Decorated with the coat of arms and crest of the MacGregors, it is topped with a large faceted citrine pommel in the revivalist style.

Fig. 4.61 (right): *The Fancy Dress Ball*

This illustrative plate appeared in a professional tailoring manual compiled by Joseph Couts in Glasgow in 1848. At the time, few tradesmen's publications existed that included detailed instructions on how to tailor tartan for kilts and trews. Couts noted this dearth of knowledge in the manual's preface, citing the specialist nature of Highland dress outfitting as a bar to general understanding.

(S. P. Lohia Collection)

facts, not simply in the staging of events but also in the art and print culture that sprung up around them. A striking example of this can be found in the material refashioning and visual replication of a basket-hilted broadsword, once belonging to Sir Evan John Murray-MacGregor and now in the collection of National Museums Scotland [4.60]. A family heirloom of the MacGregors, the material make-up of the sword is a complex interplay of different eras: an inscription on the knuckle-guard of the blade claims that it was cut down from a sword wielded at the Battle of Glen Fruin in 1602, prior to it being carried by a MacGregor during the last Jacobite Rising of 1745–46. In 1822, it was remodelled in preparation for the visit of George IV to Edinburgh to incorporate a silver basket-hilt, beautifully decorated with the iconography of the clan.[79] It was worn by Sir Evan John Murray-MacGregor as part of his ceremonial costume, distinguishing his role as head of the Highland guard charged with protecting the crown jewels on their removal from Edinburgh Castle.[80]

The revival style of Highland costume and weaponry worn by Murray-MacGregor during the 1822 visit was captured in a portrait by George Watson; the image was then reproduced as an engraving by Henry Dawe and published in London in 1825. More than twenty years later, in 1848, Murray-MacGregor's distinctive profile was recycled yet again into the pages of a professional tailoring manual, *A Practical Guide for the Tailor's Cutting-Room*, by Joseph Couts. Both the sword and its owner appear in a coloured plate, illustrating the iconic style of Highland dress deemed appropriate by Couts for 'The Fancy Dress Ball' [4.61].[81] Through its various translations into the media of paint, print and composite illustration, the sword was transformed from a revived ancestral object into an instructive icon for the aesthetic guidance of professionals in the trade. As noted by the author in the preface:

> *With respect to the pictorial embellishments of this work, they speak for themselves. This is the first attempt which has been made to make art subservient to the purposes of a cutting-room show-card of fashions. And the Artist, while he has carefully delineated every seam, &c., of the garments of his figures, has, at the same time, succeeded in giving a series of life-like and characteristic sketches of society and manners.*[82]

Highland dress as inspiration

Referencing extant artefacts within historically themed art and literature was a common occurrence during the early decades of the nineteenth century. Inherited objects, held in the ancestral houses of the gentry and the collections of antiquarians, were frequently written into the fabric of historical novels or repurposed as props in historical genre paintings. In studying the surviving material culture of Highland dress of the era, it is important to interrogate this relationship between fiction and reality. When used as sources of inspiration, an artefact could come to embody assumptions about the past, or gain a provenance it had little claim to.

In 1979, the National Museum of Antiquities of Scotland was bequeathed a short tartan frock coat with red velvet facings, supposedly worn by Prince Charles Edward Stuart during the last Jacobite Rising of 1745–46 [4.62]. Often interpreted as a genuine Jacobite relic, there is some reason to believe that the tartan from which it is made is actually a sett known to have been produced by Messrs Wilson of Bannockburn in the 1830s, marketed as 'Culloden'. In reassessing the provenance of the object in light of this new information, the validity of its connection with the exiled Stuart heir became harder to substantiate.[83]

Prior to its accession into the national collection, the coat was at Hawthornden Castle in Midlothian, a property that had been in the hands of the Drummond family since the sixteenth century.[84] Aside from its appearance in the *Exhibition of the Royal House of Stuart* that took place at the New Gallery in London in 1889, the only reference to the Jacobite history of the coat can be found in the related publication *The Royal House of Stuart* (1890), accompanied by an illustrative lithograph plate from the artist William Gibb.[85] A preface to the work by fellow contributor, W. H. St John Hope, admits that the relics selected for inclusion in the exhibition

Fig. 4.62: The Hawthornden coat

Jacobite relics proliferated in the late Georgian era, particularly following the publication of the *Waverley* novels by Sir Walter Scott. Many of these objects had doubtful provenance. While this tartan coat may have belonged to Prince Charles Edward Stuart, the tartan cloth from which it is made appears to date from the early 19th century.

and memorial folio sometimes lacked credibility, but justified their inclusion by stressing that 'even in the cases where doubt may be reasonably entertained as to their connection with particular persons, their value as choice and characteristic examples of the handiwork of the times to which they severally belong cannot easily be overrated'.[86]

In 1834, painter William Simson exhibited a piece titled *The Pretender* at the Royal Scottish Academy. Though the finished work remains untraced, several line drawings and preparatory oil sketches made by Simson in 1833 have appeared at auction over the last twenty years.[87] These various works all feature the same model in the guise of Bonnie Prince Charlie, sporting a blue bonnet, white cockade, and a short tartan frock coat with red velvet facings. In terms of its cut and colouration, the painted garment bears a striking resemblance to the coat from the collection at Hawthornden Castle. This substantial similarity was further underscored by the discovery of a mezzotint made after Simson's original work by the Scottish engraver John Horsburgh, which was acquired for the national collection in 2020. The crispness of Horsburgh's mezzotint allows us to appreciate the detail missing in Simson's rough sketches. From the number and placement of the buttonholes to the grid and scale of the tartan sett, the coat worn by the model is a compelling match for the Hawthornden coat [4.63].[88] Further scrutiny of the print revealed another layer of intrigue. As well as the inclusion of the Hawthornden coat, the figure of the Prince appears to be holding the Clanranald sword, discussed in Chapter 2 [2.8].[89] The distinctive eagle pommel of the ornate hilt is clearly visible, protruding from the gloved hand of the model. It therefore appears that Simson had access to the relic sword when working on the original painting and that the coat was in fact a prop costume, commissioned for use in the artist's studio using a commercially available, historically resonant tartan.

Fig. 4.63: *Prince Charles Edward Reading a Despatch from Sir John Cope,* by John Horsburgh (1791–1869) after William Simson (1800–47), mid-19th century, mezzotint on paper

This engraving by John Horsburgh, made after an original painting by William Simson, further complicates the story of the Hawthornden coat. The model who is representing Prince Charles Edward Stuart carries the Clanranald sword, a Jacobite relic known to have been captured by the Duke of Cumberland in the aftermath of the Battle of Culloden in 1746. However, the model's attire – and that of his attendant – is comparatively modern. Seen referenced in this context, the Hawthornden coat can be read as a Georgian prop costume. Jacobite relics are powerful objects, often with complex and contested histories. While revisiting their provenance may ultimately change how they are perceived and interpreted within the museum world, new information does not dilute their importance. Rather, these newly defined objects can be used to tell a different – no less interesting – story.

Notes

1. NMS H.LC 83. *Sgian dubhs* became increasingly common during the Victorian period and are now an integral part of contemporary Highland dress culture. Later examples are usually silver mounted, feature carved handles of horn, antler, ivory or wood, and are set with gemstones or cut glass. Basket weave and knotwork embellishment, as well as clan and national iconographies (such as the thistle and St Andrew), are customary design elements.
2. Hollander 1994, 90.
3. Johnston 2016, 8.
4. NMS H.TTA 21 A–C.
5. NMS H.TTA 16 and NMS H.TTA 17.
6. NMS K.2002.950 A–B.
7. *The Sun* (18 August 1808), 3.
8. Logan 1831, vol. I, 245–46.
9. NMS K.2005.16.1–4.
10. Bennett 1980, 99.
11. NMS M.1960.14.
12. The series of engravings by Johann Sebastian Müller can be found under NMS M.1966.109–111; Montgomery 2020.
13. NMS M.1966.109.
14. NMS K.1988.49 A–B.
15. The *c*.1820 dating originally ascribed by curators may be explained by the length of the coat tails. Typically, men's tailored coats from *c*.1790–1800 have longer tails than NMS K.1988.49 A. However, there are other surviving tartan jackets – held outwith NMS – known to be of a mid- to late eighteenth-century date that also exhibit tails of a shorter length.
16. See registration notes for 'Kidd', *Scottish Register of Tartans*; Trevor-Roper 1983, 30; Scarlett 1990, 75–76, 137–39; MacDonald 2012, 25–26, 35.
17. NMS K.2005.16.2; Bennett 1980, 97–99.
18. Reid 2013, 27–29.
19. Logan 1831, vol. I, 245–46.
20. There are three complete suits of Highland dress in the collection which feature tailored plaids in the Georgian revival style. See: NMS H.TTA 20 A–C; NMS A.1915.212 A–F; NMS A.1993.60 A–D.
21. *Morning Post* (21 December 1832), 3.
22. Macpherson 1883, 13–14.
23. *Morning Post* (17 October 1833), 4.
24. Gowns owned by Sarah Justina Davidson of Tulloch on her marriage to Macpherson of Cluny in 1832: NMS A.1934.386 and NMS A.1934.387.
25. Bassett 2016.
26. Logan 1831, vol. I, 198.
27. My thanks to Peter MacDonald for sharing his research on this sett.
28. Ehrman 2014.
29. NMS H.SMA 2; Quye and Cheape 2008, 2.
30. Nenadic 2007, 153–54.
31. Kennedy Johnson 2009.
32. Allan and Carswell 2004; Myerly 1996, 149.
33. NMS M.1995.15.371.
34. NMS M.1930.134 and NMS M.1930.276; the sett commonly employed by the military was considerably darker by comparison to that seen in this coat and kilt, based on extant fabric samples of the era.
35. NMS M.1935.12.3.
36. Haynes 2018, 172–73.
37. *The Inverness Journal and Northern Advertiser* (11 August 1815), 4.
38. NMS H.RHI 92.18; NMS M.1935.212.1.
39. Davidson 2019, 232.
40. d'Amour and Rodgers 1836, 157–58.
41. *British Press* (25 May 1808), 4.
42. *Reading Mercury* (13 November 1797), 3.
43. *Hampshire Chronicle* (8 October 1798), 3.
44. *Morning Chronicle* (6 November 1802), 3.
45. Campbell 2015.
46. NLS Dep. 268/24 (Minute book, 15 March 1802–25 March 1808), 171.
47. NLS Dep. 268/25 (Minute book, 7 May 1808–10 December 1814), 82.
48. NLS Acc. 13156/23 (James Hamilton to David Stewart of Garth, 4 March 1816).
49. For examples of Victorian and Edwardian Highland dress for children, see in particular: NMS H.TTA 19 A–C; NMS K.1997.1034 A–E; NMS K.2005.28.1–14. See also: Rose, 2010.
50. NMS A.1994.1334. Although the wearer is unknown, the material quality of the garment is an indication of the child's elite status within Georgian society.
51. This is not to imply that people in the past did not recognise and accommodate different stages of growth (i.e. infancy, childhood, adolescence, adulthood), but that the social and cultural conditions of previous eras meant such stages were less noticeably distinct. The privileging of childhood, as we might recognise it today, arguably did not emerge in Western Europe until the long eighteenth century. See in particular: Foyster and Marten 2012; Ewing 1977, 22–37.
52. For discussion of the clothing of regimental dependants, see: Mills and Carswell 1998, 192–93.
53. See in particular: Ewing 1977; Rose 1989; Buck 1996.
54. Rose 1989, 52–53.
55. As posted in *The London Chronicle* (31 December 1801), 1.
56. Rose 1989, 41. When NMS A.1994.1334 was first displayed in the Museum of Scotland, the kilt dress was worn fastened over a reproduction cotton tunic and drawers.
57. The original portrait miniature on which Turner's

engraving is based recently resurfaced at auction. The range of watercolours employed by James Holmes in rendering the tartan on ivory suggests that the sett represented is the Prince Charles Edward. See: *Five Centuries: Furniture, Paintings & Works of Art*, Lot 261 (Lyon & Turnbull: 23 February 2022).
58. Davidson 2019, 237; Watt and Waine 2019, 47.
59. *The Lady's Monthly Museum* 1812, vol. XII, 233.
60. NMS K.2002.1033. I would like to thank Dr Emily Taylor for introducing me to this object and for discussing these alterations with me.
61. Coltman 2010, 203–5. See also: Geczy 2013, 41–84.
62. Norman 1997.
63. For a discussion of the evolving role of fancy dress in society and culture, including its charitable applications, see in particular: Wild 2020, 1–32.
64. *Caledonian Mercury* (15 December 1834), 1.
65. *Inverness Courier* (11 February 1835), 4.
66. NLS Acc. 12898/2 (Minute book, 1827–45), 140.
67. *The Scotsman* (4 February 1835), 4.
68. NLS Acc. 12898/2 (Minute book, 1827–45), 137.
69. Parker and Wagner (eds) 2020.
70. NMS H.MCR 26 and NMS H.MCR 27.
71. NMS X.2018.6.1–3.
72. Mitchell 2000, 10. See also: Tyrrell 2003.
73. Anstruther 1986; *The Scotsman* (16 January 1841), 1; Marsden 2010, 228–34.
74. Both the Albion Cloth Company and Meyer and Mortimer are listed as suppliers in numerous newspaper accounts of the annual Celtic Fancy Ball during the late 1830s and 1840s, most often as the providers of costume and set dressing.
75. NMS H.NG 358; Campbell 2017.
76. *The Scotsman* (10 February 1838), 1.
77. *Caledonian Mercury* (30 January 1836), 3.
78. NMS Research Library, Society of Antiquaries of Scotland Records 2/7/119 (George Farquharson to Alexander Macdonald, 29 January 1841). Appended to this note is a signed receipt from George Potts, for two large swords and two shields.
79. NMS K.2002.607.1–2.
80. Caldwell 2009, 79–80.
81. Couts 1848, plate XVII.
82. *Ibid*., iv.
83. NMS K.2002.1031. My thanks to Peter MacDonald for sharing his views on the dating of this tartan, and for pointing me towards an example of the 'Culloden' sett in a sample book once belonging to the retailers Romanes & Paterson, now in the collection of the Clan Macpherson Museum.
84. The coat was previously on loan to the NMAS from Hawthornden Castle between 1974–79. The loan also contained a pair of white kid shoes (NMS K.2002.1030 A–B) and part of a cream silk dress (NMS K.2002.1032), said to have been worn by Mary Queen of Scots, and a claymore said to have been carried by Robert the Bruce (NMS H.LA 60). All these relics have since been determined to be of a later date than originally suggested, yet the supposed connection of Prince Charles Edward Stuart to NMS K.2002.1031 has not been subjected to the same level of material scrutiny.
85. Guthrie 2013, 154–57.
86. Skelton and St John Hope 1890.
87. A preparatory oil painting for *The Pretender*, signed and dated by Simson in 1833, appeared in the sale *Fine Paintings*, Lot 58 (Lyon & Turnbull: 26 May 2006). This painting was previously in the Drambuie Collection. See Nicholson 2002, 139. A further two sketches from the same studio session were also sold in 2006, appearing in *Paintings*, Lot 596 (Lyon & Turnbull: 5 May 2006) and *Drambuie Part 1*, Lot 71 (Lyon & Turnbull: 26 January 2006). Steel-engraved illustrations based on Simson's original sketches appeared in the Abbotsford Edition of Sir Walter Scott's works, published between 1842–47. On the retro-fitting of such illustrations to Romantic historical fiction during the early Victorian era, see: Mole 2017, 45.
88. NMS X.2020.40; Horsburgh's rendering of Prince Charles Edward after Simson was referenced in the design of an iron umbrella stand dated 1888, cast in the shape of Bonnie Prince Charlie (NMS H.1992.1819). This object is on display in the *Scotland Transformed* gallery of the Museum of Scotland.
89. NMS H.MCR 2.

Afterword

ON 6 September 1749, the remains of a woman and child were found in a plantation of fir trees on the outskirts of Muthill, Perthshire. It was thought that the woman had died while travelling to the Lothians in search of seasonal sheep-shearing work, as a metal hook was discarded close by. Months of exposure to weather and wildlife had rendered the pair unrecognisable; their only identifying features were the clothes they wore and the tools they carried with them. It was decided by the local authorities that the garments should be salvaged and given into the care of the beadle of Muthill church, where the bodies had been taken and buried. The hope was that the retained articles would assist relatives in their search for the deceased, should any come looking in future. A description of the clothing was printed in *The Aberdeen Journal*, alongside an account of the melancholy discovery:

Opposite: Detail of a woman's arisaid, c.1790

> *Their cloaths were as follows: The Woman a stript blue and white Gown, a blue and white Petty-Coat, a Check Apron and a Highland Plaid. The Child's a white plaiding Jacket and Petty-Coat, and a black and white Frock.*[1]

Already tattered and soiled beyond repair, it would not have taken long for these fragile textiles to further decompose and – eventually – disappear.

When engaging with a museum collection of dress, it is important to appreciate its absences. Historic clothing is delicate and quick to decay; the organic materials used in their construction are vulnerable to dirt, damp, pests and light damage. What has been kept is minute in comparison to what has been discarded or lost, particularly when one considers the biases that have traditionally ruled object preservation: privileging the unusual, the expensive, and the talismanic. The formal and voguish aspects of Highland dress culture are well represented within the collections of National Museums Scotland, while the everyday garments once owned and worn by the lower classes of Highland society are rare survivals. This imbalance can partially be explained by the circumstances that typically underpinned the dress of labouring men and women during the eighteenth and nineteenth centuries, such as the need to reuse, recycle and repurpose for reasons of basic economy. The relative durability, richness and diversity of the clothing worn by the gentry offered these wearers greater opportunity for the heirlooming of favoured garments between generations, thus leaving a more robust material legacy. With the emergence of the costume collector and the steady professionalisation of the museum world at the turn on the twentieth century, it was the inherited clothing of the better-off that provided an initial basis for studying the dress habits of the past.

The advent of Highland style in Georgian Britain is necessarily a tale of upper-class consumption. The urge to commission finely tailored kilt suits and gowns of silken plaid was fortified by a romanticised vision of Scotland's past. That vision – and the material culture it engendered – stood in stark contrast to the industrialising nature of modern Scotland. Cultivated by gentlemen antiquarians and popularised by the art, literature and music of the age, these imagined Highlands bore little resemblance to the lived experiences of the ordinary men and women who called the region home. And yet, the impulse to revive Highland dress culture that fired the Highland aristocracy at the close of the eighteenth century did not lack material inspiration. Artefacts, visual culture, and oral traditions passed down between generations provided a compelling foundation for the fashions to come. The resulting silhouette was an embellished blending of what was and what had been, part illusion and part homage.

Today, Highland dress is among the most recognisable symbols of Scotland. With deep roots in the material history of a specific region, the reinvention of Highland costume as a national emblem in the Georgian era continues to provoke debates of cultural authenticity and appropriation. As befits a living tradition, the desire to refashion and reconceptualise Highland dress to suit the needs of the moment promises to remain a powerful influence over the nature of the costume.

Note

1. *The Aberdeen Journal* (19 September 1749), 3.

Opposite: Powder horn

This cow horn has been carved with Highland scenes of a medieval boar hunt. The silver mountings and long chain are nineteenth-century additions. The horn was probably an heirloom, later refashioned into a wearable historical artefact. From the Clanranald collection of Jacobite and Family relics.

List of sources

Archival collections

- Highland Archive Centre, Inverness
- National Library of Scotland, Edinburgh
- National Museums Scotland, Edinburgh

Published sources

Allan, S. 2012. 'Scottish Military Collections' in Crang, Spiers and Strickland (eds) 2012, 776–94.

Allan, S. and A. Carswell 2004. *The Thin Red Line: War, Empire and Visions of Scotland* (Edinburgh: National Museums Scotland).

Anderson, R. G. W. 1989. 'Museums in the Making: The origins and development of the national collections' in *The Wealth of a Nation in the National Museums of Scotland* (Edinburgh and Glasgow: National Museums of Scotland and Richard Drew Publishing Ltd).

Anstruther, A. 1986. *The Knight and the Umbrella: An Account of the Eglinton Tournament 1839* (Gloucester: Sutton).

Bassett, L. Z. 2016. *Gothic to Goth: Romantic Era Fashion and its Legacy* (Hartford: Connecticut Wadsworth Atheneum Museum of Art).

Baumgarten, L. 2002. *What Clothes Reveal: The Language of Clothing in Colonial and Federal America* (New Haven and London: Yale University Press).

Bell, A. S. (ed.) 1981. *The Scottish Antiquarian Tradition: Essays to mark the bicentenary of the Society of Antiquaries of Scotland and its Museum, 1780–1980* (Edinburgh: John Donald Publishers Ltd).

Bell, B. 2011. 'The National Drama and the Nineteenth Century' in I. Brown (ed.) 2011. *The Edinburgh Companion to Scottish Drama* (Edinburgh: Edinburgh University Press).

Bennett, H. 1980. 'Sir John Hynde Cotton's Highland Suit', *Costume* 14:1 (1980), 95–109.

Brown, I. (ed.) 2010. *From Tartan to Tartanry: Scottish Culture, History and Myth* (Edinburgh: Edinburgh University Press).

Bryden, M. 2000. 'Shaping and Selling the Idea: How the Product was Presented' in Fladmark (ed.) 2000, 29–40.

Bucciantini, A. 2018. *Exhibiting Scotland: Objects, Identity, and the National Museum* (Amherst and Boston: University of Massachusetts Press).

Buck, A. 1996. *Clothes and the Child: A Handbook of Children's Dress in England, 1500–1900* (New York: Holmes & Meier).

Buckley, C. 2007. *Designing Modern Britain* (London: Reaktion Books).

Bueltmann, T. 2014. *Clubbing Together: Ethnicity, Civility and Formal Sociability in the Scottish Diaspora to 1930* (Liverpool: Liverpool University Press).

Caldwell, D. H. 2009. 'The Re-arming of the Clans, 1822', *Review of Scottish Culture* 21 (2009), 67–86.

Campbell, S. 2015. 'Work and Play: The Material Culture of Childhood in Early Modern Scotland' in J. Nugent and E. Ewan (eds) 2015. *Children and Youth in Premodern Scotland* (Woodbridge and Rochester: Boydell Press), 65–88.

Campbell, S. 2017. 'Cultural presumptions and curatorial context: reassessing the "highland brooch" of Early Modern Scotland' in T. F. Martin and R. Weetch (eds) 2017. *Dress and Society: Contributions from Archaeology* (Oxford and Philadelphia: Oxbow), 170–83.

Campbell, T. 2016. *Historical Style: Fashion and the New Mode of History, 1740–1830* (Philadelphia, PA: University of Pennsylvania Press).

Carswell, A. 2012. 'Scottish Military Dress' in Crang, Spiers and Strickland (eds) 2012, 627–47.

Cheape, H. 1993. 'Researching Tartan', *Costume* 27:1 (1993), 35–46.

Cheape, H. 1995. 'The Piper to the Laird of Grant', *Proceedings of the Society of Antiquaries of Scotland* 125 (1995), 1163–73.

Cheape, H. 2000. 'Objects as Evidence: The Evaluation of Material Culture' in Fladmark (ed.) 2000, 61–76.

Cheape, H. 2006. *Tartan: The Highland Habit*. 3rd edition (Edinburgh: National Museums Scotland).

Cheape, H. 2010. 'Gheibhte breacain charnaid' ('Scarlet tartans would be got …'): the Re-invention of Tradition' in Brown (ed.) 2010, 13–31.

Christie and Manson 1843. *Catalogue of the Interesting Collection of Beautiful Rings, Seals, and Trinkets; Highly Interesting Historical Relics; Assemblage of Exquisite Snuff Boxes; Armoury of Oriental, German, and Highland Arms; and Capital Modern Fowling Pieces, of His Royal Highness the Duke of Sussex, K.G., and Removed from Kensington Palace; Which (By Order of the Executors) Will be Sold by Auction by Messrs. Christie & Manson, at their Great Room, King Street, St. James's Square, On Wednesday, June 28th, 1843, and Four Following Days, at One O'clock Precisely* (n.p.).

Clyde, R. 1995. *From Rebel to Hero: The Image of the Highlander, 1745–1830* (Edinburgh: Tuckwell Press).

Coltman, V. 2010. 'Party-Coloured Plaid? Portraits of Eighteenth-Century Scots in Tartan', *Textile History* 41:2 (2010), 182–216.

Corp, E. and G. Rimer 2020. 'The weapons of Bonnie Prince Charlie – a new examination', *Arms and Armour* 17:1 (April 2020), 27–79.

Couts, J. 1848. *A Practical Guide for the Tailor's Cutting-Room: Being a treatise on measuring and cutting clothing in all styles, and for every period of life from childhood to old age* (Glasgow: Blackie & Son).

Cox, N. 2016. *Retailing and the Language of Goods, 1550–1820* (Abingdon and New York: Routledge).

Crang, J., E. Spiers and M. Strickland (eds) 2012. *A Military History of Scotland* (Edinburgh: Edinburgh University Press).

Cumming, V. 2004. *Understanding Fashion History* (London: B. T. Batsford Ltd).

d'Amour, M. and P. Rodgers 1836. *Memoirs of Mr. Matthias d'Amour* (London: Longman).

Dalgleish, G. 2000. 'Objects as Icons: Myths and Realities of Jacobite Relics' in Fladmark (ed.) 2000, 91–101.

Davidson, H. 2019. *Dress in the Age of Jane Austen: Regency Fashion* (New Haven and London: Yale University Press).

Dodgshon, R. A. 1998. *From Chiefs to Landlords: Social and Economic Change in the Western Highlands and Islands, c.1493–1820* (Edinburgh: Edinburgh University Press).

Drummond, J. 1881. *Ancient Scottish Weapons: A series of drawings by the late James Drummond, with introduction and descriptive notes by Joseph Anderson* (Edinburgh and London: Waterson & Sons).

Dunbar, J. T. 1949. *Old Highland Tartans: Early tartans, spinning implements, dye samples, illustrations of Highland dress, manuscripts, etc., from the collection of J. Telfer Dunbar, F.S.A.Scot., Edinburgh* (Edinburgh: n.p.).

Dunbar, J. T. 1950. *Two Centuries of Highland Dress: Exhibits from the collection of J. Telfer Dunbar, F.S.A.Scot., Edinburgh* (Edinburgh: n.p.).

Dunbar, J. T. 1962. *History of Highland Dress: A definitive study of the history of Scottish costume and tartan, both civil and military, including weapons: With an Appendix on Early Scottish Dyes by Annette Kok* (Edinburgh and London: Oliver & Boyd).

Dunbar, J. T. 1981. *The Costume of Scotland* (London: B. T. Batsford Ltd).

Duncan, J. 1807. *Practical and Descriptive Essays on the Art of Weaving* (Glasgow: James Hedderwick & Co.).

Dyer, S. 2019. 'Barbara Johnson's Album: Material Literacy and Consumer Practice, 1746–1823', *Journal for Eighteenth-Century Studies* 42:3 (September 2019), 263–82.

Dyer, S. and C. Wigston Smith (eds) 2020. *Material Literacy in Eighteenth-Century Britain: A Nation of Makers* (London and New York: Bloomsbury).

Dziennik, M. P. 2012. 'Whig Tartan: Material Culture and Its Use in the Scottish Highlands, 1746–1815', *Past & Present* 217:1 (November 2012), 117–47.

Ehrman, E. 2012. *The Wedding Dress: 300 Years of Bridal Fashion* (London: V&A).

Ewing, E. 1977. *History of Children's Costume* (London: B. T. Batsford Ltd).

Faiers, J. 2008. *Tartan* (Oxford and New York: Berg).

Fladmark, J. M. (ed.) 2000. *Heritage and Museums: Shaping National Identity* (Shaftesbury: Donhead Publishing Ltd).

Forsyth, D. (ed.) 2017. *Bonnie Prince Charlie and the Jacobites* (Edinburgh: National Museums Scotland).

Foyster, E. and J. Marten (eds) 2014. *A Cultural History of Childhood and Family in the Age of Enlightenment* (London: Bloomsbury).

Gaskell, E. 1866. *Wives and Daughters. An Every-day Story* (London: Smith, Elder & Co.), 2 vols.

Geczy, A. 2013. *Fashion and Orientalism: Dress, Textiles and Culture from the 17th to the 21st Century* (London and New York: Bloomsbury).

Gee, A. 2003. *The British Volunteer Movement, 1794–1814* (Oxford: Oxford University Press).

Greig, H. 2013. *The Beau Monde: Fashionable Society in Georgian London* (Oxford: Oxford University Press).

Guthrie, N. 2013. *The Material Culture of the Jacobites* (Cambridge: Cambridge University Press).

Hansard, T. C. (ed.) 1814. *The Parliamentary History of England, from the Earliest Period to the Year 1803. From Which Last-Mentioned Epoch it is Continued Downwards in the Work Entitled, 'The Parliamentary Debates.'* Vol.

XXIII. Comprising the Period from the Tenth of May 1782, to the First of December 1783 (London: Longman).

Haulman, K. 2011. *The Politics of Fashion in Eighteenth-Century America* (Chapel Hill, NC: The University of North Carolina Press).

Haynes, C. 2018. *Our Friends the Enemies: The Occupation of France after Napoleon* (Cambridge, MA and London: Harvard University Press).

Hollander, A. 1994. *Sex and Suits: The Evolution of Modern Dress* (New York: Alfred A. Knopf, Inc.)

Hoock, H. 2010. *Empires of the Imagination: Politics, War and the Arts in the British World, 1750–1850* (London: Profile Books).

Irvine Robertson, J. 1998. *The First Highlander: Major-General David Stewart of Garth CD, 1768–1829* (Edinburgh: Tuckwell Press).

Johnston, L. 2016. *19th-Century Fashion in Detail* (London: V&A).

Kennedy Johnson, E. 2009. 'Trans-coding Nationalism: Subjectivity and Military Themes in Regency Women's Dress' in M. D. Goggin and B. F. Tobin (eds) 2009. *Material Women, 1750–1950: Consuming Desires and Collecting Practices* (Aldershot and Burlington: Ashgate), 149–66.

Logan, J. 1831. *The Scottish Gaël; or Celtic Manners as Preserved Among the Highlanders: Being an historical and descriptive account of the inhabitants, antiquities, and national peculiarities of Scotland; More particularly of the Northern, or Gaëlic parts of the country, where the singular habits of the aboriginal Celts are most tenaciously retained* (London: Smith, Elder & Co.), 2 vols.

McClintock, H. F. 1943. *Old Irish and Highland Dress: With Notes on That of the Isle of Man* (Dundalk: W. Tempest Dundalgan Press).

McCullough, K. L. 2011. '"For the Good And Glory of the Whole": The Highland Society of London and the Formation of Scoto-British Identity' in J. A. Campbell, E. Ewan and H. Parker (eds) 2011. *The Shaping of Scottish Identities: Family, Nation, and the Worlds Beyond* (Guelph: University of Guelph), 199–214.

MacDonald, P. 2012. *The 1819 Key Pattern Book: One Hundred Original Tartans* (Creiff: n.p.).

McIntyre North, C. N. 1881. *Leabhar Comunn Nam Fior Ghael. Book of the Club of True Highlanders* (London: Richard Smythson), 2 vols.

McKean, C. 2000. *The Making of the Museum of Scotland* (Edinburgh: National Museums Scotland).

Mackillop, A. 2000. *'More Fruitful than the Soil': Army, Empire and the Scottish Highlands, 1715–1815* (Edinburgh: Tuckwell Press).

Mclean, M. 1991. *The People of Glengarry: Highlanders in Transition, 1745–1820* (Montreal: McGill-Queen's University Press).

MacLeod, A. 2012. *From an Antique Land: Visual Representations of the Highlands and Islands 1700–1880* (Edinburgh: John Donald Publishers Ltd).

Macpherson, A. 1883. *The Golden Wedding of Cluny Macpherson, C.B. and Mrs Macpherson, Twentieth December 1882* (Edinburgh: Printed for private use, R. & R. Clark).

Marsden, J. 2010. *Victoria & Albert: Art and Love* (London: The Royal Collection).

Martin, R. 1988. 'Tartan', *Scottish Quest Magazine: Quarterly Review of Travel and Leisure in Scotland* (Autumn 1988), 4–6.

Miller, L. E. 2014. *Selling Silks: A Merchant's Sample Book* (London: V&A).

Mills, N. J. and A. L. Carswell 1998, 'Wilson of Bannockburn and the Clothing of the Highland Regiments', *Journal of the Society for Army Historical Research* 76 (1998), 177–93.

Mitchell, I. R. 2000. *On the Trail of Queen Victoria in the Highlands* (Edinburgh: Luath Press).

Mole, T. 2017. *What the Victorians Made of Romanticism: Material Artifacts, Cultural Practices, and Reception History* (Princeton and Oxford: Princeton University Press).

Montgomery, A. 2020. *Classical Caledonia: Roman History and Myth in Eighteenth-Century Scotland* (Edinburgh: Edinburgh University Press).

Montgomery, F. and L. Eaton 2007. *Textiles in America, 1650–1870: a dictionary based on original documents, prints and paintings, commercial records, American merchant's papers, shopkeepers' advertisements, and pattern books with original swatches of cloth* (New York: W. W. Norton & Company).

Myerly, S. H. 1996. *British Military Spectacle: From the Napoleonic Wars through the Crimea* (Cambridge, MA and London: Harvard University Press).

National Museum of Antiquities of Scotland 1865. *Catalogue of Antiquities in the National Museum of the Society of Antiquaries of Scotland* (Edinburgh: Royal Institution).

National Museum of Antiquities of Scotland 1892. *Catalogue of the National Museum of Antiquities of Scotland* (Edinburgh: Society of Antiquaries of Scotland).

Nenadic, S. 1999. 'Romanticism and the urge to consume in the first half of the nineteenth century' in M. Berg and H. Clifford (eds) 1999. *Consumers and Luxury: Consumer Culture in Europe, 1650–1850* (Manchester: Manchester University Press), 208–27.

Nenadic, S. 2007. *Lairds and Luxury: The Highland Gentry in Eighteenth-Century Scotland* (Edinburgh: John Donald Publishers Ltd).

Nenadic, S. (ed.) 2010. *Scots in London in the Eighteenth Century* (Lewisburg, PA: Bucknell University Press).

Nicholson, R. 2002. *Bonnie Prince Charlie and the Making of a Myth* (Lewisburg, PA: Bucknell University Press).

Nicholson, R. 2005. 'From Ramsay's *Flora MacDonald* to Raeburn's *MacNab*: The Use of Tartan as a Symbol of Identity', *Textile History* 36:2 (2005), 146–67.

Norman, A. V. B. 1997. 'George IV and Highland dress', *Review of Scottish Culture* 10 (1997), 5–15.

Orr, S. 1921. 'Clothing found on a Skeleton discovered at Quintfall Hill, Barrock estate, near Wick', *Proceedings of the Society of Antiquaries of Scotland* 55 (1921), 213–21.

Osborne, B. D. 2001. *The Last of the Chiefs: Alasdair Ranaldson Macdonell of Glengarry, 1773–1828* (Glendaruel: Argyll Publishing).

Parker, J. and C. Wagner (eds) 2020. *The Oxford Handbook of Victorian Medievalism* (Oxford: Oxford University Press).

Pentland, G. 2011. '"We Speak for the Ready": Images of Scots in Political Prints, 1707–1832', *Scottish Historical Review* 90:1 (2011), 64–95.

Petrov, J. 2019. *Fashion, History, Museums: Inventing the Display of Dress* (London: Bloomsbury).

Pittock, M. 2009. *The Myth of the Jacobite Clans: The Jacobite Army in 1745*. 2nd revised edition (Edinburgh: Edinburgh University Press).

Pittock, M. 2010. 'Plaiding the Invention of Scotland' in Brown (ed.) 2010, 32–47.

Pittock, M. 2013. *Material Culture and Sedition, 1688–1760: Treacherous Objects, Secret Places* (New York: Palgrave Macmillan).

Quye, A. and H. Cheape 2008. 'Rediscovering the Arisaid', *Costume* 42:1 (June 2008), 1–20.

Quye, A., H. Cheape, J. Burnett, E. Ferreira, A. Hulme and H. McNab 2003. 'An historical and analytical study of red, pink, green and yellow colours in quality 18th and early 19th century Scottish tartans', *Dyes in History & Archaeology* 19 (2003), 1–12.

Ramsey, M. B. 2019. 'Plaiding the People: Party-Coloured Plaid and Its Use in the North American Colonies, 1730–1800', *The Journal of Dress History* 3:3 (Autumn 2019), 37–69.

Reid, S. 2013. *Scottish National Dress and Tartan* (Oxford: Shire).

Rose, C. 1989. *Children's Clothes since 1750* (London: B. T. Batsford Ltd).

Rose, C. 2010. *Making, Selling and Wearing Boys' Clothes in Late-Victorian England* (Abingdon and New York: Ashgate).

Sanger, K. and A. Kinnaird 1992. *Tree of Strings: Crann nan teud: a history of the harp in Scotland* (Temple: Kinmor Music).

Sargentson, C. 2007. 'Looking at Furniture Inside Out: Strategies of Secrecy and Security in Eighteenth-Century French Furniture' in D. Goodman and K. Norberg (eds) 2007. *Furnishing the Eighteenth Century: What Furniture Can Tell Us About the European and American Past* (New York and London: Routledge), 205–36.

Scarlett, J. 1987. 'Tartan: the Highland Cloth and Highland Art Form' in J. Butt and K. Ponting (eds) 1987. *Scottish Textile History* (Aberdeen: Aberdeen University Press), 65–77.

Scarlett, J. 1990. *Tartan: The Highland Textile* (London: Shepheard-Walwyn).

Scott, W. 1818. *Rob Roy*. 3rd edition (Edinburgh and London: Archibald Constable & Co. and Longman).

Sinclair, J. 1804. *Observations on the Propriety of Preserving the Dress, the Language, the Poetry, the Music, and the Customs, of the Ancient Inhabitants of Scotland. Addressed to the Highland Societies of London and of Scotland* (London: W. Bulmer and Co.).

Sinclair, J. 1813. *An Account of the Highland Society of London, From its Establishment in May 1778, to the Commencement of the Year 1813* (London: B. McMillan).

Skelton, J. and W. H. St John Hope 1890. *The Royal House of Stuart: Illustrated by a series of plates in colours drawn from relics of the Stuarts by William Gibb* (London: Macmillan and Company).

Smith, W. and A. Smith 1850. *Authenticated Tartans of the Clans and Families of Scotland* (Mauchline: W & A Smith).

Sobieski Stuart, J. 1842. *Vestiarium Scoticum: From the manuscript formerly in the library of the Scots College at Douay. With an introduction and notes, by John Sobieski Stuart* (Edinburgh: William Tait).

Sotheby's 1990. *Silver and Jewels, Wemyss Ware, Scottish and Sporting Paintings, Drawings and Watercolours. Gleneagles Hotel, Monday 27th and Tuesday 28th August 1990* (London: Sotheby's).

Stewart, D. C. 1974. *The Setts of the Scottish Tartans.* 2nd revised edition (London: Shepheard-Walwyn).

Stewart, D. W. 1893. *Old and Rare Scottish Tartans* (Edinburgh: George P. Johnston).

Stiùbhart, D. U. 2008. *The Life and Legacy of Alexander Carmichael* (Port of Ness: The Islands Book Trust).

Sutton, A. and R. Carr 1984. *Tartans: Their Art and History* (London: Belew Publishing).

Tarrant, N. 1982. 'Shambellie House Museum of Costume', *Costume* 16:1 (1982), 1–8.

Tarrant, N. 1996. *The Development of Costume* (London and Edinburgh: Routledge/National Museums of Scotland).

Tarrant, N. 1999. 'The Real Thing: The Study of Original Garments in Britain since 1947', *Costume* 33:1 (1999), 12–22.

Taylor, L. 2002. *The Study of Dress History* (Manchester: Manchester University Press).

Taylor, L. 2004. *Establishing Dress History* (Manchester: Manchester University Press).

Trevor-Roper, H. 1983. 'The Invention of Tradition: The Highland Tradition of Scotland' in E. J. Hobsbawm and T. O. Ranger (eds) 1983. *The Invention of Tradition* (Cambridge: Cambridge University Press), 15–41.

Tuckett, S. 2009. 'National Dress, Gender and Scotland: 1745–1822', *Textile History* 40:2 (2009), 140–51.

Tuckett, S. 2016. 'Reassessing the Romance: Tartan as a Popular Commodity, c.1770–1830', *The Scottish Historical Review* 95:2 (2016), 182–202.

Tyrrell, A. 2003. 'The Queen's "Little Trip": The Royal Visit to Scotland in 1842', *The Scottish Historical Review* 82:212 (2003), 47–73.

Waine, R. 2019. 'From rebellion to romantic appreciation: the wearing of tartan following the Act of Proscription', *History Scotland* 19:6 (November/December 2019), 8–11.

Walsh, C. 2006. 'Shops, Shopping, and the Art of Decision Making in Eighteenth-Century England' in J. Styles and A. Vickery (eds) 2006. *Gender, Taste, and Material Culture in Britain and North America, 1700–1830* (New Haven and London: Yale University Press).

Watt, P. 2021. 'The Highland Society of London, material culture and the development of Scottish military identity, 1798–1817', *Historical Research* 94:264 (May 2021), 351–79.

Watt, P. and R. Waine 2019. *Wild and Majestic: Romantic Visions of Scotland* (Edinburgh: National Museums Scotland).

Wilcox, D. 2016. 'Scottish Late Seventeenth-Century Male Clothing: Some Context for the Barrock Estate Finds', *Costume* 50:2 (2016), 151–68.

Wilcox, D. 2017. 'Scottish Late Seventeenth-Century Male Clothing (Part 2): The Barrock Estate Finds Described', *Costume* 50:1 (2017), 28–53.

Wild, B. L. 2020. *Carnival to Catwalk: Global Reflections on Fancy Dress Costume* (London and New York: Bloomsbury).

Wyld, H. and G. Dalgleish 2017. '"A slim sword in his hand for battle": Weapons fit for a Prince' in Forsyth (ed.) 2017, 79–94.

Opposite: Detail of a Royal Stewart tartan cloak, lined with red twill, c.1830

Index

Key

NMAS National Museum of Antiquities of Scotland
NMS National Museums Scotland
RMoS Royal Museum of Scotland
RSM Royal Scottish Museum
SNMM Scottish Naval and Military Museum
SUSM Scottish United Services Museum
SAS Society of Antiquaries of Scotland

A. McCallum & Son, Glasgow (cloth warehouse) 118; Fig. 3.14
Abercromby, Sir Ralph 65, 70
– commemorative tartan 70; Fig. 2.16
Aberfeldy, Perthshire
– tartan mills in 25
accoutrements (*see* Highland dress/costume)
Adolphus, Prince 175
advertisements (*see* newspapers)
Agnew, Mary 122
agriculture
– clearance 86, 98
– implements 16
– improvers 54, 63; Fig. 4.40
– sheep farming 36, 86, 191
Albert of Saxe Coburg and Gotha, Prince 182
Albion Cloth Company (Highland dress outfitter) 182–83; Figs 2.29, 4.59
Allan, Stuart (curator and military historian) 6
Allan's Masquerade Warehouse (fictional Highland dress outfitter) 88
alterations to clothing 177; Fig. 4.52 (*see also* recycling/refashioning of clothing)
America
– plantations in 32, 104, 132; Fig. 3.10
– trade with 111, 132; Fig. 3.5
– War of Independence 55
Amies, Sir Edwin Hardy (designer) 37
ancestry/ancestral
– houses 7, 41
– landscape 40, 76
– objects 136, 184
– Scottish 129
– stories 18, 31, 41
– textiles and dress 18, 54, 77, 81, 129
– weapons 185; Fig. 4.60 (*see also* weaponry)
Anderson, Joseph (curator) 16
antiquarians 77, 83, 94, 95, 183, 185, 192
archaeology 16, 29
– influence on fashionable dress 138 (*see also* neoclassical style)
arisaids 37, 158, 160–62; Figs 4.32–33
– as household plenishing 160–61
Atholl (*see also* Blair Castle, Atholl) 79
Augsburg 145
Augusta, Duchess of Cambridge 175; Fig. 4.50
Augusta of Cambridge, Princess 175; Fig. 4.50
Augustus Frederick, Prince, Duke of Sussex and Earl of Inverness
– dress sword based on Jacobite relic 60–62; Fig. 2.7
– Earl of Inverness tartan 59, 133; Fig. 2.6
– Highland dress collection of 59–62, 96; Figs 2.5–7
– presidency of the Highland Society of London 58–62, 70, 96
Australia (*see* diaspora, Scottish)
Austrian Succession, War of Fig. 4.43
axes 16, 85
– Lochaber 183

badges, plant
– (*see* clan culture: plant badges)
bagpipes (*see* pipers; pipes/piping)
Balmoral Castle, Aberdeenshire xi
bards (*see* clan culture: chiefs/chieftains; clan culture: retinues and retainers)
Barrock Estate, Caithness 18; Fig. 1.19 (*see also* excavated textiles)
battles 31, 80
– Aboukir Bay 165
– Alexandria 70, 167; Fig. 2.2
– Camperdown 165
– Culloden 16, 32, 35–36, 39, 61, 183; Figs 1.12, 2.8, 4.63
– Glen Fruin 184
– Waterloo 164; Fig. 4.37

Beaumont, Prof. Roberts (academic and textile historian) 24–26, 36; Figs 1.25–26
Beechey, Sir William (artist) 59, 60; Figs 2.5, 2.6
belts 13, 59, 86, 145, 150, 158; Fig. 1.11 (*see also* plaid/*breacan*: belted)
Bennett, Helen (curator and textile historian) 144
Benson & Forsyth (architects) 37
Blackburn, Lancashire 25
Blackhall of Blackfaulds, William 93–94
– kilt suit belonging to Figs 2.34–35
Blair Castle, Atholl 79
Blair Junior, Charles (merchant) 115–16; Fig. 3.9
Bombay 122
bonnets (*see* headgear)
boots (*see* footwear)
Bowles, John (publisher) 145
braid/braiding 40, 138, 141, 144, 168, 171, 173; Figs 4.46, 4.47
Brazil/Brazilians 126
breacan (*see* plaid/*breacan*)
Breadalbane, John Campbell, 2nd Marquess of
– fancy dress culture, patron of 180–82
– father, Earl of Breadalbane 80
– as Lord Glenorchy 52
– suit belonging to 180, 182; Figs 4.56–57
breeches 18, 56, 64, 72, 88, 150; Figs 4.20–21 (*see also* children's clothing: breeching)
Britain 16, 19, 22, 26, 32, 53, 72, 83, 94, 103, 109, 121, 125, 130, 137, 165, 167; Figs 2.3, 2.10, 2.23, 3.1, 3.10
British
– army (*see* battles; military; regiments)
– navy 165
– tailoring (*see* tailors/tailoring)
brooches
– Hunterston brooch 16
– plaid brooches I, II–III, 16, 41, 77, 183; Figs 1.33, 2.20, 4.59
Bruce, Sir Michael, 6th Baronet of Stenhouse 122
Bruce, Sir Patrick Craufurd 121–22, 123; Figs 3.17–18
Bruce, Sir William, 7th Baronet of Stenhouse 121
Brucklay Castle, Aberdeenshire 174

Buckingham Palace 182
buckles 68, 179
Bute Collection, The (Mount Stuart) 45
Bute Collection, The (NMS) 8–9, 26, 103
Bute, John Crichton-Stuart, 2nd Marquess of Fig. 3.19
Bute, John Crichton-Stuart, 4th Marquess of 8, 9, 25, 26, 103; Fig. 2.26
Bute, Lord David Crichton-Stuart of 8, 26, 103
buttons 40, 63, 64, 65, 66, 68, 69, 74, 86, 91, 127, 138, 141, 142, 150, 171, 173, 179; Figs 1.3, 2.14, 2.33, 4.4–5, 4.28, 4.29, 4.46–47
– button-holes 186

Caithness and Sutherland Friendly Highland Society 71
Caledonian Asylum, London 167
– use of Highland dress 167 (*see also* charity/charitable giving)
Caledonian Hunt 179
Cameron and Nicholson, Messrs, Edinburgh (tailors and clothiers) 77
Cameron of Erracht, Sir Alan 163
Cameron of Fassifern, Sir Ewen 79
Campbell, John (tailor) 74
Campbell of Islay, John Francis (Gaelic folklorist and antiquarian) 18
cantles/'locks' (*see* sporrans)
capes (*see* cloaks)
Carmichael, Dr Alexander (Gaelic folklorist and antiquarian) 9–10, 18; Figs 1.7–9
Castle Grant 41
Celtic Society of Edinburgh, The 178, 179; Fig. 2.23
– Celtic Fancy Ball, Edinburgh 178–80, 182–83; Fig. 4.54
– establishment of 87
– promotion of Highland dress as national costume 87–89
– satirical attack on 86–89
– Royal Visit (1822), role in 90
charity/charitable giving 54, 63, 73, 167, 177, 178; Fig. 4.56
Charles II, King 89
Charlie, Bonnie Prince (*see* Stuart, Prince Charles Edward)
Charlotte, Duchess of Richmond 165
Charlotte, Princess 167
Charleston, South Carolina 116; Fig. 3.10

Cheape, Hugh (curator; *see* tartan historians)
children's clothing 74, 167–75, 191; Figs 4.41–50
– bodices 171, 173, 174
– bonnets 91, 167, 169, 170, 171, 173, 175
– breeching 170; Fig. 4.41
– changing attitudes towards 168, 169–70
– coats 167, 168, 169, 170
– hose 169, 170, 173, 175
– jackets 191
– kilt dresses 168, 171, 173, 174–75; Figs 4.41, 4.45, 4.47–50
– military styling 167, 169, 171, 173; Figs 4.46–47, 4.49
– and patriotic displays 167
– philabegs 167, 169, 170
– plaids 169, 173, 175
– shoes 170
– skeleton suit 170, 171; Fig. 4.44
– sleeves 173
– sporrans 168, 173, 175
– trousers/trews 167, 169, 170; Fig. 4.41
– undergarments 170, 171, 173–74
– Victorian kilt suits 37, 168 (*see also* headgear; Highland dress/costume: and children; tartan: and children's clothing)
Christie and Manson, Messrs (auctioneers) 60, 92
clan culture 28, 30, 32, 41, 112, 128, 130, 131, 138, 158, 160, 178, 182, 183, 184; Figs 1.12, 4.35
– chiefs/chieftains 12, 41, 52, 53, 57, 61, 71, 73, 81, 85, 86, 88, 87, 90, 91, 136, 147, 178, 179, 182; Figs 4.1, 4.16, 4.42
– and feudalism 41, 77, 94, 182, 183
– plant badges 80, 94, 130, 138, 158; Fig. 2.36
– retinues and retainers 41, 86
– romanticisation of 182
– war cries 80 (*see also* tartan: clan/family)
Clark, Andrew
– kilt suit Fig. 4.3
claymores (*see* swords)
cloaks 31, 43, 45, 46, 64, 91, 104, 114, 120, 124–25, 126, 127, 144; Figs 1.1–4, 1.6, 1.8–9, 1.36, 3.19–22
Cluny Castle, Badenoch 79, 158

coats: 8, 40, 41, 59, 64, 65, 68, 72, 86, 91, 93, 125, 136, 138, 141, 142, 144, 147, 148, 163, 164, 168, 169, 180, 186; Figs 1.27, 2.4, 2.11, 2.13–15, 2.31–32, 2.34, 4.3–7, 4.10–13, 4.17–18, 4.22–25, 4.28–29, 4.35
- banyan/housecoat 176, 177; Figs 4.51–52
- Clanranald coat 180; Fig. 4.55
- Hawthornden coat 185–86; Figs 4.62–63
(*see also* tailors/tailoring)
cockades 41, 64, 86, 170, 175, 180, 186; Figs 1.34, 4.39, 4.45
collars 40, 46, 59, 66, 69, 122, 124, 126, 141, 142, 148; Figs 1.3, 2.13, 4.3, 4.5, 4.17–18
colonialism 32, 68, 125, 175
Cope, Sir John Fig. 4.63
Cotton, Sir John Hynde 144; Fig. 4.13
- Highland suit 144–45; Fig. 4.13
- trews 148
court 54, 58
- dress worn at 86; Fig. 4.5
- exiled Stuart court, Rome 39, 61
Couts, Joseph (tailor and author) 184–85; Fig. 4.61
cravats Fig. 3.19
Cruikshank, Isaac (artist) Fig. 4.40
Cuchullin Handloom Company 22
cuffs 59, 93, 122, 141, 142, 180; Fig. 4.5
- cufflinks 85; Fig. 2.27
Culloden Moor 16 (*see also* battles)
Cumming, William (piper) 41; Fig. 1.34 (*see also* Castle Grant; Grant, Lairds of; Waitt, Richard)
Cumming, William Skeoch (artist and collector) 6–7, 8, 9, 10, 102, 103, 163; Figs 1.1, 1.4–6, 1.9
Cumming Gordon, Helen 79

d'Amour, Matthias 165
d'Este, Sir Augustus Frederick 70, 97
d'Hardivillier, Charles Achille (artist) 179–80
Davidson of Tulloch, Henry 158; Fig. 4.31
Davidson of Tulloch, Sarah Justina (*see* Macpherson, Sarah Justina)
Davies, Dr Seivwright (collector) 25–26
Dawe, Henry (engraver) 184
diaspora, Scottish 40
Dickson, William (athlete) 53
Difell, Caroline Elizabeth Fig. 4.31
Dingwall, John Duff 174–75; Fig. 4.49

dirks/daggers 16, 41, 56, 61, 65, 76, 77, 85, 87, 88, 91, 179, 183; Figs 1.7, 2.21, 2.29–30, 4.1
Dornoch, Sutherland 163
Dovecot Studios, Edinburgh 6
Dress Act (1746) 8, 96, 162
- legacy of 8, 58, 78, 102
- repeal of (1782) 54–57, 102
Drummond, James (artist and curator) 16; Figs 1.16, 1.17, 1.38
Drummond, James, 3rd Duke of Perth 39, 61
Drummonds of Hawthornden 185
Dublin 165
Duff, Charles (piper) Fig. 2.21
Duff, John (merchant) 91
Dunbar, John Telfer (costume historian, collector) 2, 30, 31, 32, 102, 132
Duncan, Admiral Adam 165
Dunkeld, Perthshire 115; Fig. 3.9
dyestuffs/dyers 25, 31, 36, 46, 111, 121, 168

Earle, Augustine (collector) 8
East India Company 122, 125
Edinburgh International Festival 23, 35
Edinburgh Museum of Science and Art (*see* NMS)
Edinburgh 6, 10, 11, 12, 16, 20, 52, 63, 73, 74, 75, 76, 77, 86, 88, 89, 90, 91, 111, 112, 178, 179, 183, 184; Figs 4.24, 4.25
- assembly rooms 179
- Castle 91, 184: and crown jewels 91, 184
- Chambers Street (*see* NMS) 11, 34, 43
- Charlotte Square 87
- College Street 87
- council 31
- Gladstone's Land 3
- George Street 178, 182; Fig. 3.4
- High Street 100–1; Fig. 3.1
- Lady Stair's House 31
- Lawnmarket 31
- The Mound 16
- North Bridge 77, 91
- Oman's Hotel 87
- Queen Street 16
- Royal Visit (1822) 18, 40, 89–94, 131, 184; Fig. 1.32
- St Giles' Cathedral 100–1, Fig. 3.1
- Theatre Royal 74–75; Fig. 2.18
Edward, Prince, Duke of Kent and Strathearn 59, 78

Eglinton Tournament 182; Fig. 4.58
embroidery 64, 74, 147, 158
England 55, 56, 85, 109, 114, 128
Enlightenment culture 39
enslaved peoples (*see* tartan: and slave clothing)
Erskine, David, 11th Earl of Buchan (founder of the Society of Antiquaries of Scotland) 11
ethnography/ethnographers 18
Europe/European 136, 137, 169; Fig. 1.35
- costume books 12
- fashion 34, 137, 162, 176
- Romanticism 43, 45
  style 43; Scottish experience of 43, 53; Fig. 2.4
excavated textiles 18; Fig. 1.19
exhibitions 30, 31, 45
- *Britain Can Make It* (V&A, London, 1946) 23
- *Enterprise Scotland* (RSM, Edinburgh, 1947) 23, 24
  'Jenny Weave' 23–24; Fig. 1.23; Textile Hall Fig. 1.23
- *Exhibition of the Royal House of Stuart* (New Gallery, London, 1889) 185–86
- *Fabric of a Nation* (National Museum of Costume [Shambellie House], 2007) 36–37
- fashion 32–33
- Great Exhibition, The (London, 1851) 19
- of Highland dress 30, 31
- *Old Highland Tartans* (Gladstone's Land, Edinburgh, 1949) 31 restaged as *Two Centuries of Tartan* (Lady Stair's House, Edinburgh, 1950) 31
- *Prince Charlie's Tartan* (RMoS, 1995) 35
- at RSM 33
- *Tartan* 37
  at Fashion Institute of Technology (New York, 1989) 34, 35, 37; restaged at Talbot Rice Gallery (Edinburgh, 1989) 34–35, 37; Fig. 1.29
- of tartan 31
- *The Wealth of a Nation* (RMoS, Edinburgh, 1989) 35
- *Wild and Majestic: Romantic Visions of Scotland* (NMS, Edinburgh 2019) 45; Fig. 1.37

Fair Isle 23
Falkirk 63, 73; Fig. 2.17
fancy dress 12, 65, 176–85; Figs 2.29, 4.51
- balls/ballrooms 26, 177, 179, 180, 182; Figs 4.54, 4.56, 4.61
- masques/masquerades 58, 88, 177; Fig. 4.56
- in military style 178, 182
- pageants Fig. 4.54
- Plantagenet Ball, Buckingham Palace 182
- in theatre/theatricals 177; Fig. 4.53 (see also Celtic Society of Edinburgh; Highland dress/costume: and fancy dress culture)
Farquharson, Frances of Invercauld (Frances Strickland Lovell Oldham) Fig. 1.35
Farquharson, William 80
fashion periodicals 129
- *Ackermann's Repository of Arts* 129, 165, 173; Figs 3.24, 4.38, 4.48
- *Gazette de France* 164
- *La Belle Assemblée* 88
- *The Lady's Monthly Museum* 175
fashion plates 174–75; Figs 4.49–50
Fingask Castle Figs 4.28, 4.29
folklore/folklorists 9, 18; Fig. 1.7
footwear
- boots Fig. 3.19
- brogues, Highland 65, 86; Figs 4.17, 4.18
- shoes 18, 170
Forres 119; Fig. 3.15
Fort William 10, 36, 114
Fotheringham, Robert (merchant) 126
France/French 36, 59, 62, 70, 160, 164–65; Fig. 4.16
- Revolutionary Wars 102, 165
Fraser of Boblainy, Simon 52, 57, 96
Fraser of Lovat, Archibald 52, 55, 57, 96
Frederick Augustus, Prince, Duke of York and Albany 71, 96
frockcoats 176, 185; Fig. 4.52

Gaels/Gaelic
- culture 9, 53; Fig. 1.7
- history 9
- language 9, 52, 54, 72, 78, 95; Fig. 2.23
- literature 36; Fig. 1.7
- material culture 35, 41; Figs 1.7, 2.27
- mottos/inscriptions 60, 62, 63, 66, 68; Fig. 2.14
- music 72
- poets/poetry 36, 57
- scholarship 35, 36
gaiters 88
games (see Highland games)
garters 86, 110, 175
Gaskell, Elizabeth (author) 128
Gaultier, Jean Paul (designer) 37
gemstones (see jewels/jewellery)
George II, King 55
George III, King 58, 177; Fig. 2.13
George IV, King 53, 58, 71, 167
- Highland dress outfit 60; Fig. 2.30
- Royal Visit (1822) 18, 40, 60, 68, 89–95, 130, 184; Figs 1.32, 2.19, 2.28, 2.30, 2.31–35, 4.24–25, 4.60
George Fox, Covent Garden (merchant) 130
George Hunter & Co., Edinburgh (see Hunter, George)
George of Cambridge, Prince 175; Figs 2.50, 4.50
George, Prince of Wales (see George IV, King)
Gibb, William (artist) 185
Glasgow 33, 66, 70, 91, 95, 116, 118; Figs 1.28, 2.16, 2.36, 3.6, 3.10, 3.12–14, 4.61
- Jamaica Street 33
Glasgow Highland Society 70
Glenelg estate, Inverness-shire 122, 124; Fig. 3.17
Glenlyon Figs 4.24, 4.25
Glenlyon, Viscount Fig. 4.58
Glennie family 60, 96
Glenorchy, Lord (see Breadalbane, John Campbell, 2nd Marquess of)
Gordon, Duke of 165, 179
Gothic art Figs 4.54, 4.58
Gow, John (musician) 72
gowns 104, 126, 127, 128, 129, 158, 160, 175, 176, 191, 192; Fig. 4.31
Graham, Marquess of
- repeal of Dress Act, role in 54–57
Grand Tour 86, 136; Figs 2.4, 2.28, 4.1
Grant of Strathspey, John (dancer) 77
Grant, Lairds of 41; Fig. 1.34 (see also Castle Grant; Cumming, William; Waitt, Richard)
Great Exhibition, The (1851) (see exhibitions)
Greece/Grecian 138, 175

guns
- flintlock (fusee) 13, 85, 88
- fowling pieces 60, 147, 168
- pistols 15, 41, 86, 88, 91, 179, 183; Fig. 2.30
Gwyne, Mr (harpist) 72

Hadden, David (merchant) 111; Fig. 3.5
Halifax, Nova Scotia 111
Hamilton, James 69, 78, 167; Fig. 2.24
Hanover 175
Hanover, House of 8, 39, 57; Fig. 2.11
Harper, Pearce & Co., London (stationers) 82, 98; Fig. 2.24
Harvey & Co., London 133
Hawthornden Castle, Midlothian 185, 186
- frockcoat 185–86; Figs 4.62–63
Hays of Yester, East Lothian 176
headgear
- bonnets 18, 41, 53, 65, 73, 74, 86, 88, 94, 136, 147, 178, 179, 186
   regimental 102, 164–65, 169, 171, 175; Figs 4.38–39, 4.53
- forage cap 165; Fig. 4.39
- turbans 165
heraldry/heraldic 28, 41, 104
- banners 41; Fig. 1.34
- clan 77, 78, 94, 158
- crests 68, 175; Figs 4.58, 4.60
Heydon Hall, Norfolk 8
Highland Archive Centre 28
Highland Club of Scotland 52–53, 61; Fig 2.1
Highland dress/costume x, XIII, 2, 40, 45, 136, 138, 144, 145, 148, 158, 169, 170, 171, 179, 191, 192; Figs 1.28, 1.32, 3.9, 4.1, 4.3, 4.13, 4.42, 4.55
- accoutrements 12, 16, 18, 39, 41, 59, 75, 76, 87, 175, 183; Figs 1.18, 2.30, 4.49
- ban of 8, 55, 56, 57, 96; Fig. 4.13
- and children 167, 168, 170; Fig. 4.44
- as club uniforms 64–71
- and collecting 1–49, 59–60, 191–92
- culture of 1–49, 54, 58, 62, 77, 90, 104, 160, 170, 179, 185, 191, 192; Figs 2.10, 2.29, 4.54, 4.59
- etiquette regarding 65, 88, 178
- exhibitions of 30, 45 (see also exhibitions)
- and fancy dress culture 176–85; Figs 4.53–61
- in iconography 53, 192
- as inspiration 185–87

203

- military use/interpretation of 26, 31, 138, 162, 163, 164, 167, 171, 175; Figs 2.12, 4.3, 4.35, 4.38–39, 4.49
- outfitting 28; Fig. 4.61
- re-use/reinterpretation of 177
- revivalist style 89, 94, 150, 160, 168, 170, 179; Figs 2.5, 4.1, 4.22–23, 4.41, 4.44, 4.60–61
- romantic influence on 138, 158; Fig. 4.3
- silhouettes 54, 89, 138–57, 164, 168, 192; Fig. 4.2
- tailoring of 26, 124, 138, 144, 148
- as theatrical costume 177; Fig. 4.53
- use around the world 32

Highland Folk Museum 36
Highland games 52–53, 76, 86
Highlands/Highlanders 36, 41, 45, 52, 55, 57, 58, 74, 77, 79, 87, 121, 131, 136, 145, 163, 183, 192
- arms/weapons 12, 16, 31
- chiefs 77, 136, 147
- economy 36, 94
- education 178
- estates 87, 122; Fig. 3.17
- landscape 18, 55, 59, 86, 183
- relics of 16, 183; Fig. 1.18
- soldiers 55, 56, 164–65, 177
- sports (*see* Highland games)

Highland Society of London (HSL) 52–98, 122, 142, 167, 179; Fig. 3.17
- club uniform 63–71; Figs 2.13–15
- competitions: piping 73–79, 179
- collection of clan tartans 40, 48, 77–84, 136; Figs 2.24–25

Highland Society of Madras 65–66
Highland Society of Scotland 73
Holmes, James (artist) 174; Fig. 4.49
Hope, W. H. St John (antiquarian) 185–86
Horsburgh, John (engraver) 186; Fig. 4.63
hose 64, 65, 73, 74, 86, 102, 110, 164, 175; Figs 2.30, 4.17–18
Houston, John (weaver) 20, 22, 40; Fig. 1.21
Hugh Morrison & Co., Glasgow (Highland dress outfitters) 33; Fig. 1.28
Hunter, George (tartan weaver and retailer)
- as Garb Furnisher to the Celtic Society of Edinburgh 87
- and the Highland Society of London tartan collection 69–70, 80

'Hunter's Highlanders' 86–89
- and Royal Visit (1822) 60; Fig. 2.30
hunting (*see* sports)
Huntly, Marquis of 165

Inchkeith 52
India/Indian 175
Industrial Museum of Scotland (*see* NMS)
industry/industrialisation 19–24, 39, 40, 192
- unrest 94
Inverlochy 85
Inverness 28, 88, 89
Inverness Museum and Art Gallery 22, 36; Fig. 1.22
- 'tartan room' 22

J. Nutting & Co., Covent Garden (button manufacturers) 85
Jack, Richard (silversmith) 183
jackets 18, 26, 65, 66, 69, 74, 86, 97, 122, 180; Figs 2.30, 4.36
Jacobites/Jacobitism 18, 31, 10, 16, 32, 39, 40, 57, 90, 112, 144, 171, 179; Figs 2.3, 2.7–9, 2.11, 2.23, 2.27, 4.13, 4.16, 4.24–25, 4.50
- army 8, 35, 57, 96
- relics 8, 40, 53, 61, 62 185; Figs 4.13, 4.62
- Rising (1715) Fig. 4.42
- Rising (1745–46) 7, 35, 39, 55, 61, 163, 184, 185; Figs 1.6, 4.13, 4.42
- tartan, use of 8, 90
Jaffray, Alexander (auctioneer) Fig. 3.4
Jamaica 73
James and Walters, London (merchants) 125
Jennings-Clerke, Sir Philip 55–57
'Jenny Weave' (sculpture) 23–24; Fig. 1.23
jewels/jewellery
- gemstones Figs 4.60–61
- Scottish 16, 60, 97, 183 (*see also* brooches)

Kandler, Charles Frederick (silversmith) 61
Kauffman, Angelica (artist) 86, 136; Figs 2.28, 4.1
Kelso 141
Kensington Palace 60
Kilbarchan 20, 22; Fig. 1.20
- Weaver's Cottage (National Trust for Scotland) 22

kilt/kilts 35, 40, 52, 57, 59, 64, 136, 138, 141, 147, 148, 150, 163, 171, 180; Figs 2.6, 2.30, 4.10–11, 4.22–25, 4.45, 4.61
- and men's fashions 150
- regimental 55, 164; Figs 4.35–37
- suits 37, 92, 142, 192; Figs 2.34, 4.3, 4.10– 12, 4.17–18, 4.22–25, 4.28–29, 4.56
- tailoring of 59, 148; Figs 4.19–21 (*see also* tailors/tailoring)
- -wearing 89, 148
kimono 179
Kincardine 126
Kintail 72, 89
knitting/knitted 40, 88, 94, 169; Fig. 4.39

lace/lacemaking 40, 74, 118, 147, 158
Lacy, John (actor) 177; Fig. 4.53
Lanarkshire 20
Lancashire 25, 36
Lauder, Sir Thomas Dick (politician) 179
Leamington Spa 158
Leeds, University of 24; Figs 1.25, 1.26
- Department of Textile Industries 24; Figs 1.25–26
- Textile Society 24
Leith Figs 4.24–25
Leopold, Johann Christian (publisher) 145
Liége Fig. 4.34
Lismore, Isle of Fig. 1.7
Lochaber 77, 89
Logan, James (antiquarian; *see also* tartan historians)
London 23, 56, 58, 60, 61, 68, 70, 72, 73, 81, 86, 91, 111, 117, 121, 122, 125, 128, 130, 136, 145, 158, 160, 165, 167, 174, 184; Figs 1.18, 3.11, 4.40, 4.48
- Bedford Square 165
- Berkeley Square 158
- Buckingham Palace 182
- Carlton House 61, 167; Fig. 2.7
- Covent Garden 85, 125, 130
- Gracechurch Street 82
- Great Russell Street 165
- Hanover Square 158
- Mayfair 158
- New Gallery 185
- St James 54
- Theatre Royal Fig. 4.53
- Tower Hill Fig. 4.14

- Tower of London Fig. 4.16
- Upper Grosvenor Street 122

looms 19–22, 25, 28, 91, 110, 115, 118, 148, 165; Fig. 3.3
- dobby 25
- hand- 19–22, 25, 40, 160; Figs 1.20–21
- with Jacquard mechanism 20
- power 21
- silk 20

(see also weavers/weaving; Wilson of Bannockburn, Messrs)

Lothian 191
Lynch, Tom Massey (see tartan historians)

MacArthur, Charles (piper) 74
McCallum, Malcolm (piper) Figs 4.24, 4.25
McClintock, H. F. (see tartan historians)
Macdonald, Alexander 179
Macdonald, Hon. Sir Archibald 64
McDonald, Miss (milliner), London 165
Macdonald of Borrodale, Angus 36
Macdonalds of Clanranald
- Angus Roderick Macdonald, 23rd Chief of Clanranald 61
- collection of Jacobite and family relics 53, 61; Figs 2.8, 4.55, 4.63
- Ranald George Macdonald, 20th Chief of Clanranald 53, 61, 180 doublet Fig. 4.55
- tailor to 144

Macdonald of Sleat, Sir Alexander 168; Fig. 4.42
Macdonald of Staffa 178, 179
- James and Alexander, children of 168–69; Fig. 4.42
MacDonald, Peter Eslea (see tartan historians)
MacDonell, Alasdair Ruadh, 13th Chief of Glengarry ('Pickle the Spy') 147; Fig. 4.16
MacDonell, Colonel Alastair/Alasdair Ranaldson, 15th Chief of Glengarry 85, 86, 90, 136; Fig. 2.28, 4.1
MacDougall, Margaret O. (curator) 22; Fig. 1.22
MacGillivray, James Pittendrigh (artist and antiquarian) 9, 24, 25, 26, 36, 103; Fig. 1.24
MacGregor of Borrodale, Catriona 36
MacGregor, Rob Roy 15
MacInnes of Lochaber, Donald (dancer) 77

McIntyre, Alexander (merchant) 114
MacIntyre, Duncan Ban (Donnchadh Bàn Mac an t-Saoir) 57
Mackenzie of Gruinard, Captain William 87
Mackintosh, John 179
MacLean, Neil (piper) 73–74, 97; Fig. 2.17
MacLeod, Captain Jack 22
Macleod, Donald 79
MacLeod, John (dirk maker) 87
MacLeod, John Norman, 24th Chief of Clan MacLeod 87, 122
MacLeod of Colbecks, Colonel John 167
MacNab, Frances, 12th Chief of Clan MacNab 12–13, 14, 15; Fig. 1.15
Macpherson, James (see also Ossian/Ossianic) 57, 62, 96; Fig. 2.10
Macpherson of Cluny, Duncan 158
Macpherson of Cluny, Ewen (Jacobite officer and clan chief) 39
Macpherson of Cluny, Ewen, 14th Chief of Clan Macpherson 158; Fig. 4.31
Macpherson, Sarah Justina (née Davidson of Tulloch) 158–60, 188; Fig. 4.31
Macrae, Christopher (harpist) 72–73
McWalter, Mrs (haberdasher) 126
Macome, Hector 126
Maitland, George 70
Manchester 130
mantles 104, 129, 144, 162; Fig. 4.34
masonic lodges
- St Nathalan of Tullich-in-Mar 80
masques/masquerades (see fancy dress)
Mauchline-ware 40
Maxwell, Jane, Duchess of Gordon 165; Fig. 4.40
medals 53, 74; Fig. 2.1, 2.2
medievalism
- influence on fashionable dress 179, 180; Figs 4.54, 55
Meikle, Willie (weaver) 22
Melrose, Gamrie, Banffshire Figs 4.32–4.33a,b
Metcalfe, Martin Smith 81, 82; Fig. 2.24
Meyer and Mortimer, Edinburgh (cloth merchants and tailors) 182
Meyrick, Sir Samuel Rush
- collection of clan tartan 94–95; Figs 2.16, 2.36, 3.6
Mid Calder 126
migration 40, 55
military 52, 54, 58, 65, 70, 86, 104, 112, 119–21, 162, 163; Figs 4.4, 4.16

- British army 6, 8, 32, 36, 54, 55, 96, 102, 162; Figs 2.23, 4.35
- contracts 108
- Jacobite army 8, 35, 57, 61, 96
- outfitter/outfitting 102
- recruitment of Scots into 57, 162
- and patriotic fashions 162–75; Fig. 4.36
- style 163, 164; Figs 4.28–29, 4.35, 4.38–40
- uniforms 7, 8, 43, 102, 104, 119–21, 163; Figs 2.29, 4.35, 4.39
- wear 103, 108, 162–67

(see also battles; regiments)

Millar & Ewing, Glasgow (cloth merchants)
- as customers of Messrs Wilson of Bannockburn 112; Fig. 3.7
- as suppliers of clan tartan to Sir Samuel Rush Meyrick 95; Figs 2.16, 2.36, 3.6

millinery/milliners 163, 165
Moir, Mrs Fig. 3.4
Moir, Walter Fig. 3.4
Morayshire 18, 37
Mosman, William (artist) 168; Fig. 2.9, 4.42
Muirhead Moffat & Co., Glasgow (antique dealer) 66
Müller, Johann Sebastian (artist) 145; Fig. 4.15
Munro, William (merchant) 163
Murray, Lady Augusta 70, 97
Murray-MacGregor, Major-General Sir Evan John, 2nd Baronet 184
- depictions of 170–71, Figs 4.44, 4.61
- refashioned broadsword 184, 185; Fig. 4.60, 4.61
Murray of Clava, John G. 39
Murray, William Henry (theatre proprietor) 75
Museum of the Isles 147
Musselburgh, races 75, 76
Muthill 191

Napoleonic Wars 70, 165, 167; Fig. 4.39; influence on fashionable dress 165, 171; Fig. 4.3
National Library of Scotland 63, 69, 78, 102
National Museums Scotland (NMS) 6, 9–10, 19, 26, 28, 33, 34, 35, 36, 37, 38, 40, 43, 46, 53, 60, 64, 66, 81, 82, 85, 90, 93, 94, 127, 138, 148, 151,

205

158, 160, 182, 191; Figs 1.14, 1.16, 1.17, 4.19, 4.28, 4.29, 4.31
- as Edinburgh Museum of Science and Art 19
- as Industrial Museum of Scotland 19
- Museum of Scotland (Scotland Galleries) 37–43, 83, 96
- National Museum of Antiquities of Scotland (NMAS) 6, 8, 16, 18, 33, 37, 38, 39, 53, 61, 66, 185; Figs 4.22–25, 4.55 (*see also* RSM)
- National Museum of Costume (Shambellie House) 33, 36–37; Fig. 1.28
- National Museum of Scotland 11, 43, 45
- as National Museums of Scotland (NMoS) 6
- National War Museum 2, 6; Fig. 1.5
    collections 141
    as Scottish Naval and Military Museum (SNMM) 6, 8, 163; Fig. 1.1;
    as Scottish United Services Museum (SUSM) 6, 30, 141; Figs 1.6, 1.27
- as Royal Scottish Museum (RSM) 6, 19, 20, 22, 24, 33, 37, 160; Figs 1.20, 1.21, 1.23, 4.24, 4.25, 4.31
Nelson, Admiral Horatio 165
neoclassical style 138; Fig. 4.3
New York 34, 35, 111; Fig. 3.5
newspapers 48, 53, 57, 89, 144, 165, 178, 179, 165, 179, 183
- advertisements 74, 91, 93, 124–25, 129, 178; Fig. 2.33
North, Charles Niven MacIntyre (artist) Fig. 1.18
Norwich 130
Nutter, Tommy (designer) 37

object labelling 2, 6, 21; Fig. 1.4
Ogilvie, Lord 80
oral traditions 41, 54
Order of the Thistle Fig. 2.6
Ossian/Ossianic (*see also* Macpherson, James) 54, 57, 62, 89, 96; Fig. 2.10
- 'Malvina wigs' 88
Outer Hebrides 8; Figs 1.8, 1.9

Paisley 126
Palace of Holyrood 90, 91
pantaloons 150; Figs 4.20, 4.21
Paris 164, 165; Figs 4.37, 4.48

Paterson, John 77
patriotism/patriotic 52, 53, 54, 59, 70, 72, 75, 79, 80, 90, 94, 141, 148, 162, 163, 165, 168, 175, 177; Figs 2.5, 2.14, 4.3
patrons/patronage 8, 9, 52, 57, 58, 59, 60, 66, 71, 72, 73, 86, 167, 178, 182; Figs 2.5, 2.18, 4.56
pelisses 125, 129
Perthshire 31, 182, 191; Figs 2.28, 3.9, 4.24, 4.25, 4.28, 4.29
Phoenix Park, Dublin 165
pipers 41, 59, 73, 74, 75, 86, 87, 145, 158, 182 (*see also* Cumming, William; Duff, Charles; MacArthur, Charles; McCallum, Malcolm; MacLean, Neil)
pipes/piping 16, 41
- competitions 63, 73, 74, 76; Figs 2.10, 2.17–18
Pitlochry 31
plaid/*breacan* 18, 34, 40, 41, 52, 56, 57, 58, 64, 65, 73, 77, 80, 90, 91, 94, 105, 117, 125, 126, 130, 141, 144–45, 150, 160, 162, 165, 169; Figs 1.1, 2.3–4, 2.22, 2.30, 2.34, 3.11, 3.24, 4.13, 4.26, 4.27, 4.34–35
- barred Figs 4.32–33a,b
- belted 41, 65, 86, 136, 145, 147, 150, 151, 160, 170; Figs 1.34, 4.26–27
- fringed 93, 175; Fig. 4.30
- ribbons 110
- tailored 59, 150, 151; Figs 4.22–30
- -wearing 145; Figs 4.14, 4.15, 4.34 (*see also* tartan)
pockets 148, 150; Figs 4.20, 4.21
Poland/Polish 175
Port Glasgow 20
Potts, George 183
powder horns 16, 76, 86; Figs 1.5, 2.30
Prince Edward Island Caledonian Society 120–21; Fig. 3.16
purses 13–14, 15, 18, 58, 65, 86, 179, 180; Figs 1.11, 1.13, 1.14 (*see also* sporrans)
Purse, William (merchant) 119; Fig. 3.15

quaichs 37

R. Menzies & Co., Carmarthen (merchant) 129
Raeburn, Sir Henry (artist) 136, 170; Figs 1.15, 2.22, 3.19, 4.1

recycling/refashioning of clothing 12, 46, 160, 177, 192 (*see also* alterations to clothing)
regiments 6, 43, 104, 112, 119, 121, 169, 171
- 15th Light Dragoons 142
- 22nd Light Dragoons 142
- 42nd Regiment of Foot (Black Watch) 163, 180; Figs 4.14, 4.35
- 72nd Regiment of Foot 87
- 79th Regiment of Foot (Cameron Highlanders) 120, 163
- 81st Regiment of Foot 171
- 91st Regiment of Foot (Argyllshire Highlanders) 165
- 92nd Regiment of Foot (Gordon Highlanders) 120; Fig. 4.40
- grenadier officers Fig. 4.35
- Loyal MacLeod Fencibles 167
- Royal Écossais (Royal Scots) Fig. 14.16
- Royal Perthshire Militia Figs 4.28, 4.29
- voluntary yeomanry cavalry 119–20
  (*see also* battles; military)
revival/revivalism 32, 62
    style 61–62, 89, 94, 136; Fig. 2.5
ribbons 45, 59, 91, 94, 110, 127, 138, 147, 150, 164, 165, 169, 170, 171, 175, 180; Figs 3.22, 4.3, 4.19, 4.39, 4.45, 4.57
Rio de Janeiro 111
Robertson & Wigham, Glasgow (merchant) 117–18; Figs 3.12–13
Robertson, Andrew (portrait miniaturist) 77, 79; Fig. 2.22
Robertson of Struan, Alexander 79
Romanes & Paterson, Edinburgh (tartan retailers) 28, 91, 112, 114–15, 189; Fig. 3.8
Romans
- Highland dress, debated influence on 145
- occupation of Scotland 145
Romantic movement 35; Fig. 4.54
- in Europe 45, 53, 179
- in Scotland 45, 75, 129, 158, 192
- influence on fashion 60, 86, 179
Rome 39; Fig. 4.1
rosettes 40, 64, 150, 171
Ross, Donald Munro 40; Fig. 1.32
Ross-shire 18
Rousseau, Jean-Jacques 169
Rowatt, Thomas (curator) 20

Royal Company of Archers 178
- tartan uniform 64; Fig. 2.11
Royal Scottish Academy 186
Royal Scottish Museum (see NMS: RSM)
Royal Visit (1822) 18, 40, 60, 68, 89–95, 130, 184; Figs 1.32, 2.19, 2.28, 2.30–35, 4.24, 4.25, 4.60
Rugends, George Philipp (artist) 145; Figs 4.14, 4.15

St Andrew 37, 91, 188
St Lucia Fig. 2.23
Saltire Society, The 31
saris 34
sashes 70
Satchwell Leney, William (artist) 73; Fig. 2.17
satire 56, 86, 88–89, 164; Figs 2.3, 4.37, 4.40
Scarlett, James (see tartan historians)
scarves 91, 162
Scotland/Scottish 45, 52, 54, 55, 56, 57, 58, 65, 68, 72, 73, 74, 76, 81, 85, 87, 89, 90, 91, 114, 144, 145, 162
- and colonialism 32
- and commerce 109, 126, 130, 192
- culture 22, 36, 37, 43, 130, 192
- diaspora 40
- heritage 24, 37, 46
- history 37, 38, 93, 192
- iconography 68, 137, 192
- identity 25, 37, 45
- land 37, 124
- military/soldiers 167, 171, 175; Fig. 4.43
- mythology 38
Scott Douglas, Sir John James, 3rd Baronet of Springwood Park ('Captain Douglas') 141–42; Figs 4.4, 4.5, 4.6, 4.7
Scott, Sir Walter 15, 86, 88, 179, 186
- commemorative tartan for 108
- *Ivanhoe* (1819) 179
- *Rob Roy* (1817) 15
- Royal Visit (1822), role in 90–91
- *Waverley* (1814) 179
- Waverley novels 186
Scottish Naval and Military Museum (see NMS: SNMM)
Scottish Register of Tartans 29
Scottish Tartans Authority, The 60; Fig. 2.7
Scottish United Services Museum (see NMS: SUSM)

setts (see tartan setts)
sgian dubh 16, 136; Fig. 4.2
Shambellie House (see NMS: National Museum of Costume)
shawls 112, 115; Fig. 3.8
- Indian 175
Shetland 18
shields (see targes/shields)
shirts 170; Figs 4.17, 4.18
Siddons, Harriet (actress and theatre manager) 75; Fig. 2.19
Simson, William (artist)
- *The Pretender* 186; Fig. 4.53
Sinclair, Sir John, 1st Baronet of Ulbster 63, 64, 65, 68, 87, 96, 124; Fig. 2.10
SINDEX (Sett Index) 28–29
- card Fig. 1.27
Six Foot Club 179
skeleton suits 170, 171; Fig. 4.44
Skene, W. F. (curator and historian) 81, 98
Skye, Isle of Fig. 4.42
sleeves 93, 126, 127, 141, 148, 158, 173, 180; Figs 2.31, 4.5
Small, Colonel John 58
Smith, Andrew (see tartan historians)
Smith, William (see tartan historians)
snuff mulls 77
Sobieski Stuart brothers (see tartan historians)
Society of Antiquaries of Scotland (SAS) 11–18, 183
- Purchasing Committee 66
Society of True Highlanders 85, 87, 90; Figs 2.27, 2.28
Sommers, John (merchant) 126–27
Sotheby's (auctioneers) 60
spencers 164; Fig. 4.38
spinning 31
sporrans VIII, 12–15, 16, 23, 40, 41, 59, 76, 77, 168, 175, 180; Figs 1.12, 2.6, 2.30, 4.35 (see also purses)
- antiquarian illustration of Fig. 1.16
- for children 168, 173, 175; Figs 4.42, 4.48, 4.49
- closure, styles of (cantles, clasps, locks) 12–15, 168; Figs 1.13, 1.14
- in fancy dress 180; Figs 4.57, 4.58
- military use Fig. 4.35
- as prizes 76–77
- weaponised 12–13, 15, 16; Figs 1.10
sports 168
- golfing 168
- horse racing 75, 76

- hunting 168
  (see also Highland games)
Springwood Park, Kelso 142
- collection 141
Stafford, Lady 79
Stewart, Donald Calder (see tartan historians)
Stewart, Donald William (see tartan historians)
Stewart, Duncan 82
Stewart of Bonskeid, Dr Alexander 53
Stewart of Garth, Major-General David 69–70, 97, 98, 188; Fig. 2.23
- and the Celtic Society of Edinburgh 87, 90
- and the Highland Society of London, tartan collection 77–83; Fig. 2.25
stockings (see hose)
Stonehouse 20
Stonyhurst College 36
Strathbogie Ploughmen Society 70
Strathglass 89
Strathspey 77
Stuart, House of 7, 8, 31, 35, 39, 53, 55, 185; Figs 2.8–9, 4.16
- exiled court in Rome 39, 61
Stuart, Prince Charles Edward 8, 31, 35, 39, 53, 60, 61, 90, 112, 185, 186; Figs 2.7–9, 4.16, 4.63
- 'Bonnie Prince Charlie' persona, creation of 112
- Borrodale fragment 35–36, 39; Fig. 1.30
- clothes allegedly worn by 8, 31; Fig. 1.6
  Hawthornden coat 185–86; Figs 4.62–63
- gift of Highland dress and accoutrements 36, 39–40; Fig. 1.31
Stuart, Prince Henry Benedict 39
- gift of Highland dress and accoutrements 39
Sussex, Duke of (see Augustus Frederick, Prince)
Sutherland, John 33; Fig. 1.28
swords 77, 183
- basket-hilted 53, 85, 136; Fig. 4.35
- broadswords 41, 61, 136, 179, 184; Figs 2.8, 4.35
- claymores 37, 76, 94, 183
- dress 59, 60, 62; Fig. 2.7

T. & L. Tuck, Haymarket, London (jewellers and cutlers) 60–61

207

tailors/tailoring 26, 31, 40, 48, 69, 73, 74, 93, 97, 124, 126, 136, 138, 141, 142, 144, 145, 147, 148, 150, 151, 170, 180, 184–85, 192; Figs 1.2, 2.13, 2.15, 2.34, 3.22–23, 4.8–12, 4.20–23, 4.26–29, 4.44, 4.61
– kilts 148, 150; Figs 4.19, 4.20, 4.21, 4.28, 4.29
– manuals 184–85; Fig. 4.61
Talbot Rice Gallery, Edinburgh 34
Taplow Lodge, Buckinghamshire 122, 124
targes/shields vi, 39–40, 41, 49, 53, 61, 85, 136, 147, 179, 183
Tarrant, Naomi (curator and textile historian) 33–34, 124
tartan (*also* plaid/*breacan*; tartan setts)
– and children's clothing 74, 167–75
– clan/family 26, 31, 40, 52, 69, 77, 79, 82, 83, 88, 94, 104, 105, 108, 114, 115, 120, 127–28, 129, 130, 131, 136, 138, 179, 182; Figs 1.35, 2.5, 2.24–26, 2.30, 3.9, 3.22–23, 4.3
– collection of 1–49, 77–83, 94–95, 136
– commemorative/celebratory 70, 108; Fig. 2.16
– and commerce 40, 102, 104, 105, 129, 130
– consumers/customers of 100–33; Figs 3.1, 3.4–5, 3.11, 3.14–15
– contemporary relevance 37, 43
– design of 101–33
– diagrams/drawings of 117–24; Figs 3.11–16, 3.18
– exhibitions of (*see under* exhibitions)
– in fancy dress 105, 176–85
– as fashion fabric 26, 34, 45, 104, 105, 124–28, 129, 171; Figs 3.2, 3.4, 3.20–21, 3.24
– and identity-making 32, 35, 54, 89, 105, 124, 129, 160
– manufacture/making of 29, 31–32, 101–33, 128–31; Fig. 3.23
– in the military 34, 108, 103, 167 military style Fig. 4.38; regimental 108, 119–21, 163; Fig. 4.36; uniforms 103–4, 119–21
– mills 25, 28
– mythologising of 29, 30, 104
– pattern books 102, 110
– and Prince Charles Edward Stuart 8, 39, 61
fragment 35; Fig. 1.30; kilt 35; romanticisation of 112

– research/scholarship of 29, 30, 35, 77, 102, 104, 129
– retail/merchandising of 101–33; Figs 3.6, 3.8, 3.10, 3.23
– and romanticism 35, 77–83, 89–95, 129
– samples/offcuts/fragments/remnants of 102, 103, 104, 105, 109–16; Figs 1.25–26, 3.4, 3.7, 3.12–13, 3.23
– and Scotland 37, 43
– and slave clothing 32, 116, 148; Fig. 3.10
– tailoring of 68–69, 141; Figs 2.15, 4.8, 4.9, 4.12, 4.61 (*see* tailors/tailoring)
– trade/trading 101–33
– in Victorian era 32
– weaving of 29, 108 industry 22, Figs 1.24, 4.50 (*see also* weavers/weaving)
– in world market 103, 111, 126; Fig. 3.4
tartan historians 102, 104
– Cheape, Hugh (curator) 11, 34, 35, 36
– Logan, James (antiquarian) 120–21, 130–31, 144, 150, 151; Figs 3.16 and p.131
– Lynch, Tom Massey 36
– McClintock, H. F. 2, 30, 31
– MacDonald, Peter Eslea 30, 36
– Scarlett, James 28, 29
– Smith, Andrew 28
– Smith, William 28
– Sobieski Stuart brothers 32 controversy over *Vestiarium Scoticum* 32
– Stewart, Donald Calder 28–29, 32, 69
– Stewart, Donald William 28
tartan setts 25, 28, 29, 30, 32, 69, 71, 79, 80, 83, 91, 102–33, 148, 150, 158, 171, 186; Figs 1.27, 3.5, 3.9, 3.12–13, 4.17–19, 4.62
– Abercromby/Abercrombie 70, 95; Fig. 2.16
– Atholl 79, 115–16; Fig. 3.9
– Black Watch Figs 4.35, 4.56
– Buchanan 127; Figs 3.22–23
– Caledonia 95, 112, 148; Figs 2.16, 4.17, 4.18
– Cameron of Erracht 163; Fig. 4.36
– Campbell of Argyll 118; Fig. 3.14
– Chisholm 117; Fig. 3.11
– Clanranald 120

– Colquhoun 95, 111
– Culloden 185
– Cumming 93; Fig. 2.34
– Douglas 97, 126
– Drummond Figs 4.24, 4.25
– Drummond of Strathallan 114
– Farquharson 80; Fig. 1.35
– Glenorchy 93, 111; Fig. 2.34
– Gordon Fig. 3.4
– Graham 95
– Grant 126
– Hunting Stewart 19, 20, 40; Fig. 1.21
– Inverness, Earl of 59, 133; Fig. 2.6
– Kidd 112, 148; Figs 4.17, 4.18
– Macdonald 71
– McDuff 118, 125–26
– MacGillivray 24–26
– MacGregor 80, 105 kilt suit 142, 144; Figs 4.10–12
– McKay 71
– Mackenzie 81, 95; Fig. 3.24
– Mackintosh 81; Figs 4.20–23, 4.26–27
– MacLean Fig. 4.3
– Macleod 119, 167; Fig. 3.15
– McNab 81
– Macpherson 79–80, 112, 148, 160; Figs 3.6, 4.17–18
– Murray of Atholl Figs 4.28–30
– Ogilvie 80, 114
– Prince Charles Edward 71, 96, 111, 112, 168, 171, 175; Figs 3.7, 4.50
– Regent 108
– Rob Roy 105
– Robertson Figs 4.24–27
– Royal Stewart/Stuart 40, 43, 66, 69, 70, 112, 124, 141, 142; Figs 1.36, 2.13, 2.25, 2.30, 3.19–21, 4.4–5, 4.8–9, 4.34
– Stewart 23, 112, 126
– Sutherland 79
– Walter Scott 108
– Waterloo 108
tassels 144, 168, 180
Taymouth Castle, Perthshire 182
Theatre Royal, London Fig. 4.53
theatre/theatricals (*see* fancy dress)
Thriepland, Sir Patrick Murray, 5th Baronet Figs 4.28, 4.29
thistles
– cups 37
– insignia/motifs 53, 59, 60, 61, 66, 68, 74, 93, 141, 179, 188; Figs 2.13–14, 4.3–5

Tieleman, Melchior Gommar (artist) 175; Fig. 4.50
Trevor-Roper, Hugh (historian) 35, 104
trews/trousers 8, 65, 170; Figs 4.13, 4.53, 4.61
turbans 175
Turkey/Turkish 175
Turner, Charles (artist) 174; Fig. 4.49
Turner, Joseph Mallord William (artist) 100–1; Fig. 3.1

undergarments 173, 174
uniforms (*see* military: and uniforms; tartan: in the military: uniforms)

Victoria and Albert Museum, London 23
Victoria, Queen 60, 182
– tour of Highlands (1842) 182
Vieillevoye, Barthélemy (artist) Fig. 4.34

waistcoats 64, 66, 72, 74, 91, 122, 147, 148–50, 168; Figs 4.3, 4.17–18
Waitt, Richard (artist) 41; Fig. 1.34
Wales/Welsh 72, 73, 129
– flannels 133
– triple harp 72
Walker, Messrs, of London (cloth merchants) 117; Fig. 3.11
Walker's Warehouse, Covent Garden, London (cloth warehouse) 125
Watson, George (artist) 184
weaponry 12, 15, 16, 39, 41, 53, 58, 59, 60, 61, 73, 74, 96, 136, 183, 184; Figs 2.5, 2.27, 2.29, 4.35
weavers/weaving 19, 20–21, 22, 26, 28, 29, 87, 91, 102, 104, 108, 115, 103; Figs 1.20–21
– handloom 19–22, 30, 40
– pirn wheel 21
– Spitalfields 165, 182
– Weaver's Cottage (Kilbarchan) 22 (*see also* Wilson of Bannockburn, Messrs)
Wedderburn, John 81, 98
West Highland Museum 10, 36
West Highlands 26
West Indies 73, 148
– plantations in 148
West, Sir Benjamin (artist) 66; Figs 2.2, 2.12
Westwood, Vivienne (designer) 37
Wilkie, Sir David (artist) 60
William, Prince (later William IV) 58
William, Prince, Duke of Cumberland 61; Fig. 4.63
William Steven & Co., Edinburgh (clothiers and hatters) 91, 93
Wilson, William (weaver) 102
Wilson of Bannockburn, Messrs 26, 31, 32, 40, 70, 71, 91, 102–33, 148, 160, 163, 185
– agents of 109–10
– archive (at NMS) 26, 40, 45, 102–33; Figs 3.2–18, 3.20–23
– and clan tartans 26, 120
– customers of 105–31, 163; Figs 3.4–18
– exporting of tartan 32, 111, 126
– and the Highland Society of London, clan tartan collection 79
– and James Logan 120–21, 130–31; Fig. 3.16
– liquidation of (1924) 26, 102
– and military dress 26, 103, 119–21, 163
– samples/fragments/offcuts/remnants, use of 45, 110–16, 163; Figs 3.4–10
– and Scottish Romanticism 112, 129
– patterns, Wilson, transcription by James Pittendrigh MacGillivray 26; Fig. 1.24
– and uniforms of Highland clubs and societies 70–71, 120–21
Wilson Stow & Co., Glasgow (cloth merchants) 116; Fig. 3.10
Wright, John Michael (artist) Fig. 4.53

Acknowledgements

National Museums Scotland would like to thank the William Grant Foundation for funding the research, conservation and photography which made this book possible.

The author would like to thank the following individuals for offering their expertise and support in the preparation of this book: Stuart Allan, Jack Barton, Hugh Cheape, David Forsyth, Anna Groundwater, Matt Knight, Sarah Laurenson, Darren Layne, Clara Low, John McLeish, Peter MacDonald, Madeleine Pelling, Calum Robertson, Emily Taylor, Georgia Vullinghs, Patrick Watt and Helen Wyld.

Grateful thanks are also extended to the conservators, photographers and collections services staff of National Museums Scotland, and to the picture library and publishing staff of NMS Enterprises Limited.

The publisher would like to thank the following institutions for consenting to the reproduction of images:

- Armadale Castle, Gardens and Museum of the Isles
- The British Museum
- Brown University Library
- The Bute Collection at Mount Stuart
- City of Edinburgh Council
- The Clark Art Institute
- The Fishmongers' Company
- Glasgow Museums Collections
- Highland Archive Centre
- The Lewis Walpole Library, Yale University
- Lohia Foundation
- Los Angeles Public Library
- National Galleries of Scotland
- National Trust for Scotland
- Royal Collection Trust
- SCRAN
- Shutterstock
- Yale Centre for British Art